TA886551

THE CURIOHAUS TRIALS

'At his best, man is the noblest of all animals; separated from law and justice he is the worst.'

Aristotle

THE CURIOHAUS TRIALS

BRINGING THE NAZIS TO JUSTICE 1945–1949

RUSSELL KENT

Pen & Sword
MILITARY
AN IMPRINT OF PEN & SWORD BOOKS LTD.
YORKSHIRE – PHILADELPHIA

First published in Great Britain in 2025 by
PEN AND SWORD MILITARY
An imprint of
Pen & Sword Books Limited
Yorkshire – Philadelphia

Copyright © Russell Kent, 2025

ISBN 978 1 03611 175 5

The right of Russell Kent to be identified as Author of this work has been asserted by him in accordance with the Copyright, Designs and Patents Act 1988.

A CIP catalogue record for this book is available from the British Library.

All rights reserved. No part of this book may be reproduced, transmitted, downloaded, decompiled or reverse engineered in any form or by any means, electronic or mechanical including photocopying, recording or by any information storage and retrieval system, without permission from the Publisher in writing. No part of this book may be used or reproduced in any manner for the purpose of training artificial intelligence technologies or systems.

Typeset in Times New Roman 11.5/14 by
SJmagic DESIGN SERVICES, India.
Printed and bound in the UK by CPI Group (UK) Ltd.

The Publisher's authorised representative in the EU for product safety is Authorised Rep Compliance Ltd., Ground Floor, 71 Lower Baggot Street, Dublin D02 P593, Ireland.
www.arccompliance.com

For a complete list of Pen & Sword titles please contact
PEN & SWORD BOOKS LIMITED
George House, Units 12 & 13, Beevor Street, Off Pontefract Road,
Barnsley, South Yorkshire, S71 1HN, England
E-mail: enquiries@pen-and-sword.co.uk
Website: www.pen-and-sword.co.uk

or

PEN AND SWORD BOOKS
1950 Lawrence Rd, Havertown, PA 19083, USA
E-mail: uspen-and-sword@casematepublishers.com
Website: www.penandswordbooks.com

MIX
Paper | Supporting responsible forestry
FSC® C013604

CONTENTS

LIST OF ILLUSTRATIONS

Every effort has been made to contact all copyright holders. The publishers will be glad to make good in any future editions any errors or omissions brought to their attention.

ABBREVIATIONS

1WCIT	No.1 War Crimes Investigation Team
2WCIT	No.2 War Crimes Investigation Team
3WCIT	No.3 War Crimes Investigation Team
AEL	*Arbeitserziehungslager* – work education camp
ARP	Air Raid Police (*Luftschutzpolizei*)
BAOR	British Army of the Rhine
BBC	British Broadcasting Corporation – a British television company
CBS	Columbia Broadcasting System – a US television company
CIC	Civilian Internment Camp
CROWCASS	Central Registry of War Criminals and Security Suspects
DCOS	Deputy Chief of Staff
DJAG	Department of the Judge Advocate General
FRG	Federal Republic of Germany or West Germany
GHQ	General Headquarters
Gestapo	*Geheime Staatspolizei* – Secret State Police
GOC	General Officer Commanding
GOC-in-C	General Officer Commanding-in-Chief
HQ	Headquarters
IMT	International Military Tribunal
JAG	Judge Advocate General
KdF	*Kraft durch Freude* – strength through joy
KG	*Kriegsgefangener* – prisoner of war
Kripo	*Kriminalpolizei* – Criminal Police
KZ	*Konzentrationslager* – concentration camp
MTB	Motor torpedo boat
NCO	Non-commissioned Officer

NSDAP	*Nationalsozialistische Deutsche Arbeiterpartei* – National Socialist German Workers' Party (Nazi Party)
NWE	North West Europe
OKW	*Oberkommando der Wehrmacht* – the high command of the German armed forces
POW	Prisoner of war
RAF	Royal Air Force
RE	Royal Engineers
RMP	Royal Military Police
RSHA	*Reichssicherheitshauptamt* – Reich Security Headquarters
RSM	Regimental Sergeant Major
SA	*Sturmabteilung* – 'Storm Division' or Storm Troopers
SD	*Sicherheitsdienst des Reichsführers-SS* – Security Service of the *Reichsführer-SS*
SHAEF	Supreme Headquarters Allied Expeditionary Force
Sipo	*Sicherheitspolizei* (Security Police)
SOE	Special Operations Executive
SS	*Schutzstaffel*
SSRF	Small Scale Raiding Force
Stalag	*Stammlager* – general prisoner of war camp
TNA	The National Archives at Kew, London
UK	United Kingdom
UNWCC	United Nations War Crimes Commission
US	United States
USHMM	United States Holocaust Memorial Museum
WCIT	War Crimes Investigation Team
WW1	The First World War, 1914–18
WW2	The Second World War, 1939–45

ACKNOWLEDGEMENTS

My greatest debt of gratitude is to the British military legal staff who documented the details of the trials described in this book. The British Army Department of the Judge Advocate General gathered together the many statements, affidavits, photographs, maps, diagrams and trial records without which this book would not have been possible.

Thank you to the many colleagues in Germany who offered assistance without reservation: Dr Reimer Möller and Franciska Henning from the KZ-Gedenkstätte Neuengamme Archiv, Nicole Mattern of the Vereinigung Kinder vom Bullenhuser Damm eV, Tim Hölschermann of the Hamburg Curiohaus, Anika Kindereich from the Stadtarchiv Celle and Detlef Boick, Editor of *Elbe-Jeetzel-Zeitung* were outstanding.

Staff of many libraries, archives and collections have been kind and helpful, particularly The National Archives at Kew, The Wiener Holocaust Library, The Cambridge University Library, The Imperial War Museum Collections and The Liddell Hart Centre for Military Archives at King's College, London.

Dr Marc Buggeln (University of the Bundeswehr Hamburg), Roberta Baskin (former investigative reporter for CBS) and Miriam Kleiman (Program Director for Public Affairs at the US National Archives and Records Administration) were supportive and encouraging. I am also grateful that Philip Collins found time to apply his expert technical eye to find the many errors I missed. Any that remain are my own.

I am lucky to have a professional, friendly and enthusiastic publishing team at Pen and Sword. Thanks particularly to Harriet Fielding, Jon Wilkinson and Stephen Chumbley.

Finally, I thank my wife, Lindi, for tolerating the many days I spent researching away from home and lovingly accepting my long silences when I was engrossed in reading or typing on our dining table.

INTRODUCTION

Lead prosecutor Colonel Backhouse looked up from his notes, 'Was there no gas chamber there before you arrived?' Josef Kramer gave a one-word answer, 'No.' The Colonel continued, 'Was it constructed under your instructions and did you quite deliberately gas 80 prisoners in that gas chamber?' With no hint of shame, Kramer said, 'Yes, on the orders of *Reichsführer* Himmler.'[1]

Many people think there was one war crimes trial in Nuremberg after the Second World War, but the testimony above did not occur there. The trial of SS Captain Josef Kramer, the commandant of Auschwitz-Birkenau, Natzweiler and Belsen concentration camps, took place weeks earlier over 500km away in a Lüneburg gymnasium.

The so-called 'Nuremberg Trial', more properly the International Military Tribunal (IMT), tried just twenty-two defendants in the Nuremberg Palace of Justice from 20 November 1945 to 1 October 1946. They represented the most senior Nazis from a range of Reich ministries, German armed forces, governors of German-occupied countries and Nazi organizations, but no concentration camp commandants were prosecuted. The Gestapo, the SD and the SS were declared to be criminal organizations. Furthermore, the IMT proclaimed the leaders of the Nazi Party (the *Nationalsozialistische Deutsche Arbeiterpartei* or NSDAP) to be criminals. Twelve were sentenced to be hanged, three to life imprisonment and four to long prison terms. Three were acquitted.[2]

But what of the other Nazis, the hundreds of thousands who had mistreated, mutilated and murdered in the name of the Third Reich? The Americans led twelve further trials in Nuremberg and many more in Dachau. There were Soviet trials, Polish, French, Yugoslavian, Czech, and Hungarian trials. And there were British trials.

Immediately after the war ended, British military trials were held in several different towns. But it quickly became obvious a central location was needed where several trials could be held simultaneously, court personnel could be housed and where there were holding facilities for the many accused Germans. Although over 60 per cent of housing in Hamburg had been damaged or destroyed, there were sufficient suitable buildings still standing to accommodate legal staff, including the world-famous Hotel Atlantic on the Altersee. A far less comfortable facility could house the accused prisoners – the former concentration camp in Neuengamme, a few kilometres south-east of the city. Renamed the Civilian Internment Camp No. 6, it was here that former guards, policemen and doctors awaited their date with justice.

The British held the trials in an intact Hamburg concert hall called the Curiohaus. Numerous wood-panelled rooms allowed several courts to sit at the same time. In the main courtroom (Court One), members of the court sat on one side of the hall behind a table draped with a Union Jack. Opposite, and slightly lower, was the dock where the accused sat. If there were several accused, they often wore numbered placards around their necks to ease identification. In front of the dock were tables for the defence. The prosecution occupied a table to the side. The ends of the former concert hall had seats for Allied spectators and journalists, but the stage was reserved for VIPs. German spectators occupied a gallery above the judging panel.

A few academic articles have accurately bemoaned the lack of attention given to the British military war crime trials by historians and legal scholars, noting the trials have been labelled 'minor' or 'forgotten'.[3] Even the precise number of British trials in Germany remains uncertain, but the most reliable figures come from Kartrin Hassel's *Kriegsverbrechen vor Gerichte* – 328 trials with 937 people charged.[4] The effort made to hear all these trials was enormous. Although the Hamburg Curiohaus was the venue for most, there were trials too in Celle, Braunschweig, Wuppertal, Osnabruck, Hannover, Recklinghausen and many other towns. Depositions often needed to be translated and not just from German, but from Polish, Czech and other languages. Copies had to be made and distributed. Exhibits needed translation, duplication and collation. When the case was ready, court members had to be appointed, notified, transported and housed. This included the court president, members of the judging panel, ushers, guards, interpreters and often a Judge Advocate (a legal advisor). Prosecution and defence lawyers spent many days in preparation. Victims, witnesses and accused persons often needed to be transferred from their homes or prisons to somewhere near the courtroom, where they too required accommodation. A long paper trail was generated.

You might think these records represent a valuable seam for historians to mine, but there are problems. Chief among these is that there are few published trial transcripts. In the late 1940s, William Hodge & Company produced a few volumes in its *War Crimes Trials* series, but these are now difficult to find outside university libraries. They are useful, but they do not contain full transcripts – this would have been impossible as the trials sometimes went on for months, producing hundreds of pages of evidence often in several languages. The largest of these volumes (by number of pages) is *The Belsen Trial*, but even this book covers just the first trial, neglecting to inform the reader that there were several further Belsen trials.[5] There are many War Office and Foreign Office files in the British National Archives, probably at least one for every trial, but these are of varying quality. The best are large box files containing details of the War Crimes Group (North West Europe) investigations and comprehensive reports to the Department of the Judge Advocate General (DJAG). There are depositions from victims, witnesses and the accused, details of the court, longhand transcripts of the trial, petitions and accounts of reductions to sentences. Where present, some of the most revealing documents are summary statements from the prosecution, defence and Judge Advocate. But most files hold crumbling pages of the bare minimum: court proceedings (meaning the court composition, charges, pleas, findings and sentences), petitions for those convicted from their families, friends, priests and German politicians (most of which were roundly rejected) and masses of 'chits' – small pieces of paper requesting supplies, transfers, and expenses. Some files have just a few pages, which are often copies of documents to be found in other places. The shortage of quality paper available after the war is wholly evident with depositions typed on cheap, brittle sugar paper or handwritten on transparent onionskin stock. This has resulted in some dilapidated files, which have proved tough for The National Archives to maintain and are challenging to handle.

This book does not attempt to cover all the Curiohaus trials – there were 150 and it would not be possible in a single volume. Many trials are poorly documented with sparse information and the terse details would soon become repetitive. Instead, the trials are broadly categorised by subject and each is illustrated by a few cases.[6] These expose some common fallacies used to excuse the crimes of the Third Reich including the fairytale that the German population knew nothing of the camps or the conditions in them. Within these pages, you will discover Hamburg alone had several subcamps of Neuengamme where people were kept in appalling conditions and whose job was to clear rubble after Allied bombing raids. The locals could not have missed these ragged, emaciated unfortunates toiling in the streets. You will also find a case where a *prisoner* refused an order to kill other prisoners and yet survived the war, exposing the lie that all orders had to be followed on pain of death. In the final chapter, you will see that many ordinary German soldiers of the Wehrmacht were not innocent of the Holocaust and there were millions of committed Nazis for the Allies to deal with at the end of hostilities in May 1945.

1

THE BEGINNING OF WAR CRIMES TRIALS

A war crime is said to have occurred when there is a violation of the standards of allowed behaviour in an armed conflict by a person or group. The rules were largely laid down in the Hague Conventions of 1899 and 1907 – a series of international declarations negotiated at two peace conferences and signed by most of the belligerents involved in the two world wars.

When peace returned to Europe at the end of the First World War (WW1), there was pressure to bring those guilty of war crimes to judgment. Justice may have been served quickly if there had been a clause in the Armistice itself which demanded the handover of accused men. Unfortunately, in the prevailing atmosphere of hate, indignation and overriding thirst for retribution, such a section was overlooked. Thousands of men were allowed time to escape justice by changing their names and fleeing to other countries. A petition to extradite a long list of suspects was not made until the 1919 Paris Peace Conference. A commission at the conference tried to establish a way to prosecute war criminals and their report added articles 228, 229 and 230 to the Treaty of Versailles. The treaty came into force on 10 January 1920, over a year after the surrender.

Article 228 of the Treaty of Versailles bound the Germans to, ' . . . hand over to the Allied and Associated Powers . . . all persons accused of having committed an act in violation of the laws and customs of war . . .'. Furthermore, the Allied courts demanded that the Germans provide all the relevant evidence and eyewitnesses. The former German high command and government, including Kaiser Wilhelm II, topped the Allied wanted list. But the Dutch refused to give up the Kaiser, who was in exile in the Netherlands. This may have been an expression of their neutrality, but there is evidence to suggest they did not recognize any court as having the legitimacy to try the former German Head of State.

The Germans also argued against arresting all the other senior military officers and politicians that the Allies wanted to prosecute. Such action, they contended, might bring down their unstable government. The Allies could do little to compel the Germans as they had no occupying forces, but the compromise reached would prove disastrous: the former enemy themselves would prosecute the accused before the Supreme Court of Leipzig. Sceptical, but willing to see whether the proposal would work, the Allies handed a list of forty-five test cases to the court. German lawyers worked to prepare as they would ordinary criminal cases. The result was the first trial did not begin until 23 May 1921. Two and a half years had elapsed since the November 1918 Armistice. In this time, witnesses had disappeared, some had died, and evidence for crimes that had occurred at the start of the war was almost seven years old.

In the end, a mere twelve Germans were tried in nine trials; five brought by the British, one by the Belgians and three by the French. The other cases were dismissed for lack of evidence and the trials were over by 16 July 1921, within two months of beginning. Of the few convicted, the longest sentence was four years' imprisonment. The two men sentenced to this term were helped by their fellow countrymen to escape and to flee Germany. The Germans accepted neither their sole guilt nor the fairness of trials against their soldiers alone. Many believed an equal number of war crimes had been committed by the Allies and wondered when the victorious countries would try their own war criminals. Rather than humility, the German public showed widespread support for the accused and cheered in court when men were acquitted.[1]

The Allies realized they had made a big mistake. Hundreds, perhaps thousands, had escaped justice for war crimes and the unfairness felt by the Germans had not been eased. During the next war, the Allies pledged to do better, promising to improve upon the miserable legacy of the Leipzig trials. Despite initial Foreign Office reluctance, Churchill began to make public announcements saying that at the end of the Second World War (WW2) there would be a proper reckoning. In his speech on the German invasion of Russia, Churchill said:

> Any man or State who fights against Nazism will have our aid. Any man or State who marches with Hitler is our foe. This applies not only to organized States but to all representatives of that vile race of Quislings who make themselves the tools and agents of the Nazi regime against

> their fellow-countrymen and against the lands of their births. These Quislings, like the Nazi leaders themselves, if not disposed of by their fellow-countrymen, which would save trouble, will be delivered by us on the morrow of victory to the justice of the Allied tribunals. That is our policy and that is our declaration.[2]

But the policy amounted to little and the Foreign Office seemed determined to keep it that way. Over 80 years on, it is difficult to imagine how isolationist many countries were. If atrocities were being committed against foreign people by other foreign people in distant countries, the prevailing mood of many Allied governments was that they should be left to sort it out themselves. This is precisely how the British Foreign Office behaved. Careful denunciation was allowed, but they were most reluctant to commit to any firm action against war criminals.

The occupied nations themselves were the first to notify Germany formally that it would be made to answer for war crimes. In the Inter-Allied Declaration signed at St James's Palace in London on 13 January 1942, representatives of Belgium, Czechoslovakia, Free France, Greece, Holland, Luxembourg, Norway, Poland and Yugoslavia placed among their principal war aims the punishment of those guilty of or responsible for violence against their countrymen. The gears slowly began to turn. President Roosevelt's press statement of August 1942 in which he wrote, '. . . the time will come when they shall have to stand in courts of law in the very countries which they are now oppressing and answer for their acts',[3] showed the way. But courts of law were not everyone's preferred form of justice for war criminals.

Churchill proposed a curious mixture of drumhead court martial and summary execution. German leaders would be declared 'world outlaws'. When captured, their identity would be verified by an officer after which they would be shot. The Americans supported this position. Unlikely as it may seem, the impetus for trials came from the Soviets who had experienced the positive (for them) political effect of terror trials in the 1930s. Eventually persuaded, Churchill wrote to Roosevelt, 'There must be no executions without trial; otherwise the world would say we were afraid to try them . . . if there were no trials there must be no death sentences.'[4] Churchill was doubly convinced of the justice of trials shortly after the Tehran Conference in late 1943. Relaxing over drinks, Stalin had teased Churchill that the German General Staff of about 50,000 officers and technicians should be rounded up and shot. Shocked, Churchill retorted, 'The British Parliament and public will never tolerate mass executions. Even if in war passion they allowed them to begin they would turn violently against those responsible after the first butchery had taken place.' 'Fifty thousand must be shot,' continued the mischievous Stalin. 'I would rather be taken out into the garden here and now and be shot myself than sully my own and my country's honour by such infamy,' replied Churchill.[5]

On 7 October 1942, the US and UK committed to a United Nations Commission for the Investigation of War Crimes announced in the House of Lords by Lord Chancellor John Simon. The Allies argued amongst themselves about which countries would form the Commission and who their representatives might be. After more than a year of procrastination, the Commission had its inaugural meeting at the Foreign Office in London on 20 October 1943. Even then, the Soviets did not attend and they never did, stating they had their own agency collecting evidence of war crimes in the Soviet Union. Lord Simon, the chairman, declared the Commission would aim to investigate and record evidence of war crimes and to identify the individuals responsible where possible. When the Commission thought the evidence adequate, this would be reported to the Allied government concerned. Simon emphasised the Commission should not concern itself with how suspects would be tried.[6] This was partly clarified a month later when Churchill, Roosevelt and Stalin finally formalized their proposals on post-war justice in The Moscow Declaration of 1 November 1943.

The Allied governments had received a steady supply of information about atrocities. They knew crimes were being perpetrated by Germans and people sympathetic to Nazi aims in occupied countries against prisoners of war (POWs), Jews, Roma, Sinti, Slavs, homosexuals, priests, Jehovah's Witnesses and other civilians on an enormous scale. Everybody knew who the chief criminals were: the leaders of the NSDAP and state, the high command of the German military, leaders of the various police organizations, the senior diplomats, bankers, judges and civil servants. This relatively small group, however, could not have carried out the large-scale extermination of the people mentioned above. Some estimated this would involve 80,000 people supported by the German military, an efficient bureaucracy and a transport system all sustained by many ordinary people.[7] It was becoming clear there would be two categories of war criminals: the majority would belong to the many thousands of Axis guards, police, paramilitary units and troops involved in specific crimes in identifiable locations. A smaller number would be held accountable for offences without geographic location. These would be the 'major war criminals'. Each group would be handled differently.

The United Nations Commission for the Investigation of War Crimes (later renamed the 'United Nations War Crimes Commission' or UNWCC) had no team of detectives scouring Europe for war crimes. Instead, the UNWCC relied on each country submitting evidence to it for investigation. Its Committee One was a legal group which concentrated on facts and evidence to decide whether there was a *prima facie* case (sufficient evidence to form a legal claim). Where there was, names and particulars were added to a list for distribution among the UNWCC governments.[8] But by May 1944, over six months after its first meeting, there were few names on the list. Most believed they could produce a longer list based on their own knowledge of Nazi politicians and the German high command. The problems suffered by the UNWCC in 1944 are well covered in Tom Bower's *Blind Eye To Murder* where he reveals in-fighting between departments, mechanisms inserted to delay names of alleged war criminals being added to the UNWCC list and doubts about whether international law could prevail against German national law. Neither the British Foreign Office nor the US State Department could agree on how to treat the accused or even who the suspects were. By the end of 1944, it became obvious the military, who had so far avoided the war crimes saga, would need to be involved in the legal effort. They were the only force in the theatre of war that could hunt down, detain and, ultimately, prosecute suspected war criminals.

As parts of Europe were liberated in 1944 and 1945, the Central Registry of War Criminals and Security Suspects (CROWCASS) began compiling three lists: all German POWs, all men detained for specific crimes and all wanted men. Given the tens of thousands of names on these lists, it was clear the plan to identify, find and return the greater number of war criminals to the place where they had committed atrocities to be tried by locals would not be practical. In addition, as the British and Americans conquered areas of Germany, it was obvious the plan could not survive the liberation of the concentration camps whose staff had often perpetrated crimes in more than one country. When the war ended on 8 May 1945, Germany was divided into four zones of occupation: Soviet, French, British and American. If rapid justice was required (and it was as witnesses died following liberation or fled the camps to return home) each of the Allies would have to be responsible for the crimes committed in its zone of occupation and military courts were going to be needed. For the British, this required a Royal Warrant.

The warrant, signed by King George VI on 14 June 1945, established that British military courts would be authorized to prosecute and sentence persons charged with 'violation of the laws and usages of war'. Normal court-martial procedures would apply and all personnel would be from the British military. A president and at least two others would be the judging panel. At least one should be legally trained, otherwise a Judge Advocate would be appointed to advise the court on the law and make sure the trial was conducted properly. International law (in its infancy) would apply, but the normal English legal rules regarding the types of evidence allowed would be loosened. The court could hear any statement, read any document and even receive secondary evidence of statements made by or attributable to such witnesses (usually called 'hearsay evidence'). It was the court's duty to decide how heavily the evidence presented weighed upon the charges made. Critically, for many of the British trials, section 8 (ii) of the Royal Warrant allowed that evidence given against any member of a unit or group of men could be received by the court as evidence of the responsibility of each member for a crime. British military tribunals could decide that staff with responsibility for a concentration camp formed a group. If any of that group committed a crime against the prisoners, all individuals in the group were equally guilty of it whether or not they were present. Acquittals by the court would be final, but guilt and sentences were to be confirmed by the British Army General Officer Commanding-in-Chief (GOC-in-C). A convicted criminal had two weeks from the end of the trial to submit a petition against conviction or sentence to the confirming officer, but there was no right of appeal.[9]

The British military courts would adopt the usual British adversarial system where one party represents the prosecuting state and another the accused person. Each side would present evidence and argue their case before a neutral judging panel acting like umpires. The panel of judges would then choose whether the accused person was guilty of the charge. In the adversarial system, the prosecution must prove their case – a fundamental principle in British criminal law. We are familiar with what is called 'the burden of proof' (also referred to in law as the legal or persuasive burden). This is where the prosecution must put before the court evidence to prove the facts as they see them. Moreover, the evidence presented must be sufficient to meet a high standard of proof. In a criminal case, the standard of proof required for prosecuting evidence is 'beyond a reasonable doubt'. Usually, reasonable doubt is defined as, 'any doubt which would make a reasonable person hesitate in the most important of his or her affairs'. But the legal burden is not the only obligation. The 'evidential burden' requires the prosecution to put before the court sufficient relevant evidence to make an issue 'live'. It must allow the court to conceive facts and introduce evidence that convinces the court these facts are true.

The rules of evidence determine what material can be introduced; it must be relevant, admissible and have weight. The weight of evidence is, to a degree, governed by its type. Two specific types of evidence were relied upon by the British military courts. The first was direct evidence that could stand alone to prove an assertion, such as eyewitness testimony given under oath (perhaps the most powerful). The second type was demonstrative evidence – a document, photograph, film, audio recording or similar that directly establishes a fact. This includes an affidavit – a written declaration of facts signed by a person who swears the information included in the document is accurate to the best of their knowledge. An affidavit is witnessed and signed by a notary public or other legal official authorized to do so. Once signed, the document becomes legally binding. The British military courts also relied on circumstantial evidence, used to infer something based on a series of other facts that can be proven. Such evidence cannot stand alone because it requires logical reasoning to prove.

Surprisingly, little physical evidence such as a weapon or other item from a crime scene was used. Bodies were often exhumed and examined, but this seems to have been mostly to afford them decent reburial rather than to collect evidence. Details of postmortem examinations are in some case files, but testimony from pathologists is rare. Unusually, however, hearsay evidence was sometimes allowed. The common understanding of hearsay evidence is the repetition in court of a statement made to a witness by a third party. When it occurred, the British military court was advised to be careful on judging whether the statement was uttered and mindful that the third party could not be questioned on its veracity.

The British legal team tried to head off the defences they anticipated would be raised during the trials. The most expected of these was the defence of superior orders, as this had been a common feature of the WW1 Leipzig Trials. In 1921, two submariners were accused of shooting at the lifeboats of the steamer *Llandovery Castle*, which their U-boat had sunk by torpedo.[10] The defence case was that the U-boat Commander Helmut Patzig, not himself tried by the court, ordered the shooting and others followed his superior orders. The German court rejected this defence, saying, 'Patzig's order does not free the accused from guilt'. Furthermore, the court found, ' . . . the subordinate obeying such an order is liable to punishment, if it was known to him that the order of the superior involved the infringement of civil or military law'. The court found this applied to the accused and sentenced them to four years in prison.[11] The *Llandovery Castle* case was often cited by the British prosecutors in the Curiohaus trials as invalidating the defence of acting under superior orders.

The defence of *Nullem crimen sine lege, nulla poena sine lege*, which is there should be no crime without a preceding law and no punishment for an act committed before it was illegal to do so, was claimed in the first large Curiohaus trial – 'The *Peleus* Trial'. The court decided, however, that it did not apply as the seafaring code of not killing shipwrecked persons who have taken refuge in lifeboats was well-known by all seamen and it had already been dismissed as a defence in the *Llandovery Castle* trial. One principle behind the *nulla poena sine lege* defence is that the person committing an act must be doing so in good faith, thinking what they are doing is legal (or at least not illegal). It is hard to accept anyone committing the acts tried by the British could have assumed this. Few people believed crimes had not been committed, even if international law had not caught up and defined some acts of the accused Germans as illegal. Even fewer thought a legal technicality should exonerate the perpetrators.

The childish logical fallacy of trying to defend your position merely by indicating the same weakness in your opponent – the *Tu quoque* defence (you did it too)– was attempted by several defendants during interrogation and when on trial. An illegal act, however, cannot become legal just because an opponent has committed the same illegal act. There is no doubt the Allies also committed war crimes, during wartime criminals fight in all armies, but there was a difference. The Allies fought a defensive war – there would have been no war had the Germans not invaded other countries. Of course, the Allies engaged in fierce combat, but their aim was not to take other countries' territory for 'living space', to enslave people or to exterminate those they considered inferior. Additionally, the German government always had the option to sue for peace, while people in the occupied countries, the slaves in Germany and the wretches in the camps had no such recourse. As Robert Jackson said prior to the IMT, 'We must make clear to the Germans that the wrong for which their fallen leaders are on trial is not that they lost the war, but that they started it'.[12]

Many orders were given during the war, which resulted in the deaths of thousands of civilian men, women and children. At least on the Allied side, however, orders were expressed in such terms that military men could follow them, believing there was a legitimate war aim. The Allied bombing campaign extended to whole cities and populations only when it became clear the accuracy needed to hit individual targets could not be achieved. The German Luftwaffe had realized the same and acted similarly. British airmen were told area bombing was required to knock out the enemy's ability to manufacture war materials or to prevent the movement of troops and supplies.[13] The Allies knew there would be many civilian casualties, but at least there appeared to be a rightful wartime requirement. Some historians claim that such bombing, knowing it would kill numerous women and children, was itself a war crime. But it was different – it was combat. German fighters and anti-aircraft weapons battled the Allied aircraft. The bombings of German cities were missions carried out *under fire* and 38 per cent of Royal Air Force aircrews were killed in action. A further 11 per cent were wounded or taken prisoner.[14]

Allied war crimes were rarely the result of written orders and were usually committed by maverick soldiers ignoring the rules. Most of the examples in Sean Longden's *To The Victor The Spoils* are of this type. Even the Bascari massacre where Sergeant Horace West of the US 180th Infantry Regiment murdered thirty-seven Italian and German POWs falls into this category. Additionally, West was court-martialled and sentenced to life imprisonment.[15]

The IMT in Nuremberg is the trial everyone brings to mind when the words 'war crimes trial' are spoken. This was the trial of the most senior Nazis the Allies could round up and whose crimes had no specific geography. But even this was a small sample of those the Allies could have tried. The IMT indicted a mere twenty-four Nazis. In the end, twenty-one took a seat in the dock. German industrialist Gustav Krupp was included in the original indictment, but was too ill to be tried. Head of the German Labour Front, Robert Ley, committed suicide on the eve of the trial. Hitler's deputy, Martin Bormann, could not be found – he was tried *in absentia*.

The IMT did not prosecute the largest group of accused, nor did it take the longest time to prepare, but it captured the contemporary international public interest more than any other trial. And yet in 1945, once the furore caused by visual evidence of atrocities in the concentration camps through the film *Nazi Concentration and Prison Camps* ebbed away, public interest diminished rapidly. The dry nature of a trial by document revealed itself as unworthy of regular news reporting. Public interest reignited only when twelve of the defendants were sentenced to death by hanging. Bormann still could not be found to face the noose and Göring evaded it by committing suicide, but ten were hanged on 16 October 1946. Seven were sent to Spandau Prison to serve various sentences and three men were freed to re-join German society.

The trial generated a 42-volume record, *Trial of The Major War Criminals before the International Military Tribunal*, but this was just the beginning. Even now, there are more books, academic papers and television programmes covering the IMT than any other war crimes trial. This is perhaps rightly so as the IMT practically founded the field of international law. More importantly in the immediate post-war period, it established categories of crimes that could be tried in subsequent Allied courts. Crimes against peace were defined as planning, preparation, initiation or waging of a war of aggression, or a war in violation of international treaties, or participation in a common plan for the accomplishment of such a war. War crimes were described as violations of the laws or customs of war. Such violations would include, but not be limited to, murder, ill-treatment or deportation of the civilian population to slave labour or for any other purpose, murder or ill-treatment of POWs or persons on the seas, killing of hostages, plunder of public or private property, wanton destruction of cities, towns, or villages, or devastation not justified by military necessity. The British had a list of thirty-two acts which it considered to be war crimes.[16] Crimes against humanity were identified as murder, extermination, enslavement, deportation, and other inhumane acts committed against any civilian population, before or during the war, or persecutions on political, racial, or religious grounds whether or not in violation of domestic law of the country where perpetrated. Defendants could also be accused of leading, organizing, instigating or being accomplices in the formulation or execution of a conspiracy to commit these crimes during the years preceding 8 May 1945.

It had been planned that there would be many trials led by the IMT, but several factors precluded it. The trial of the major war criminals took six months to prepare and lasted over ten months. By the time it finished in October 1946, the four major powers had become weary of the process and the definition of 'Allies' had begun to look dubious. Even as the Soviets tried the Nazis for war crimes and crimes against humanity, they were performing similar acts in some of the Eastern European countries they occupied. The French, British and Americans were worried that the validity and legacy of the IMT might be tarnished by further Soviet participation in international trials. Cooperation between the Allies cooled to such an extent that another international trial became an impossibility.

Fortunately, the Allied Control Council had issued Control Council Law No. 10, on 20 December 1945, which empowered any of the occupying authorities to try suspected war criminals in their respective occupation zones.[17] The Americans continued for a further twelve trials in Nuremberg. They intended to arrange trials of the complex Nazi system of inhumanity and to bring some of its most prominent supporters to justice. These twelve later trials became known as the 'Subsequent Nuremberg Trials'. Between 1946 and 1949, 185 high-ranking leaders of German doctors, judges, industrialists and police organizations were indicted. Thirty-five were acquitted and the others received sentences ranging from death to long-term imprisonment.[18] But even these trials brought to justice few of those directly involved in millions of individual atrocities.

The British military courts in Hamburg and other cities, began to sit before the IMT, but did not concern themselves with indictments for crimes against peace and crimes against humanity. The definition of these crimes had kept the Allies spinning their wheels for months. The British were increasingly interested only in war crimes perpetrated against Allied persons. This meant that the British prosecuted no senior Nazi industrialists, scientists or members of the judiciary. Perhaps the most abhorrent feature of Nazism, racist murder, was also not a specific feature of British trials. As the military courts and IMT began their work, the UNWCC faded away. They may have provided dossiers on war criminals to prosecutors, but their major legacy is the volumes of law reports that it compiled, and the record of its institutional history.[19]

For the British trials, the Royal Warrant was adopted on 18 June 1945. It broadly stated that a war crime was 'a violation of the laws and usages of war,' but did not detail the principles of liability or allowable defences. It did not even include specifics of exactly what was a war crime – this came later.[20] The 21st Army Group was renamed the British Army of the Rhine (BAOR) and made responsible for the occupation and administration of the British Zone in north-west Germany. The BAOR established War Crimes Investigation Teams (WCITs) to examine the many accusations of war crimes in the zone and to pursue suspects. Despite limited resources and a constant churn of personnel as men were demobilized, the teams did their best. However, often the evidence they collected after visiting crime scenes, interrogating suspects and deposing witnesses was paper-thin. Once a WCIT closed its investigation, the materials were sent to the British Army DJAG in London where, if justified, a formal accusation was drafted. The case files were then returned to HQ BAOR, which prepared for a trial to be held as near as practicable to the scene of the crime and the location of witnesses.

If the DJAG had all the cases they wanted to try prepared in advance, they would certainly have attempted to establish some case law built up from precedent – the decision of an earlier court could have been binding on a later court deciding a similar case. This would have saved courts from arguing similar points in law and enabled a defendant's counsel to advise their client more safely on defence strategies. The binding force of judicial precedent is possible, however, only when there is good law reporting (where lawyers and judges can read the results of trials) and a settled judicial hierarchy (where judges in lower courts can rely on judgements in higher courts).[21] The British military courts in the Curiohaus trials had neither. There was no central publication of trials to which the court members could refer and there was no hierarchy. The preferred position of being able to refer to decisions in earlier trials regarding culpability, acceptable defences, sentencing and petitioning was unworkable. Sometimes the same presiding judge was appointed to similar trials, but each appears to have been heard in relative legal isolation. It may have been entirely fortuitous, therefore, that one of the earliest trials beginning in October 1945 would establish that the defences of 'operational necessity' and 'following superior orders' could not be made.

The *Peleus* Trial

German submarine *U-852* was given orders to patrol the Indian Ocean and left Kiel on 18 January 1944. Just south of the equator about 480km off the west coast of Africa, at about 7:20pm on 13 March, *U-852* encountered the Greek freighter *Peleus*. Without warning, *U-852* engaged the unescorted steamship, sinking her with two torpedoes. The U-boat captain, Heinz-Wilhelm Eck, would have been expected to use full speed to escape the area rapidly before submerging to avoid detection. The area was known to be in range of Allied land-based aircraft capable of sinking his submarine – four sister submarines had disappeared without a trace here already. But he took a different approach and searched for survivors. About twelve of the thirty-five men on board the *Peleus* had jumped into the sea and were clinging to various rafts and flotsam. Eck took Third Officer Agis Kefalas and a Russian sailor aboard to interrogate. After questioning the men, he returned them to their raft assuring them that the English would pick them up. *U-852* then disappeared into the darkness.

About 1km from the survivors, Eck ordered weapons and hand grenades onto the bridge, mounted a machine gun onto the railings and announced the wreckage was to be destroyed. Second Lieutenant Hans Richard Lenz protested this was illegal as the survivors would also be killed, but he was overruled by his captain and went below. Shockingly, it was the submarine's doctor, Walter Weisspfennig, who opened fire with the machine gun, but it soon jammed. Second Lieutenant August Hoffmann cleared the gun and continued firing, but the rafts were not sinking. So, *U-852* moved closer and, shining its manoeuvring lamp onto the wreckage, hand grenades were dropped. When Seaman Wolfgang Schwender came onto the bridge for his midnight watch, there were still sufficient targets for Eck to order him to fire the machine gun, which he did until it jammed again. Returning to the bridge, and despite his earlier protests, Lenz cleared the stoppage and fired a few bursts himself. After over five hours, Eck ordered his submarine to leave the scene and reassured his crew they had done the right thing. Despite their ordeal, four of the *Peleus* crew survived: Chief Officer Antonios Liossis, Agis Kefalas, Rocco Said and Dimitrios Argyros. After 25 days adrift in two rafts, Kefalas died from his wounds. After 32 days, the remaining three men were picked up by a Portuguese steamer.

U-852 continued its mission, torpedoed a British cargo ship off Capetown on 1 April, rounded the Cape and sailed north, transmitting its position to German headquarters. Its signals, however, were decrypted and on 2 May, two British planes of 621 Squadron RAF dropped depth charges onto the surfaced submarine just off the Cape Guardafui. Eck crash-dived to 130m, but an explosion caused water to reach the submarine's batteries, giving off choking chlorine gas. Forced to the surface, the crew fought off successive attacks from British aircraft, but Eck ran aground at dusk and decided to abandon ship. The crew that went ashore was rounded up by the Somaliland Camel Corps, perhaps the only submariners to be captured by a desert unit. Those who remained to detonate scuttling charges were arrested by the Royal Navy. *U-852*'s log was discovered and the British finally uncovered the story of the *Peleus*.

A British military court convened in the Curiohaus on 17 October 1945 to hear 'The *Peleus* Trial'. This early trial was heard by a panel of seven judges, which is unusual as most courts comprised just four.[22] Two panel members were from the Greek Navy. *U-852* Captain Eck and three of his crew, Weisspfennig, Lenz and Schwender, in full uniform, were charged with 'committing a war crime in that you in the Atlantic Ocean on the night of 13/14 March 1944, when Captain and members of the crew of Unterseeboot 852 which had sunk the steamship *Peleus* in violation of the laws and usages of war were concerned in the killing of members of the crew of the said steamship, Allied nationals, by firing and throwing grenades at them.' This was the form in which all subsequent war crimes charges would be framed. The Judge Advocate immediately had to make it clearly understood that the phrase 'in violation of the laws and usages of war' qualified the words following it ('the killing of members of the crew by firing and grenade') and not the words proceeding it (the sinking of the *Peleus*).[23] In future charges, the phrase would form a clause and be enclosed in commas. All the accused pleaded 'not guilty'.

Before the prosecution could open their case, British barrister Major Lermon, who was acting for Lenz, asked the court for an adjournment. He stated the defence counsellors had been briefed just four days previously. They needed access to German naval documents and time to prepare expert witnesses who had not yet arrived in Hamburg. He also wanted a chance to refer to relevant textbooks, explaining they had received a book on international law only the previous night. Additionally, Lermon explained, the German counsellors needed time to appreciate and prepare for the adversarial nature of an English court. He argued that it would be unfortunate for a court, which might expect to set a precedent and may want to sentence the accused to death, to proceed knowing the defence was unprepared. This lack of time for the defence to prepare was a feature of all too many Curiohaus trials. But there were so many accused to prosecute and the pressure to do so quickly only got stronger over the years of the trials, they had to progress regardless. The prosecutor, Colonel Robert Halse, objected to the defence request, but Judge Advocate Melford Stevenson found a compromise: the prosecution would continue to the end of their case. If by that time the defence witnesses were not in court, the defence application for an adjournment could be renewed. As lack of time was at the heart of the defence problems, Lermon agreed.[24] He may have rued this decision as the prosecution took just one day.

Halse presented the case for the prosecution and read the affidavits of the surviving sailors to the court. Before Halse got to the end of the first affidavit (that of Antonios Liossis), Lermon objected again. The defence did not have a copy of the affidavit. He emphasised that without it, the defence could not follow the reading to see whether the prosecution was being faithful to the document. In addition, defence counsel Todsen, acting for Eck, stated the defence could not make notes about what was said in the affidavit and, as the trial continued, they might forget a point which may be important to the accused.[25] The Judge Advocate suggested Halse skipped this affidavit and read the second, which had also been sworn by Liossis. The third affidavit read by Halse was that of Rocco Said towards the end of which Said related a story told to him by Agis Kefalas before he had died. Lermon objected again, saying the evidence was third-hand. The prosecution relied on regulation 8(i)(*a*) of the Royal Warrant which read, 'If any witness is dead or is unable to attend or to give evidence or is, in the opinion of the Court, unable to attend without undue delay, the Court may receive secondary evidence made by or attributable to such witness'. There was a discussion regarding whether the court had the power to receive such evidence. The Judge Advocate agreed that in a court which was bound by ordinary English law, such evidence could not be admitted, but *this* court could do so if it wished. The court decided to admit the statement which concerned what happened when Kefalas and a Russian seaman had boarded *U-852*.[26]

The prosecution then examined several of the crew of *U-852* whose names were kept out of the record so they could not be reported in the

German press. Each witness told what he had seen of the shooting. Some identified one or more of the shooters, but said it was too dark to see whether men were amongst the wreckage. This was disingenuous as Eck had interrogated two survivors and returned them to the sea, so the crew knew there were men amidst the debris. One crewman gave evidence he had marked the track chart of *U-852* with the place where the *Peleus* was sunk by writing the date over the position. This clinched the question whether it had been this particular submarine which sunk the steamship.[27]

Next Halse examined John Mossop, a solicitor from the Supreme Court and temporarily working at the Admiralty, who read to the court a statement that he had witnessed Lenz make at the London District Cage, the main British interrogation centre for captured German officers. In it Lenz recounted how he had objected to Eck's order to fire on the wreckage, 'I then heard the captain had decided to eliminate all trace of this sinking. I assumed from this that it was intended to kill the survivors.' Mossop also told the court he had spoken to Eck, but Eck had declined to make a statement about the shooting. Eck did, however, want to make a statement about superior orders. He was warned it would be written down and might be used in evidence against him. Nevertheless, he made this sworn statement, 'Neither before sailing or on passage did I at any time receive orders to shoot or otherwise to eliminate survivors from any vessel that my boat might sink.'[28] It seemed while his crew might depend on the defence of superior orders, Eck would rely on a different defence. After half a day, the prosecution rested their case.

The defence counsellors were hard-pushed to complete their case before the court reopened the next day. Professor A Wegner, acting on behalf of all the accused on matters of international law, first spoke about Eck's defence of operational necessity. In his opinion, the captain's order to eliminate wreckage was just that, and should not have been interpreted by Lenz to mean they should fire upon survivors. Second, Wegner thought a defence of superior orders should be allowed, but agreed it should be examined from three points of view: justification, exculpation and mitigation. He also raised the defence that there should be no punishment for an act committed before it was illegal to do so, reminded the court that hearsay evidence should be judged carefully and suggested the men might not have intended to kill the survivors.[29] This final point was important as in English Law, to prove murder, the prosecution must show the accused committed the act (*actus reus* – guilty act) and had the intention to kill or cause grievous bodily harm (*mens rea* – guilty mind). These are no small tasks.

The first defence witness was Eck who was questioned by his counsel, Dr Todsen. He let slip twice that he knew there were survivors amongst the wreckage and yet had given the order to fire on it. Todsen asked, 'Was it not clear to you that through sinking the wreckage and the rafts that you would also sink the survivors?' to which he answered, 'It was clear to me that the possibility of saving their lives disappeared'. The Judge Advocate asked, 'The decision of which you have spoken was a decision to destroy among other things, survivors, was it not?' Eck answered, 'It was clear that through destroying the rafts and wreckage survivors would also die'.[30]

On the third day of the trial, Hoffmann and Weisspfennig were examined by defence counsel Dr Pabst. Both admitted to firing on the wreckage as they were ordered to do so.[31] Lenz gave an extraordinary account of why he had eventually fired the machine gun at the wreckage, having initially opposed the order. He told his defence counsel, Lermon, that he had pushed Schwender aside and taken the gun from him. Asked why, he said, 'I did not want that a man should be hit and killed by bullets which had been fired by a seaman who was in my view a bad character.' It was not the shooting he objected to, but the man firing.[32] Schwender told Pabst he had been ordered to fire on the wreckage, which was clear to him, and he saw no men. Moreover, he would not have fired at human beings if there were any.[33] The fourth day of the trial consisted of closing speeches for the defence and prosecution and a careful summing up by the Judge Advocate. Melford Stevenson explained the shooting of unarmed enemies was forbidden. He said, 'To fire so as to kill helpless survivors of a torpedoed ship is a grave breach against the law of nations. The right to punish persons who break such rules of war has been equally recognized for many years. There is no difficulty or complication about it.' He referred to the *Llandovery Castle* case, tried in Leipzig, where the German court itself found, 'The firing on boats [containing survivors of the sinking] was an offence against the law of nations.' He reminded the judging panel it was their duty to acquit any defendant over which they had a reasonable doubt of guilt.

Melford Stevenson spent some time discussing the two defence pleas. First, on operational necessity, Eck's claim that he wanted to protect his submarine against attack by Allied planes by destroying every trace of *Peleus*. While it was unfortunate survivors died, Eck maintained 'he was under the paramount necessity of protecting the boat and his crew'. The Judge Advocate asked why Eck had not considered the futility of trying to obliterate every trace of wreckage or the oil patch that would have been left. Why had he not instead sped away from the area under the darkness of night? Second, on the defence of following superior orders, Melford Stevenson told the court, 'Members of the armed forces are bound to obey lawful orders only, and that they cannot, therefore, escape liability if in obedience to a command they commit acts which both violate unchallenged rules of warfare and outrage the general sentiment of humanity'. Furthermore, he added, 'is it not fairly obvious to you that if in fact the carrying out of Eck's command involved the killing of these helpless survivors, it was not a lawful command, and that it must have been obvious to the most rudimentary intelligence that it was not a lawful command, and that those who did the shooting are not to be excused for doing it upon the ground of superior orders?'[34]

On 20 October 1945, the court found all five of the accused to be guilty. Eck, Hoffmann and Weisspfennig were sentenced to death by firing squad. Lenz was sentenced to life imprisonment and Schwender to 15 years. This was the first conviction under the Royal Warrant for offence of war crimes in the European theatre.[35] On 11 November 1945, the sentences were all confirmed by BAOR GOC-in-C Field Marshal Sir Bernard Montgomery. While awaiting his execution, Eck was visited in his prison cell by prosecution and defence representatives preparing the case against Grand Admiral Karl Dönitz. After Hitler had committed suicide, on 1 May 1945 Dönitz became the head of the German Reich and set up a government in Flensburg. He was to be tried at the IMT in Nuremberg and the legal staff wanted to clarify whether Eck had received orders from Dönitz sanctioning the shooting of survivors. Eck told them what he had told the British court – the decision had been his alone and Dönitz had nothing to do with it.

Eck, Hoffmann and Weisspfennig's death warrants were signed by Montgomery on 12 November 1945 and they were executed by firing squad on 30 November 1945 at Lüneburg Heath. This was the place where Montgomery had on 4 May 1945 accepted the German high command's unconditional surrender of all German armed forces in Holland, north-west Germany (including all islands),

Schleswig-Holstein and Denmark. It is also the site of *Reichsführer-SS* Heinrich Himmler's unmarked grave. Lenz's life sentence was reduced and he walked free from Werl Prison on 27 August 1952. Schwender was released on 21 December 1951.[36]

The Zyklon B Trial

Zyklon B was the trade name of a cyanide-based pesticide invented in Germany in the early 1920s. It consisted of hydrogen cyanide (prussic acid), a cautionary eye irritant and one of several adsorbents (the surface of which the chemical coats). In the case of pellets, the adsorbent was probably small cubes of calcium sulphate.[37] The supply chain of the pesticide was complex, but the distribution and usage rights for Zyklon B were awarded to two companies one of which was Tesch & Stabenow GmbH (Testa) in Hamburg. It was Testa that supplied the German military and SS.[38]

Initially, Zyklon B was used to fumigate warehouses, ship holds and to delouse clothing, but from 1941 the SS used it to kill people. The gas killed by blocking the cellular production of adenosine triphosphate (ATP). ATP provides energy to drive processes in cells, such as muscle contraction and nerve impulse transmission. Without ATP, heart muscle cells and nerves quickly stop working. Inhalation of 100–300 parts per million of gaseous hydrogen cyanide causes death within 10 to 60 minutes, with death coming more quickly as the concentration increases.[39]

The first Belsen trial in Lüneburg revealed that a huge number of people had been killed in the Auschwitz gas chambers. Here small-scale testing using the gas to kill Soviet and Polish prisoners began in August 1941. Block 11, where the initial tests were conducted, was not suitable for gassing larger numbers, so the SS moved the facility. The crematorium morgue could hold hundreds of prisoners. The first 900 Soviets were gassed there in September 1941. In 1942, two further gas chambers were added in converted farmhouses. Between March and June 1943, four larger custom-built gas chambers and associated crematoria went into operation at Auschwitz-Birkenau – each could gas many hundreds of people at a time. The two former farmhouses were decommissioned, but one returned to its murderous use in 1944.[40] Between 1941 and

1945, Testa supplied Zyklon B *by the ton* to Auschwitz where over a million were murdered using it.[41]

Initially, the British had been content to try those who participated in the gassings or selecting people to be killed. A former Testa employee, however, revealed he had seen evidence senior personnel in the company where he was previously employed were aware their product was being used to kill innocent people in concentration camps. Former bookkeeper Emil Sehm wrote twice to the British authorities in the summer of 1945. Part of his second letter read:

> Dr TESCH reported about an invitation he received to a conference at the OKW BERLIN. He stated to which members he was introduced and in which way and form. About the subject of the conference he wrote that the speaker explained that the execution of the Jews by shooting has developed in a mass execution and furthermore it is very unhygienic. Dr TESCH was asked to submit any suggestion, whether and how Jews could be exterminated by using hydrocyanic acid. Afterwards technical points about the application of hydrocyanic acid were discussed and amongst other suggestions one way was suggested that all Jews detailed for extermination should be taken into a barracks previously prepared (gas-tight). During the night, a trained man (using a respirator) should enter the barracks and place hydrocyanic acid plates in the rooms. In future, instead of getting buried, dead bodies will be cremated. Dr TESCH offered himself to SS men who will be selected by the OKW and put at his disposal to train on courses for this purpose (using hydrocyanic acid).[42]

Number Two War Crimes Investigation Team (2WCIT) detained Dr Bruno Tesch, the sole proprietor of the firm in September 1945. Together with Sehm, 2WCIT raided Testa's offices. They found the file room had been burned out in March 1945. As only this room had been damaged and it was in the centre of the building, the team was sceptical that it alone had been destroyed in an air raid. Amongst the remains of many burnt papers, they could not find the travel report referred to by Sehm. Under interrogation by Major Anton Walter Freud, Tesch admitted being an NSDAP member since 1933 and accepted he had been a 'supporting member of the SS', but denied any suggestion he had been aware the SS used his product to kill people. Sehm's statement was not sufficient grounds to hold Tesch and Freud was forced to release him. Convinced Tesch knew what he had done and was a war criminal, however, Freud and his team lobbied the British high command to let them continue investigating. In October 1945, Tesch was re-arrested and held for questioning. Karl Weinbacher, Tesch's deputy in complete charge of the company during his frequent business trips, and Dr Joachim Drosihn, the firm's chief gassing technician, were also detained. The prosecution built a case to test the principle that commercial transactions conducted by civilians who knowingly contribute to war crimes will expose the civilians themselves to being charged with a war crime.

On 1 March 1946, the 'Zyklon B Trial' opened in the Curiohaus.[43] Tesch, Weinbacher and Drosihn were accused of committing a war crime by 'putting the means to commit the crime [mass extermination of Allied civilian nationals] into the hands of those who actually carried it out'.[44] This violated Article 46 of the Hague Regulations of 1907, which the German and British governments had signed. This article specifically stated the lives of persons in occupied countries must be respected.[45]

The prosecuting counsel, Major Gerald Draper, decided that he had to prove three points. First, show that Zyklon B gas was used in concentration camps to kill people. Second, convince the court that the quantity of the gas supplied, particularly to Auschwitz, was out of all proportion to the requirements for clothing disinfection and increased in proportion to the killing in the camp. Third, show Tesch knew (and by association Weinbacher and Drosihn must also have known) Zyklon B was used to murder people in gas chambers.

On day two of the trial, Draper called Wilhelm Bahr, a former SS Sergeant at the Neuengamme concentration camp. In 1942, Bahr attended a three-day course run by Tesch on the use of Zyklon B, presumably as a pesticide. There was no mention of Tesch suggesting the gas could be used to kill people, but Bahr had been warned it was deadly. He said the gas was used in two chambers in the camp for delousing clothes. He also confessed he had used a 200g tin of the gas pellets to kill twenty Russian prisoners. Emphasising he was under orders, he had locked the men in a bunker, poured in the gas pellets and then gone to lunch.[46] Bahr was tried later in March 1946 for his activities in Neuengamme, sentenced to death and hanged on 8 October.

Draper called Dr Charles Bendel a Romanian doctor deported to Auschwitz in December 1943. He was transferred from the main camp to Auschwitz-Birkenau at the end of February 1944 and worked there as a doctor in a crematorium next to the gas chambers. Bendel had already given evidence of murderous daily occurrences there to the first Belsen trial in 1945. In the Curiohaus, he repeated his evidence that while he was in Auschwitz-Birkenau about a million people had been gassed using Zyklon B. He estimated 1,000g (two medium-sized tins each holding 500g) were used to kill 1,000 people. From this, Draper extrapolated that a tonne of Zyklon B (1,000,000g) was sufficient to kill a million people. A summary of Exhibits HG and HH showed that Testa had supplied over 7 tonnes of Zyklon B to Auschwitz in 1942 and over 12 tonnes in 1943 – more than enough to kill everyone murdered there during the camp's existence and to fumigate all their clothes. But the point was did Tesch, Weinbacher and Drosihn know?

Sehm was questioned by Draper and asked to tell the court, as accurately as he could, what he had read in the 1942 Tesch travel report. He quoted, ' . . . the shooting of Jews is growing more and more frequent and the burial of the great number is proving to be more and more unhygienic. To change this it is proposed that the extermination of the Jews should be done now through the effects of prussic acid. Dr Tesch is asked to give concerning this idea some propositions.' He added that Tesch, 'proposed to use prussic acid just as it is used for the extermination of vermin, to use it now for the above-mentioned purpose'. In addition, Sehm said the report contained the following sentence, 'I, Dr Tesch, take now those orders or propositions to train SS personnel in the proceedings concerning prussic acid gas'.[47] Sehm confirmed that he had written down the details of the report and showed the note to his friends Kate and Wilhelm Pook who suggested he should burn it. In 1942, in their opinion, it was too dangerous to be caught with such a document. Sehm tore the note into pieces and burnt it in his friend's ashtray.[48] With evidence this thin on the ground, Draper knew he needed more to convince the court. He had to satisfy the panel members that the note existed and contained the wording claimed by Sehm.

Erna Biagini, a Testa shorthand typist, confirmed she had worked on a document regarding Zyklon B that read, ' . . . it might be used for human beings as well'. Anna Ünzelmann, a typist and clerk, testified the travel report had been dictated to her. After Tesch had finished dictating she said, 'I took the papers on which I had taken the dictation and wanted to leave the room and he spoke a few words to me inasmuch as he said to me that our Zyklon B had been used for the killing of human beings'.[49]

In their defence testimonies, Tesch, Weinbacher and Drosihn denied all knowledge that the products they supplied had been used to kill people. Dr Zippel, Tesch's defence counsel, argued that the labels on the tins of Zyklon B found in Auschwitz were not contemporary with the ones being used by Testa in 1942 and 1943, and other agents may have supplied the cans. But this was contrary to the evidence in Testa's control books, which revealed the tonnage of Zyklon B that it had supplied to Auschwitz and other concentration camps.[50]

The Judge Advocate, barrister C L Stirling, carefully guided the court. He said that he thought the strength of the prosecution's case rested on whether it had been shown that senior Testa managers were the kind of men who would have known 'every little thing' about the business. He suggested they were. He asked whether such men would have known the huge deliveries of Zyklon B to Auschwitz were far more than needed for delousing and concluded they would. Tesch and Weinbacher were found guilty and hanged on 16 May 1946. Regarding Drosihn, Stirling stated the general evidence suggested he had no say in the supply of Zyklon B. The strong implication was that Drosihn was blameless in this matter and he was acquitted.[51]

2

TRIALS FOR MURDERING CAPTURED BRITISH SOLDIERS

In battle, when a man throws up his hands in capitulation, it is not surprising that occasionally he's shot by an enemy whose blood is running hot. Similarly, immediately after combat, surrendering troops who moments earlier had been killing their foes' comrades have suffered the same fate. Allied and Axis soldiers were both guilty of murdering defeated opponents during the war. But only the Axis powers and the Soviets ordered the killing of captured enemy troops on a massive scale, far from the battlefield and long after combat had ended.

Soldiers on all sides should have been given some protection from the 1899 Hague Convention signed by Germany. Declaration II, *Laws and Customs of War on Land*, contained many articles relating to the treatment of surrendered belligerents and POWs. It broadly stated they must be handled with mercy.[1] Further safeguards should have been afforded by the Geneva Conventions, four treaties and three additional protocols, some of which were established before WW2. The 1929 conference in Geneva led to the adoption of a *Convention relative to the Treatment of Prisoners of War* by many countries, including Germany and most Allied states. Article 2 of the Convention states, 'Prisoners of war are in the power of the hostile Government, but not of the individuals or formation which captured them. They shall at all times be humanely treated and protected, particularly against acts of violence, from insults and from public curiosity. Measures of reprisal against them are forbidden.' The Soviet Union was not a signatory to the Convention, but Germany was and this should have protected Soviet troops from the barbaric treatment they received as POWs. It did not, nor did it always offer protection to captured soldiers from other Allied nations who had signed the Convention.

Le Paradis

In May 1940, German troops began to push west to overrun and occupy Luxembourg, the Netherlands and Belgium. When they continued their offensive through the Ardennes into France, the British Expeditionary Force (BEF) was sent to meet the onslaught. The Germans fought ferociously and gradually pushed the British back towards the sea. The BEF eventually found itself in a U-shaped pocket as the Germans flanked, attacking from north, south and east. The only escape was by sea at the port of Dunkirk. Between 26 May and 4 June 1946, over 338,000 troops were evacuated from the harbour and beach in Operation DYNAMO. The success of the operation was partly made possible by troops staying behind to fight the Germans and keep the retreat corridor open. Some of these soldiers were the men of the 2nd Battalion Royal Norfolk Regiment and 1st Battalion Royal Scots.

The Norfolks along with the 8th Lancashire Fusiliers were ordered to hold a line at the villages of Riez du Vinage, Le Cornet Malo and Le Paradis. On 27 May 1940, troops from the German 3rd Company 1st Battalion 2nd *SS Totenkopf* Rifle Regiment engaged the Norfolks at Le Cornet Malo and pushed them back to their company headquarters at Cornet Farm. Here they dug in with the Royal Scots around the farmhouse on the Rue de Paradis, which was soon destroyed by a combination of German mortar, tank and artillery fire. The men fell back to a cowshed where they fought until they ran out of ammunition and were ordered to surrender. In 1940, the murderous reputation of SS divisions was not well known and the British troops did not realize that after fighting them, surrender was perilous.

After some brutal treatment where some lost teeth, the ninety-nine British POWs were marched along the Rue de Paradis, through a small gate and into a meadow.[2] Alongside a brick barn on the Creton Farm, they were fired on by two SS machine guns. Those not immediately killed were finished off by bayonets, rifle butts and more bullets. Remarkably, there were two survivors, William O'Callaghan and Albert Pooley. They had quickly dived for cover and then been shielded by the bodies of their friends. Although injured, later in the evening they made their escape. After four days, however, they were forced to surrender to a regular German army unit. They spent the rest of the war in a succession of POW camps and, in Pooley's case, hospitals. Pooley's wounds were so bad that he was repatriated in October 1943. While in convalescence, he reported the shooting, but was not believed by the investigating officers. O'Callaghan too reported the murders in a form he completed when he returned to England in 1945. But the form was lost and has never been seen again.

The shooting was first investigated by a Supreme Headquarters Allied Expeditionary Force (SHAEF) court of inquiry ordered to look into the crime in March 1945. Led by Lieutenant Colonel J H Boraston, the court visited the Creton Farm and sketched the area. A week later, the court convened at the Hotel Royal in Lille to hear witnesses.[3] Simone and Georges Brams told the court they had seen about 100 British soldiers machine-gunned in the meadow by the farm. Monsieur Brams said the officer in charge had two 'pips' on his shoulder, but he doubted he would recognize the German soldier again. The Mayor of Lestrem, Desire Leleu, told the court that ninety-seven bodies had been exhumed from the site of the massacre in 1942 and reburied in the graveyard of Le Paradis church. Several witnesses were heard who testified to the state of the British bodies upon exhumation including that some were bound and had fractured skulls. Witness Eugene Lecomte told the court there were two survivors, although he didn't know their names, which came as a surprise to the British who had not known that anyone had escaped the killing. The court of inquiry report was eventually published on 9 May 1945. It listed the dead men and stated they were POWs killed by an unknown division of the SS. It recommended the responsible individuals be tried for murder.

Anyone arrested in the British Zone in occupied Germany and found to have been a member of the *SS Totenkopf* was sent to the London District Cage for interrogation.[4] This is where SS Captain Fritz Knöchlein, commander of No.2 company of the 2nd Regiment of the *SS Totenkopf*, and SS Sergeant Theodore Emke, leader of a machine-gun platoon in No.4 company of the 2nd *SS Totenkopf*, found themselves shortly after the end of the war. Questioned by Lieutenant Colonel Alexander Scotland and others, Emke stated he had not been involved, but he thought Knöchlein had given the order to fire upon the POWs. The British decided to prosecute the more senior man alone. Knöchlein was charged on 28 August 1948 with committing a war crime in that he, 'in the vicinity of Paradis, Pas De Calais, on or about May 27th 1940, in violation of the laws and usages of war, was concerned in the killing of about ninety POWs, members of the 2nd Battalion The Royal Norfolk

Regiment, and other British Units'. He pleaded not guilty and the court was adjourned until Monday 11 October 1948 when it reconvened in Court Five of the Curiohaus.[5]

Pooley was the first witness called by the prosecuting barrister, Field-Fisher. After giving his account of the shooting, he was asked whether he could identify the German officer standing by the gate of the meadow where the murder occurred. Pointing to Knöchlein, he said, 'I think that is the man'.[6] Pooley's identification was less than positive; he felt uncertain about it as the man in the dock was not in uniform. The court accepted a prosecution request that Knöchlein attend court wearing an SS uniform so that Pooley could attempt identification once more. Pooley remembered the man as wearing a German officer's cap with 'silver braid around it'. The type of hat worn by Knöchlein became central to the case against him with two other prosecution witnesses describing the hat in the same way as Pooley. Knöchlein accepted he had such a hat, but said it was in his personal kit, which he did not take into battle.[7]

In the spring of 1946, before there had been any sign there would be a war crimes trial of those responsible for the massacre at Le Paradis, Pooley had returned to the scene and spoken to many witnesses including the Cretons. In hindsight, this may not have been a wise move. Defence counsel Uhde attempted to persuade the court that Pooley had returned to France to 'get his story straight' before making an official statement. Pooley did himself no favours when he said, 'I wanted to see for myself just where it happened, and make sure in my own mind that it was actually a fact and not a dream'.[8] Attempting to further weaken Pooley's credibility, Uhde asked whether he had identified Knöchlein in an impromptu identity parade at the London District Cage. Pooley said he thought he had. Uhde pushed him, 'But were you absolutely certain?', to which Pooley answered, 'Not at that time'.[9]

On the second day, the court heard 'ear-witness' testimony from Mme Romanie Castel. She said that after the fighting had died down, she heard machine-gun fire from the direction of the Creton Farm followed by loud groaning. Later she saw the dead British soldiers. Castel said she was threatened by a German officer whom she identified in court as Knöchlein.[10] This was a weak prosecution attempt to link Knöchlein to the crime and could only identify him as being in the area at the time. Witness Emil Stuerzbecher, of the 2nd *SS Totenkopf*, added a little weight to the prosecution's case. He said in the evening of 27 May

1940 rumours had spread around the regiment that Knöchlein had been responsible for the murder of many British soldiers in retaliation for their use of dum-dum bullets.[11] Stuerzbecher, however, expressed doubt that the dum-dum bullets sent with a report of the incident to senior German command were genuine.[12]

The question of whether the British had used dum-dum bullets during the battle for Le Paradis came up several times during the trial. It was never fully explored, but as Judge Advocate Honig explained, trying to justify breaking conventions by claiming the British did so too (the *tu quoque* form of the *ad hominem* fallacy) could not be a defence. In his summing up, he told the court, 'As far as the allegations and counter-allegations concerning the use of irregular methods of warfare by the British are concerned, there is no need for you to worry about this in the least, because whether or not they were used is entirely immaterial'.[13]

Day three of the trial was an important day for the prosecution. Max Schneider, of No.4 company the 2nd *SS Totenkopf*, testified he saw the British prisoners being shot and Knöchlein was in command. He had assumed there had been a court martial before the shooting, but there was no evidence of this. Crucially, he told the court twice that Knöchlein had given the order to fire.[14] Shortly after this evidence, Pooley returned to the court. Four men in SS uniform were escorted into the court individually and Pooley wrote down the one he recognized as being the German officer in charge in Le Paradis. Not surprisingly, as he had seen him two days previously in the dock, Pooley identified Knöchlein.[15] Prosecution witness August Leitl added little to the case but did tell Field-Fisher he had not seen any dum-dum ammunition. He believed the large head injuries suffered by some of his German comrades had been caused when the bullets went through their helmets and became flattened. The resulting wounds showed the characteristics of a dum-dum bullet strike, but were not caused by one.

Next to give evidence was Theodore Emke who was lucky not to be on trial himself as it was his machine-gun platoon that fired upon the POWs. In his October 1946 statement at the London District Cage, Emke claimed his platoon commander Petri had usurped his command and he merely stood by while the slaughter took place. He witnessed Knöchlein give the order to fire which was simultaneously relayed to the machine-gunners. He repeated this in court and claimed to have heard Knöchlein shout the order to shoot.[16] Under cross-examination, he was asked whether he was afraid he might be called to answer for the incident, but insisted he was not. Whatever the truth here, it seems the British at the time were content with trying the bigger fish, Knöchlein, and were satisfied justice was best served by using Emke as a prosecution witness. This technique was also used in other trials.

On 15 October 1948, O'Callaghan was in the Curiohaus to give evidence. He gave the court roughly the same account of the shooting as Pooley. He supported Pooley's testimony that Knöchlein had worn a peaked cap on the day of the murders.[17] Hoping for a more reliable recognition of Knöchlein, as he had not seen him previously in court, Field-Fisher took O'Callaghan through the identification process which had been used for Pooley on the 13th. O'Callaghan identified Knöchlein as the German officer who appeared to be in command.[18] The Judge Advocate revealed, however, that O'Callaghan had by chance passed Knöchlein on the stairs outside the courtroom before giving evidence. As Knöchlein was under guard, perhaps in handcuffs, the defence alleged it was not surprising he was later able to identify the defendant in court. In an anxious attempt to get a solid identification, the Judge Advocate asked O'Callaghan, 'Quite apart from what this man may or may not have done are you certain that you saw him on that day?' O'Callaghan answered, 'I am almost certain he is the man who stood just inside the gate'.[19]

The prosecution exhibits included documents from US legal representatives. These contained a photostat copy of a translated covering letter from German General Staff XV1 Army Corps to Sixth Army HQ.[20] The contents of the letter established the outrage felt by some in the German military about the atrocity and how their investigation into the murders had been frustrated. Attached to the covering letter was an account by Anti-Gas Officer of General Staff XVI Major Freiherr von Riederer who reported the shooting as a 'summary shooting'.[21] The handwritten corrections to the translated document in The National Archives, however, add a level of uncertainty. It seems the original translation had included the sentence, 'Close examination proved that it was obviously a case of prisoners who had been shot following a standing court decision'. Whereas the hand-corrected version reads, 'Close examination *showed* that it was *apparently* a case of prisoners who had been *shot by way of summary shooting*' and seems to suggest the word '*standrechtlicherschossen*' (summarily shot) had been wrongly translated from the original. Since the original German document is not in the archives, it is impossible to say whether Riederer reported the shooting as following a standing court (court martial) decision or as a summary shooting.

The defence case opened on 18 October 1948 with Knöchlein in the witness box where he denied everything. He claimed he was not present at the shooting and not close enough to give any orders. Under cross-examination, he did admit not knowing whether a court martial had taken place.[22] Field-Fisher was at pains to point out that as a commanding officer, Knöchlein would have known if it had. Knöchlein complained that his treatment at the London District Cage amounted to torture, but his complaint was not upheld. It seems certain, however, that prisoners were treated harshly. They were put on short rations, sleep-deprived and given heavy-duty tasks to carry out. They were probably subjected to stress positions and given work details similar to those used as punishment in the British Army. Whether the line into torture was crossed is debatable.

To find Knöchlein guilty, the court had to believe Emke, the only person who claimed to have seen and heard the order to fire, and trust the identification by Pooley and O'Callaghan. Perhaps both should have raised reasonable doubt. Emke's evidence was constructed to absolve himself of guilt and was obtained in the London District Cage. Despite Pooley and O'Callaghan having seen Knöchlein in London, neither was certain and their identifications in Hamburg were both botched. At 11:30 on 25 October 1948, however, the court found Knöchlein guilty and a few hours later sentenced him to death by hanging.

In his case review letter to GOC-in-C BAOR, Lord Russell of Liverpool from the DJAG outlined three other pieces of circumstantial evidence he found important, but now appear to be weak. Hearsay evidence of Knöchlein's 'great excitement' at the capture of the British soldiers, hearsay evidence of a 'heated interview' between Knöchlein and his battalion commander on the adverse effect the murders may have on his military advancement and hearsay evidence of a deceased officer who considered the treatment of the POWs to be dishonourable.[23] The sentence was confirmed and Knöchlein was executed on 21 January 1949.

Heavy Water Raids

In 1942, Chief of Combined Operations Lord Louis Mountbatten formed the amphibious Small Scale Raiding Force (SSRF), also called

No.62 Commando. The force would strike the enemy in small, specialised groups on raids that would be difficult to anticipate or defend against. Commando units had first been organized in June 1940 when British military moralc was at a low point following thc cvacuations at Dunkirk. Based upon the tactics of the Boer commandos that the British had faced at the end of the nineteenth century, British commandos would attack German forces in occupied Europe with a 'hit and run' policy.

To help prepare for a large-scale amphibious assault, the Allies desperately needed intelligence on the state of German defences along the French coast, the effectiveness of enemy equipment and the morale of German troops. On 3 October 1942, the SSRF attacked the island of Sark in the Channel Islands. The main purpose of Operation BASALT was to bring German prisoners back to the UK for interrogation. A twelve-strong commando team landed on Sark at night, taking five German soldiers prisoner from a hotel where they slept. In the scuffle to detain them, two ran off to raise the alarm. The commandos, determined to achieve their aim, tied the hands of at least one of their remaining captives. One still managed to escape and a third was shot at close quarters. A single German soldier was taken back for interrogation.

Hitler wanted a way to fight back at this new tactic. Feigning fury at the small-scale breach of the Geneva Conventions, the alleged shooting of a bound POW by British troops, he issued the secret Commando Order (*Kommandobefehl*) on 18 October 1942. It instructed his military that commandos were, 'to be annihilated to the last man'. Even though the Germans had practically invented contemporary commando raids with their glider-borne attack on the Belgian fort of Ében-Émael in 1940 and they knew the Commando Order was in breach of the Geneva Conventions, the order went out.[24] Army Chief of Staff Alfred Jodl distributed copies with an appendix stating the order was, 'intended for commanders only and must not under any circumstances fall into enemy hands'.[25]

Spurred on by the mission success of Operation MUSKETOON in September 1942, which closed the German-held Norwegian power plant at Glomfjord for the rest of the war, a commando raid was planned on the Vemork hydroelectric power plant close to the town of Rjukan.[26] But this time it was not the ability to produce electricity that the British wanted to curtail.

German scientists needed a 'moderator' to slow down the movement of neutrons in their primitive nuclear reactors so that they were more likely to react with fissile uranium-235 and produce energy. They had almost exclusive access to the ore containing the 235 isotope of uranium, what they desperately needed was a moderator. Two were available: graphite and heavy water. The German scientists preferred heavy water and craved as much as could be manufactured. The Norwegian Vemork plant, which the Nazis controlled, produced several litres a day.

Similar nuclear experimentation was also happening in other countries and the British feared the Germans might achieve a breakthrough allowing them to engineer a devastating 'atomic' bomb before the Allies. The facility producing heavy water in Norway had to be destroyed so the Nazis could not make weapons of mass destruction and win the war and it had to be done quickly. Bombing was considered, but the site was difficult to hit with precision by high-altitude bombing raids as it was built on a ridge enclosed by steep mountains. The storage containers, deep underground, were unlikely to be damaged by bombs anyway. The risk to Norwegian civilian lives was also considered too great. Commando raids were the answer.

Infiltration of a force by submarine, as had been done for MUSKETOON, was not an option as Vemork was about 130km inland from the Norwegian coast. Three methods of attack were considered instead: flying boat, parachute and glider. A Catalina flying boat could have landed a force of twenty-five commandos on a lake above the plant, but by the time the plan was ready, the lakes were frozen for the winter. Parachute attack had too many disadvantages – paratroopers often found themselves scattered over many kilometres and unable to join up with their comrades. Parachuting onto thickly wooded mountain slopes was also not relished. The biggest problem with a parachute drop, however, was being seen by the enemy. This left the final option and so Operation FRESHMAN became the first British airborne glider raid. Two Halifax bombers would each tow a Horsa Mark 1 glider flown by men from No.38 Group RAF and the Glider Pilot Regiment. The gliders would be filled with Royal Engineers from the 9th (Airborne) Field Company and the 261st (Airborne) Field Company carrying sufficient explosives to close the Vemork plant for good.

The gliders were to be guided in to land by ground-based Norwegian SOE agents who had parachuted in a month before as Operation GROUSE.[27] These experienced men had already faced trouble surviving the harsh Norwegian winter on a high, snow-covered plain called the Hardanger, and they realized the men in the gliders were in for a tough time.[28] The plan was for the commandos to attack the plant at Vemork, remove their battledress under which they wore civilian clothing, ditch everything connecting them to the British Army (including weapons) and escape as best they could to neutral Sweden. The GROUSE Norwegians would have known this to be suicide. Attempting to cross hundreds of kilometres in polar conditions, without specific training, proper clothing, shelter, rations and especially skis was a ludicrous proposal. None of the commandos spoke Norwegian or Swedish and there were other problems.

Three formerly 'MOST SECRET' documents in The National Archives tell an alarming story about the preparation for FRESHMAN. On 29 October 1942, Mountbatten wrote to Air Marshal A S Barratt, Air Officer Commanding-in-Chief, Army Co-operation Command, emphasising the urgency of attacking Vemork. Furthermore, Mountbatten stressed the operation must take place, 'during the November moon period' of 1942.[29] Perhaps unknown to him, this would be when the weather on the plateau would be at its worst.

In a letter from Barratt to Mountbatten dated 31 January 1943, he explained that 38 Group RAF were equipped with Whitley planes which could not tow a Horsa glider and so they had been provided with three Halifax bombers. However, 'the state of serviceability of the three Halifaxes provided was exceedingly low'. Only two could be sufficiently repaired for the operation. He also pointed out that his crews were not fully trained to operate Halifaxes. Had it not been for the extreme importance of the operation, Barratt would have tried to veto it.[30]

Barratt's letter contained a report by Group Captain Norman commanding 38 Wing RAF. The report stated that the Halifax aircrews managed to get only nine and a half hours of flight training over the minimum 50 hours due to 'difficulties of serviceability'. Although both aircraft carried first and second pilots, the first pilot alone was considered competent to tow gliders at night.[31] Norman explained the Halifaxes had to be fitted with Rebecca airborne transceiver and antenna for which the maintenance crews had no technical instructions inferring that the equipment may not have been properly installed. The Rebecca/ Eureka transponding radar was a short-range radio navigation system comprising two parts: the Rebecca airborne transceiver with antenna and the Eureka ground-based transponder (activated by the GROUSE Norwegians).[32] The correct functioning of this equipment was vital to navigating the Halifaxes to the correct glider landing zone.

Despite these problems, around 6pm on the evening of Thursday 19 November 1942, the planes took off from RAF Skitten at the northern tip of East Scotland.[33] The men of GROUSE were ready to mark the dropping area with a triangle of red lights and guide the aircraft into the area with Eureka. The first Halifax-Horsa combination made brief contact with the Norwegians, but hit bad weather and lost it again. Unable to find their landing zone, reluctantly, they turned for home. While still over Norway, the towing rope for glider DP349 broke and it crashed into the mountains around Fyljesdalen overlooking Lysefjorden east of Stavanger. Eight of the seventeen men on board were killed outright, the remaining nine men were all injured, four severely. The towing Halifax just made it home. The second tug-glider group fared even worse. Having never contacted the ground-based Eureka, they also apparently turned for home. Either the tow plane released the glider or its tow rope also broke and glider HS114 crash-landed in the mountains between Helleland and Bjerkreim. Three men were killed and the surviving fourteen were injured to varying degrees. Their towing Halifax crashed into a mountain at Hestadfjell, killing the whole crew instantly.

The survivors of glider HS114 surrendered to the Germans and were taken to the Slettebø camp near Egersund. An over-enthusiastic interpretation of the *Kommandobefehl* resulted in them being shot almost immediately without prior interrogation. Their bodies and those of the dead from the glider were taken to the dunes at Brusand and thrown into a hastily-dug trench. In July 1945, Royal Engineers from the 1st Parachute Squadron exhumed the bodies and reinterred them with full military honours in the Eiganes churchyard near Stavanger.[34]

The Trial of Behren

Following the liberation of Norway, several suspects for the murder of the men of glider HS114 were sought by war crimes investigators. The German doctor who had examined the injured soldiers was Staff Surgeon Günther and the firing squad that shot the men appeared to have been commanded by Corporal Wagner, but neither could be found. Further statements from German prisoners showed Captain Walther Schrottberger had given the order to shoot the prisoners, but he too was missing. Preparation for the trial of Paul von Falkenhorst (former commander-in-chief of the German armed forces in Norway) revealed

Colonel Erwin Werner Probst had given orders that the Commando Order must be followed and the Royal Engineers handed over to the SD (*Sicherheitsdienst*). Before this could be put to Probst, however, he died of heart failure.[35] Probst's senior, Lieutenant General Karl Maria von Behren, the commanding officer of the 280th Infantry Division at Stavanger, however, was in custody.

His trial by the British began at the Curiohaus on 28 May 1946 presided over by Major General N A Coxwell-Rogers of the Royal Engineers which was perhaps fitting, but hardly impartial.[36] Behren was charged with committing a war crime in that in Norway on or about 20 November 1942, in violation of the laws and usages of war, he was concerned in the killing of fourteen unidentified British POWs at Slettebø. He pleaded not guilty. The prosecution was keen to clarify the men of glider HS114 were in uniform and so should have been treated as POWs. The men had specifically worn battledress so the Germans would be in no doubt this was an Allied military attack. If the Germans had suspected a local operation, there was a risk of severe reprisals against the people in the area. Each commando had worn the usual khaki battledress with civilian clothes beneath (to be worn during the proposed escape to Sweden).

Norwegian witness Trond Hovland, a 40-year-old *lensman* from Helleland, testified that the soldiers wore khaki trousers with a long pocket, khaki shirts and caps.[37] He remembered one cap having initials, 'I noticed that one of the Englishmen had a metal cap-mark with the initials of R.F. or R.E.'.[38] A second witness, nurse Guinevere Benestad, went to the crash site to offer medical assistance. She was able to corroborate Hovland and say the men were all dressed alike in uniform.[39] Farmer Kristoffer Varden testified to having seen bodies buried in Brusand.[40]

When Behren took the stand he was asked in detail about the Commando Order. Wriggling, he suggested the words of the order could be interpreted loosely. He said he had called a meeting of his officers where he instructed them to kill in battle the sort of men mentioned in the order. If they took prisoners, they were to be handed to the SD. After doing so, he claimed, he did not know what the security services would do with such prisoners.[41] But the men had not been handed over to the SD and so Behren had not followed the order to the letter. The morning after the murders, Behren claimed he could not believe Probst's report that the men had been shot and he stated there should be an investigation. Judge Advocate Barnett asked, 'Was an investigation made into the case?', whereupon Behren squirmed again. He answered,

'Colonel Probst answered and said we had to wait for a report about the facts first and I said, "All right, but see to it that this report comes into our possession."' Barnett enquired whether the report actually did come into his possession and Behren answered, 'No'.[42] His claim to have been overburdened with work may have been true, but the real reason Behren never ordered any kind of inquiry was that he feared arrest by the SD for not following the Commando Order. Proof of this is Behren's reaction on the evening of 20 November 1942 when SS Lieutenant Colonel Friedrich Wilkens, the Stavanger SD commander, came to see him. When Wilkens told Behren he had been down to Egersund to interrogate the captured British prisoners only to find they had been taken out and shot, Behren said he was very frightened – the SD knew he had not followed the order.[43]

After less than half an hour of deliberation, the court found Behren not guilty and he was acquitted. This is odd because he had admitted to passing on an order which caused a war crime to be committed. Many others were convicted and even hanged on flimsier evidence. We do not know the deliberations the judges made or why they decided Behren was not guilty, but perhaps we can guess. At a time when opinion was turning against war crimes trials, a guilty verdict may have forced the hand of the British. Justice would have demanded that all senior German officers suspected of passing on the Commando Order be prosecuted, which would have significantly increased the required number of trials when the establishment favoured a reduction.

The Trial of Seeling, Hoffmann and Feuerlein

There was no justice for the fourteen British commandos of glider HS114, but what of the men in glider DP349? Nine had survived the impact, all were injured, but three managed to stagger through the snow to a house in Fyljesdalen. Martin Fylgjesdal explained in his statement after returning from work:

> Three slightly wounded English soldiers were in my home. The others were in the glider. Later in the evening a Norwegian Doctor Bjonness, Leif Espedal, and a policeman from Stavanger arrived. We all went up to the glider. The glider was very badly damaged except the cabin where

> I observed three seriously wounded Englishmen and eight dead ones. The wounded ones were brought to my house where they were looked after by the doctor. The Englishmen were dressed in khaki and under their uniforms they wore white ski-dress.[44]

The Norwegian rescuers could not keep the crash secret from the Germans and, the day after, nine survivors were arrested. The Stavanger Gestapo initially held them all in prison. Statements by Dr Finn Bjonness, Leif Espedal and Norwegian Civil Air Defence worker Sigmund Stangeland all confirmed the British men were wearing military uniforms and so should have been protected by the Geneva Conventions. Rather than being treated as POWs, however, the five fittest men, Frank Blackburn, Frank Bonner, Wallis Jackson, Wilfred Walsh and William White, all sappers from 9th Airborne, were transferred to the police detention camp at Grini near Oslo.

Four injured men remained in the prison for interrogation. Their wounds were partly described in a statement by Dr Bjonness. He said, 'One of them was so badly wounded that I feared for his life. I suppose he had got an internal haemorrhage. One very big man had his arm out of joint and some ribs broken. The third had one arm broken and broken ribs.'[45] It is probably safe to infer from this the fourth man was similarly wounded. What had happened to the four men, Corporal James Cairncross, Driver Peter Farrell, Lance-Corporal Trevor Masters and Sapper Eric Smith (also from the 9th Airborne)[46] was publicly unknown until a British military court was convened in the Oslo Law Courts on 10 December 1945.[47] Unfortunately, a full transcript of this trial is not available. One was almost certainly made for the court as there were three shorthand staff taking notes and four interpreters, but their records were never formalized and so there is no transcript in the archives. This is true of many war crimes trials. It probably reveals an absence of sufficient personnel rather than a lack of enthusiasm.

Luftwaffe Captain Dr Werner Seeling, SS Battalion Sergeant Major Erich Hoffmann, a driver for the Gestapo, and SS Sergeant Fritz Feuerlein, a gaoler, were charged in that they at Stavanger, on days unknown in or about November 1942, in violation of the laws and usages of war, were concerned with the killing of four unidentified British POWs. All pleaded not guilty.[48] Two others had been sought in connection with the killing: SS Sergeant Max Sachse, a former prison guard, and SS 2nd

Lieutenant Luitpold Kuhn, a former Gestapo detective superintendent, but they were not in custody. Not knowing whether the other accused men would ever be found, the British went ahead with the Oslo trial without them.

Each of the accused gave a different account both in pretrial statements and in court – all were keen to absolve themselves. The court heard the injured British men were taken to Gestapo headquarters where SS Lieutenant Colonel Friedrich Wilkens, the Stavanger SD commander, gave an order that, after interrogation, the men were to be executed according to the Commando Order. But Wilkens's men refused to shoot seriously injured men. In an attempt to declare the men fit to be shot, Wilkens ordered them to be examined by Seeling who claimed to have told him they required hospital treatment. Wilkens had no authority over Seeling and the doctor could have seen to it that the men went to a hospital. Instead, he did nothing. About a day later, Wilkens sent for Seeling again and told him the men were to be shot as saboteurs. Seeling protested and so it was suggested the prisoners be poisoned. Once more, Seeling said he protested. Wilkens was never captured and may have been killed in Norway, so he was not available to comment on Seeling's story who claimed he had injected all four men with morphine to relieve the pain of their injuries and that he regretted being unable to save them.

Seeling graphically described the torture of one injured man. He told his defence lawyer, Captain L Irving, 'Then I saw the second injured man lying in the second room. He was lying on his stomach. There was a noose around his neck. Two or three men were standing around; one was standing at his head and had a string in his hand . . . He pulled up the body and just let it down again and pulled the body up again. I was frightened when I saw that.' The doctor also told the court that he had seen Hoffmann step on the throat of an injured soldier with the entire weight of his body and 'where the Adam's apple is to be seen it was all squashed'. He continued to tell the court that, out of disgust, he had tried 'to feel for it with my foot, but it was only a matter of seconds'. Astonishingly, the doctor maintained that he had examined the man's wounds with his foot *while wearing his boot*. But, of course, Seeling had actually confessed to standing on the man's throat himself.

Feuerlein in his statement admitted moving two men to the room where they were killed and, although he knew it was wrong, he made no protest. He further said Seeling, aided by Sachse, had strangled one man with a rope tied to a radiator. Feuerlein admitted putting his foot onto the chest of a man when ordered to do so, which would have been excruciating for a man with rib injuries. He demonstrated to the court how he had seen Seeling inject at least one of the men with air. The Judge Advocate was persuaded Feuerlein was being truthful as he doubted whether a former house painter could have given such an accurate description of air being injected without having seen it.

Hoffmann verified that Seeling had stood on the throat of one man. He claimed SS 2nd Lieutenant Otto Petersen shot the fourth trooper. Petersen was dead by this time, having committed suicide in November 1945, and so he could not confirm or deny this accusation. Hoffmann, however, admitted he had also shot at the fourth man, but could not say for sure whether his shot had hit him. Hoffmann may have thought this cleared him, but he had confessed to having the *mens rea* (guilty mind) for murder. Witness Schneider told the court that Hoffmann had admitted to him that both he and Petersen had shot the fourth British soldier in the back of the head.

Whatever had occurred in the prison, the Germans had denied the men proper hospital care, tortured and then murdered them. They loaded the bodies onto a truck, transferred them to a boat on the Stavanger quay, took them out to sea, weighed them down with stone slabs and cast them overboard. The men are commemorated on the Brookwood Memorial in Surrey and with a separate memorial stone in Stavanger.

On 13 December 1945, the court found Seeling and Hoffmann guilty of the charge and sentenced them to death. A firing squad shot Seeling at 9:05am on 10 January 1946 in Akershus, Oslo. Hoffmann was doubly condemned – a Norwegian court had already sentenced him to death for his part in the murder of seven Norwegian patriots. British executioner Albert Pierrepoint hanged him in Hameln Prison on 15 May 1946 at 3:20pm.[49] The British military court also found Feuerlein guilty and sentenced him to life imprisonment, but the British handed him to the Russians to answer for crimes against their countrymen. What happened next to him is unknown.

First Trandum Trial

The fate of the five uninjured sappers not murdered in Stavanger was gradually uncovered by War Crimes Investigation Team E assigned to Norway under the command of Major John Humphries. The British men had eventually been executed by firing squad. On 4 December 1945, a military deputy of the JAG, Brigadier H Shapcott, sent the case of the murder of British POWs at Trandum to the GOC of Norwegian Allied Land Forces. He explained that of the thirty-four accused, the British had twenty men in custody in Norway and were seeking the other fourteen. Shapcott said he saw no reason to delay the trial of the twenty while the British hunted for the others. He inferred the trial should be held in Oslo as soon as possible, but for an unknown reason, the British transferred the case to the Curiohaus.[50]

By the time the trial opened in the Curiohaus Court One, there were fewer names on the list of those accused.[51] The DJAG had decided SD Captain Oskar Hans, who had commanded the firing squad, would be tried separately. Hans Behnke had suffered a mental breakdown and was unfit for trial. Erwin Morio, Rudolf Schubert, Hans Fischbach and Emil Clemens were being tried on other charges in Norway. Wilhelm Esser was not prosecuted, but appeared as a witness in a later trial. This left thirteen to face the charge of committing a war crime for being concerned in the killing of six British POWs, Able Seaman Evans, Lance Corporal Jackson, Sapper Bonner, Sapper Blackburn, Sapper Walsh and Sapper White.[52] It is not clear from the documents in The National Archives, but it seems the trial progressed based largely on statements the accused had given under oath. The proceedings contain no transcript.[53]

The Germans had given the sappers civilian clothes before they were transferred to Grini. Although they kept some military clothing, which may have identified them as soldiers, it became harder for them to prove their entitlement to POW status. Conditions were harsh in the camp, but did not stray into the barbaric inhumanity that was a feature of concentration camps. The men were interrogated by the Gestapo, Luftwaffe and SD. Although there is no evidence they were tortured, these sessions cannot have been friendly. After two months in the camp, the Germans knew most of the details of the mission and had decided the fate of the British men – they prepared a grave in Trandum forest.

The night of 18 January 1945 was freezing with snow on the ground when the Germans loaded the five Royal Engineers and British sailor Evans onto trucks bound and blindfolded. After two bone-chilling hours, the convoy of two cars and two trucks halted in a forest to get permission from the administration to proceed. The prisoners had expected a detention facility where they would face a military commission to be questioned about where they had proposed to lay their explosives in Vemork. But Trandum was not a camp, it was a tank shooting range and an execution site. In total the Germans killed 173 Norwegian, 6 British and 15 Soviet citizens there.[54] The execution squad (*Sonderkommando*) led the British POWs to the edge of the grave while the drivers remained with the convoy. The shooters lined up in two ranks and, on the command '*Achtung*' from Hans, the execution squad shot the POWs and filled the grave.[55] The SD swore to secrecy all those that had taken part under a 'special obligation statement'.[56] Several affidavits mentioned that the British men had been given fur coats to wear to protect them from the freezing night. This was probably a lie to garner some sympathy from the court – nobody mentioned the removal of the coats prior to the shooting and the Oslo Police found no fur coats when the bodies were exhumed.[57]

The Judge Advocate, Sir Shirley Worthington-Evans, ensured the court followed the proper legal procedure for judging whether the thirteen accused were guilty. The court discussed the identities of the six men executed and their missions. They gave much time to establishing that the men were entitled to POW status: they were in uniform and had laid down their arms. The statements of the accused were vital in verifying that the killing was unlawful – none of them mentioned knowledge of any trial before the execution. SD Sergeant Major Josef Schneider said in his statement,

> I and several other members of the Sonderkommando marched off in order to enlarge the grave. Later on, Hans detailed the members of the execution squad to which I was also appointed. Who apart from myself was so detailed I cannot say. Hans then declared to us that only a very short fire order would be given, that is to say that the rifles were to be made ready on a sign from the arm and that we were to fire on a single word of command.[58]

Hermann Bölck and Erich Penning were also clear about being part of the firing squad. Six other men were less forthcoming in their statements, but admitted being present at the grave when the execution took place.[59] Ludwig Bieber explained in his statement he had taken part in five executions, but as he had not joined Hans's execution squad until the summer of 1943, he could not have taken part in this shooting. Alexander Etling, Peter Göttling and Willi Korneffel were drivers in the convoy.

Dr Walter Grimm, on behalf of all the accused, had three lines of defence. First, he argued they all acted under military orders. To strengthen this defence, he noted, 'In 1943, when the execution took place, the accused would have been regarded as innocent by the English law because they acted under orders'.[60] Here he was relying on paragraph 443 of the 1929 British *Manual of Military Law* which explained soldiers who committed violations of the recognized rules of warfare (such as ill-treatment of POWs) under orders to do so were not war criminals and could not, therefore, be punished by the enemy. The British had amended the paragraph in April 1944 so that violation of the rules of warfare under superior orders could be regarded as a war crime. Grimm seemed to have a point.

Second, the execution squad, Grimm explained, had acted under unavoidable necessity and were therefore not responsible for their act. He appeared to have been relying on the defence of duress. For this to be successful, however, Grimm would have to have shown that during the entire act, the firing squad was compelled by threats of death or serious physical injury. The prosecution may have accepted Hans 'had an exceptionally nasty and brutal character' as Grimm claimed, but he had handed out brandy and cigarettes immediately *before* the execution, which probably did not sound to the court like the continued threat of harm.[61] Grimm's third pillar of defence was, as he accepted, the weakest. He argued the shooters had not known their action to be a war crime. But none of the accused knew for sure whether there had been a trial and conviction of those they executed, so they could not have been sure the shootings were legal.

On 26 August 1946, the court found Josef Schneider, Hermann Bölck, Erich Penning and six others guilty and sentenced them all to 14 years in prison.[62] They acquitted Bieber, Etling, Göttling and Korneffel. In November of the same year, a BAOR review accepted the firing squad may not have known the British men were POWs and determined the prosecution had failed to prove that no trial had taken place before the men were shot. It recommended the findings of the trial and the sentences should not be confirmed.[63] After a reduction of the sentence to 10 years, the British released all the guilty men from Werl Prison between December 1951 and February 1952.

Second Trandum Trial

Perhaps there was justice for the commandos and Able Seaman Evans when the SD officer in charge of the Trandum execution squad appeared in court? Oskar Hans was first tried in Norway for killing 312 Norwegians of whom 68 were executed without trial. In January 1947, a *Lagmannsrett* court found him guilty and sentenced him to death. The Norwegian Supreme Court, however, reviewed the case later that year and found Hans may have believed the executions to be lawful. Based on this, they quashed his conviction and released him.[64] It looked like Hans might get away with his crimes, but he did not escape the British. Rearrested, they tried him in the Curiohaus Court Three for murdering the British men in Trandum forest.[65]

Prosecutor Olson, in his opening speech on 18 August 1948, clarified that he sought to show the men killed were wearing uniforms and should have been treated as POWs upon capture. The first Trandum trial, held two years earlier, had provided ample evidence both the commandos and sailor were in uniform when captured. Additionally, Trond Hovland's sworn statement of 26 June 1945 had even mentioned a man from the crashed glider had a cap badge with the letters RF.[66] It was probably RE (Royal Engineers), but Hovland can be forgiven for this slight mistake. Olson's larger goal, however, was to prove the Germans had not tried the British men before execution. He said, '

> . . . the Hague Convention provides in the clearest terms that anyone who falls alive into the hands of the enemy is not to be punished in any way, let alone killed, for any offence, unless before he is killed or punished, he has a proper and fair trial. That is a right which, under the provisions of the Hague Convention, even a spy is entitled to, and I anticipate that the one thing that will be abundantly clear in this case is that there was no sort of trial and no sort of investigation before these six members of the British forces were taken out and shot at Trandum.[67]

Wilhelm Esser, who was present at the execution but not tried, was questioned in court by Olson. He told the prosecutor he had interrogated the British men, taken statements and issued a report, but he had heard nothing about a trial. Had there been a trial, of course, the interrogating officer would have been called to give evidence. This was powerful proof of its absence. It was reinforced when Hans took the stand to be questioned by his defence counsel, Dr Schoen. He told Schoen the British men 'had been sentenced for sabotage and espionage, and were sentenced to death by shooting. The sentence had been confirmed, the petition had been refused and the execution by shooting had to be carried out the following day . . . '[68] But by mentioning sentencing and nothing else, Hans had given the game away. There never was a trial, the petition was a sham and the execution was a war crime.

In his summing up, Schoen accepted the men from FRESHMAN were in uniform when captured. He argued, however, that since the evidence in the case was so similar to Hans's Norwegian trial where his conviction had been quashed, the British court should also find him not guilty (as he had pleaded). In particular, since Hans had claimed to think the executions had been legal, the Norwegian court had found reasonable doubt he had the *mens rea* for murder. Olsen rejected this, telling the court there was no evidence of a trial prior to the shootings and the British soldiers had been victims of the Commando Order. As further evidence for this, the prosecutor used the German Manual of Military Law which stated a representative of the court that passed a sentence must read it in the presence of the accused immediately before execution. This was not the case for Evans, Jackson, Bonner, Blackburn, Walsh and White whom the SD deceived into thinking they were to appear before some kind of German panel. They knew nothing of their specious sentence.

On 25 August 1948, the court found Hans guilty and sentenced him to death by judicial hanging. The GOC-in-C BAOR confirmed the sentence a month later. But on 1 October 1948, the British commuted his sentence to 15 years' imprisonment. Hans was released from Werl Prison on 23 April 1954. The convicted murderer of six British men served less than a year in prison for each.

Stalag Luft III Case – 'The Great Escape'

Between 20 and 21 March 1946, Sir David Maxwell-Fyfe, the British Chief Deputy Prosecutor at the Nuremberg IMT, cross-examined *Reichsmarschall* Hermann Göring. A large part of his examination focussed on the murder of fifty Allied airmen who escaped from Stalag

Luft III. There are more British War Office files containing more data on the Stalag Luft III case than any other war crime tried at the Curiohaus. The case obsessed post-war Britain more than any other. If you enter the search term 'Stalag Luft III' on The National Archives search page, it returns a list of 864 files. This is more than the combined total of files for the concentration camps Belsen, Ravensbrück and Neuengamme where the Germans killed tens of thousands and clearly shows the focus for investigation and prosecution by the British authorities.[69] Such a huge amount of information deserves more attention than can be given here. As it was a large part of the effort to bring justice for crimes against captured Allied soldiers and perhaps the only war crimes case about which the British public felt strongly at the time, however, a brief account follows.

Most people with a passing interest in WW2 and a familiarity with the film *The Great Escape* will know the basic facts. During the night of 24 March 1944, seventy-six Allied officer airmen escaped from the POW camp Stalag Luft III in a tunnel they had dug under the compound and almost to the forest outside the fence. The plan had been for many more to escape, but the German guards discovered the tunnel exit before most could get away. The day after the escape, an enraged Hitler gave orders for every recaptured officer to be shot. Göring, head of the Luftwaffe, apparently pointed out to Hitler that a massacre might bring about reprisals to German airmen in Allied hands. Hitler agreed, but insisted 'more than half' were to be shot and issued the relevant order. *Reichsführer-SS* Heinrich Himmler, chief of state security, fixed the total at fifty and organized the killing of the men. Head of the criminal police (Kripo), SS Major General Arthur Nebe, selected those to be executed.

As the Kripo recaptured the escapees, they were interrogated for any useful information and then handed over to the Gestapo. Sometime later, in many different locations and in small groups, the fifty selected were collected by the Gestapo in cars on the pretext of returning them to a POW camp. After stopping for a comfort break, they shot the POWs at close range from behind. The bodies were left for retrieval, after which they were cremated and the ashes returned to Stalag Luft III. Field Marshal Wilhelm Keitel, head of the German high command, believed this might deter further escapes.

Camp commandant Lieutenant Colonel Erich Cordes informed the POWs in Stalag Luft III that forty-one of the escaped men were shot while attempting to evade arrest, but the POWs collated the names of forty-seven prisoners who they thought may have been murdered. The Senior British Officer, Group Captain Douglas Wilson, surreptitiously passed the list to a visitor from the Swiss Red Cross. They in turn informed the British government and Foreign Secretary Anthony Eden announced the news to the House of Commons on 19 May 1944.[70] Subsequently, the Senior British Officer of Stalag Luft III at the time of the escape, Group Captain Herbert Massey, was repatriated and briefed the Government about the fate of the escapees. Eden updated Parliament on 23 June 1944, promising that, at the end of the war, those responsible would be brought to 'exemplary justice'.[71] Eventually, the number of escapees killed was revealed to be fifty.

Shortly after the end of the war, a team from the Special Investigation Branch of the Royal Air Force Police, headed by Wing Commander Wilfred Bowes, hunted down the killers.[72] Like all the other war crimes investigation teams, they were working against the odds on what are now called 'cold cases' – crimes committed more than a year previously. But worse still the very people they sought had been in the perfect department to give themselves new identities prior to the German surrender. They had easily melted away incognito into the general population. Despite this, the investigators arrested twenty-one people accused of the crime and an attempt was made to bring them to justice in two trials.[73]

The British held the first trial in Court One of the Curiohaus between 1 July and 3 September 1947.[74] They charged eighteen men with two counts of conspiring to kill the Stalag Luft III escapees.[75] Former Head of the Breslau Kripo, Max Wielen, was charged only with these two counts. The other seventeen were charged with extra counts (three to nine) individual to their involvement in the killings.[76] All pleaded not guilty.

Originally, Dr Wilhelm Scharpwinkel, Head of the Breslau Gestapo, was also to be charged. His name was stricken from the charge sheet, however, with the note that he was not present and not charged.[77] This was because the Russians had him in custody. After much negotiation, in Autumn 1946 they let Captain M S Cornish, an Intelligence Corps interrogator from the London District Cage, speak with Scharpwinkel in a Moscow prison. He told Cornish he had travelled to Berlin with Wielen to meet with Gestapo head Heinrich Müller and Kripo head Nebe who ordered him to cover up the shootings. He admitted being part of a group involved in killing six of the escaped airmen, but denied firing a weapon himself.[78]

Colonel Robert Halse for the prosecution sought to prove Wielen was involved in the conspiracy to kill the fifty escaped POWs. He had several strong points to rely upon, beginning with the fact that Wielen knew the Allied men were POWs because he had ordered the nationwide 'hue and cry' when informed of the mass escape. Wielen could not claim to be ignorant of their fate as the RSHA had summoned him to Berlin where Nebe showed him Hitler's order regarding the escaped POWs. Wielen's office then put together a list of the escape ringleaders and sent it to Nebe. The prosecution submitted there was 'perfect co-operation between the Gestapo and the Kripo on the top level at the RSHA, i.e. between General Müller and General Nebe, and it was an irresistible inference that unless there had also been such co-operation on the next lower level between regional headquarters of the Gestapo and Kripo, the smooth execution of the Hitler order would have been impossible'.[79]

The prosecution further claimed Wielen had helped to cover up the crime. His office had sent the urns containing the ashes of the murdered officers back to Stalag Luft III with the explanation that the Gestapo had shot the POWs when they had attempted to escape. Also, shortly after the news of the crime had been announced in the House of Commons, Müller and Nebe had ordered Wielen back to Belin for a meeting. There they commanded their subordinates to whitewash the shootings by faking evidence and reports. The Gestapo revisited the execution sites to manufacture evidence including making detailed false reports, sketches of the scenes and firing more shots into trees. They fabricated teleprinter messages suggesting a vehicle had broken down before an escape attempt, there had been fighting or that some of the POWs had died while being taken to hospital.[80]

Wielen's defence was that he played an insignificant part and 'even by sacrificing his life' he could not have prevented the shooting of the POWs.[81] The summing up by Judge Advocate C L Stirling, however, was more persuasive of Wielen's guilt. The Judge Advocate said, 'It seems to me an irresistible inference that this scheme of Hitler's to shoot secretly these 50 officers could not go through without the connivance and cooperation of the Kripo and the Gestapo and, Gentlemen, why should that cease when you come down to the lower stage of the "Leitstellen" [regional headquarters] level?'[82] The court found Wielen guilty of the first and second charges and sentenced him to life imprisonment. He served just over five years and was released in October 1952.

The court found the remaining accused not guilty of the two conspiracy charges largely as the RSHA had not ordered them to Berlin, they had not been shown Hitler's order or necessarily been aware of what was happening outside their areas.[83] They were, however, all found guilty of the murders of the POWs either directly or as accessories. In the first Stalag Luft III trial, unusually, the trial judges left an explanation of the sentences they gave. The court summarised the common features of the evidence; receipt of the Hitler order, arrangements made for its execution and the actual shooting. It noted the prosecution's case rested entirely on the depositions of the accused and the defence was that some had been acquired under duress (meaning it might be unreliable). In court, however, all had admitted they were present during the killings (except for Gmeiner and Schimmel who had ordered the shootings in their separate cases). What the court had to decide, it therefore stated, was what part each of the accused played in the shootings and whether they knew their prisoners were POWs.

Charges 7 and 8 against Kiel Gestapo members Johannes Post, Hans Kähler, Artur Denkmann, Oskar Schmidt, Walter Jacobs and Wilhelm Struve are illustrative of the way the court operated.[84] The court accused these men of killing Squadron Leader James Catanach (Royal Australian Air Force), Flight Lieutenant Arnold Christensen (Royal New Zealand Air Force), Pilot Officer Halla Espelid (Royal Air Force), and Pilot Officer Nils Fuglesang (Royal New Zealand Air Force). Their story was typical of what happened to the murdered men.

The airmen were arrested by the Kripo in Flensburg on the German border with Denmark and held in the city's police prison. After a couple of days, the Kiel Gestapo collected them in two cars. Post, Kähler and driver Denkmann took the Australian Catanach. Franz Schmidt,[85] Oskar Schmidt, Jacobs and driver Struve took the other three airmen and drove south deeper into Germany. About 16km outside of Kiel, the cars stopped and the airmen got out, expecting a quick break. What happened after that is difficult to clarify since the accounts were from those on trial and each gave a different story. Common to all, however, was shooting the airmen.

In his statement to Lieutenant Colonel Alexander Scotland in the London District Cage, Oskar Schmidt said the airmen were still handcuffed during the shooting. He did not believe he had fired his pistol, but he could have. He said Post used a rifle to shoot all the airmen in the head after the pistol shots.[86] In his defence testimony to

Dr H Lappenberg, Oskar Schmidt said he had a mental blackout, but did not shoot. He told Lappenberg he did not see Kähler shoot, but Jacobs and Franz Schmidt may have. He explained how Post grabbed a rifle from Kähler to shoot the prisoners in the back of the head.[87]

Jacobs told Scotland the four airmen were shot with Franz Schmidt, Oskar Schmidt and Post all holding pistols. Then, Post had taken Kähler's rifle and shot all four twice in the back of the head.[88] Later, when giving evidence to his defence counsel, Dr G Adler, Jacobs admitted to shooting an airman himself.[89]

SS Major Johannes Post led the execution party. He was a committed Nazi, having joined the NSDAP and the Brownshirts of the SA (*Sturmabteilung*) in 1930. Showing clear premeditation, Post told the court he and Schmidt had previously driven into the countryside to reconnoitre an execution site.[90] He said his superior, Friedrich (Fritz) Schmidt, had ordered him to form a squad to shoot the four airmen. Post was in the first car to arrive at the site. He said he had uncuffed Catanach and, after he got out of the car, shot him once in the back. Then the second car arrived and the three remaining airmen got out still handcuffed. Post shouted at his Gestapo colleagues to shoot the men, Franz Schmidt, Oskar Schmidt and Jacobs drew their pistols and did so. He then ordered Kähler to use his rifle to deliver a *coup de grâce* to at least one man, but Kähler stood frozen. So Post grabbed the rifle and did it himself.[91]

All the accused relied on the defence of acting under superior orders. The Judge Advocate read to the court from the contemporary British *Manual of Military Law* that the accused could not escape liability, 'if in obedience to a command they committed acts which both violated unchallenged rules of warfare and outraged the general sentiment of humanity'. He said, 'I think there can be no doubt apart from any other matter, that none of the accused in this case would be outside those concluding words, if he really knew that he was taking part in the killing of recaptured POWs who had done nothing else but escape'.[92]

The accused had further relied upon the defence of duress, meaning they felt threatened with serious physical injury either at the time or in the future if they did not commit the killings. The prosecutor quoted again from the British *Manual of Military Law*: 'An act may also be excused if committed by a person acting in subjection to the power of others providing that he is compelled to act as he does by threats of death or serious physical injury continued during the whole time that he so acts and that the part taken by him in the unlawful act or acts is throughout strictly a subordinate part.' He argued that, apart from the drivers Denkmann and Struve, none of the accused had played a strictly subordinate part.

Dr Meyer-Labastille, lead defence counsel, tried to argue the accused did not know it was illegal to shoot the men as they claimed to believe a Hitler order was law. The attempts by the Gestapo to hide what they had done put the lie to this. Regardless, the court rejected the plea on the legal principle that a person cannot escape liability for their illegal action by claiming they thought it was legal (*ignorantia juris non excusat* – 'ignorance of the law excuses not'). The defence also suggested the accused did not know their prisoners were POWs thinking them to be spies or saboteurs. But even spies and saboteurs were entitled to a trial and the defence could only be valid if the accused honestly believed the men had been tried and they were carrying out a lawful execution. The court felt the prosecution had proven otherwise.

The defence tried hard on behalf of the accused men with two further defence pleas. The first was that the accused could not be expected to resolve a conflict between German law and international law. The accused claimed any order emanating from the Head of State was a legal order and disobeying it would have been a criminal offence in German law. Thus, they were in an impossible position: either they disobeyed a German law or an international law. Although the Judge Advocate did not deal with this point, the court held it invalid probably because there was no statute or decree that a spoken command of the Head of State had legal force and the defence produced no evidence to support it. The second plea was that only combatants could commit war crimes. The prosecutor explained that the term 'war crime' was a technical expression only and referred to illegal acts committed by soldiers *or civilians* during war. The court agreed and supported the rule, 'Anybody who commits a war crime can be punished by a military court, regardless of his status'.[93] Earlier war crimes trials in Hamburg had also sustained this principle. In the Zyklon B Case in March 1946, the court had decided, 'any civilian who is an accessory to a violation of the laws and customs of war is himself also liable as a war criminal'.[94]

The court decided those charged with Counts 3 to 9 were all guilty; the accused took part in the shootings and knew the airmen were POWs.[95] C L Stirling, the Judge Advocate, explained the term 'concerned in the killing', which formed part of Charges 3 to 9, should be interpreted as, 'carrying out some performance which went on directly to achieve the killing' and further, the performance 'would not have been so effective or been done so expeditiously if that person had not contributed his willing aid'.[96] The prominence of the parts played by the guilty men was reflected in the sentence each was given. The court sentenced thirteen of the accused, including Post, Kähler, Schmidt and Jacobs, to death. Pierrepoint hanged them in Hameln Prison in February 1948. The court sent two to prison for life (Boschert and Breithaupt). They sentenced Denkmann and Struve (the Kiel Gestapo drivers) to 10 years' imprisonment.[97]

The second Stalag Luft III trial against Erwin Wieczorek, Richard Hänsel and Reinhold Bruchardt opened in the Curiohaus on 28 August 1948 to beat the 1 September 1948 cut-off date issued by the Cabinet's Overseas Reconstruction Committee. It adjourned the same day. Proceedings resumed on 11 October 1948 and concluded on 6 November 1948.[98]

The three accused were all charged with count one: 'Being concerned together and with *SS-Gruppenführer* Müller and *SS-Gruppenführer* Nebe, at diverse places in Germany and German-occupied territory, between 25 March, 1944, and 13 April 1944, in the carrying out of an order to kill prisoners of war who had escaped from Stalag Luft III as a result of which said order 50 such prisoners of war were killed.' The court charged Wieczorek with two further counts (two and three) that he killed a total of ten named airmen. It further charged Hänsel on count three with killing six named airmen and Bruchardt on count four with killing four named airmen.[99]

Wieczorek was head of the counter-intelligence department of the Breslau Gestapo. He told his defence counsel, Dr Hübbe, he had heard but not seen the shootings. Critically, on cross-examination by Lieutenant Colonel G Barratt, he revealed his suspicion that prisoners were not spies, but POWs from Stalag Luft III as he had heard Scharpwinkel interrogating them. Hänsel was a department head of the Görlitz Gestapo. He knew about the escape from the POW camp through a teleprinter message. He too heard shots, but saw nothing. Bruchardt was in the Danzig Gestapo. The case against him was more complex. He claimed to have visited the execution site only after the killings, but according to the statements by two drivers, Bontenbroich and Reimer, he was there with his superior when the airmen were murdered.[100]

The court found Hänsel not guilty on all charges. They found Wieczorek guilty on counts 1 and 3 and sentenced him to death by hanging. The Deputy Judge Advocate General, in reviewing the case wrote, ' . . . there is no evidence that I can find in the proceedings of his [Wieczorek] aiding and abetting Scharpwinkel, who was head of the Breslau Gestapo, by making arrangements; guarding the prisoners; commanding the firing party; keeping a look-out or in any way at all'.[101] Wieczorek's sentence was, therefore, quashed. The court found Bruchardt guilty on counts 1 and 4 and sentenced him to death by hanging. Parliament had, however, voted for an experimental suspension of the death penalty in the UK and extended it to the British Zone in Germany. Bruchardt's sentence was changed to life imprisonment and eventually reduced to just 20 years. He was released from Werl Prison on 16 November 1959 after serving 11 years.

3

TRIALS FOR KILLING AND MISTREATING FORCED LABOURERS

Between 1941 and 1944, the Nazi regime was desperate for workers to support wartime production of weapons, equipment and food. The Eastern Front continued to consume German soldiers by the tens of thousands and replacing them meant the available workforce in the Reich dwindled just as increased output was needed. A typically complex bureaucracy attempted to replace German men recruited to the armed forces with forced labour from the homeland and the occupied countries. When SS Lieutenant General Fritz Sauckel became General Plenipotentiary for Labour Deployment in 1942, the Germans transported millions against their will to be forced labourers in Germany. At the peak of the war, one of every four workers in the economy of the Third Reich was a slave.[1]

The Nazis ignored most international law regarding the treatment of POWs, but they completely dismissed it concerning slave labour. The very act of taking forced labourers from occupied countries was prohibited by Article 52 of the *Laws and Customs of War on Land* (Hague IV, 1907), which Germany had signed. It reads,

> Requisitions in kind and services shall not be demanded from municipalities or inhabitants except for the needs of the army of occupation. They shall be in proportion to the resources of the country, and of such a nature as not to involve the inhabitants in the obligation of taking part in military operations against their own country. Such requisitions and services shall only be demanded on the authority of the commander in the locality occupied.

Rather than follow the convention to which they had bound themselves, as the Germans occupied a territory, they applied the principle of taking slaves to the Fatherland with two objectives: first, to solve the massive need for production to back their war aims and second, to support their racist doctrine of exterminating those they regarded as *untermenschen* (subhumans). Millions of people were compulsorily moved to Germany and many thousands died.

The Nazi hunger for slave labour became insatiable. Each time a country was subjugated, more people were forcibly transported to the Reich to join the myriad already toiling in the fields and factories. A 1943 study concluded that there were 6.5 million slave labourers or POWs working in Germany. By 1944, this had risen to 8.6 million. Before the end of the war, the number had likely grown even larger.[2] Slave labourers from the east, particularly the Soviet Union and Poland, were often kept in fenced and guarded camps annexed to their place of work. They were inadequately housed, fed and clothed and little attention was paid to their medical needs.

Neugraben/Tiefstack Case

The first prisoners held at the Hamburg-Neugraben subcamp of Neuengamme, however, were not from the eastern German-occupied lands, but from Italy. Between 1943 and 1944, 500 Italian POWs were forced to work for a construction company building prefabricated panel houses for those made homeless by the Allied bombing. In the summer of 1944, the men left and it became a camp for 500 Czech Jewish women.[3]

Anita Landsberger's story of how she came to the subcamp via other concentration camps was typical. She was Jewish, born on 29 September 1909 in Hamburg. She trained as a kindergarten teacher at the Fröbel Seminar and opened her own kindergarten for children of all religions in 1929. When the Nazis came to power, she was forbidden to care for non-Jewish children and her business shrank. Fearing for her future in Germany, in 1933 she emigrated to Prague to work as a governess for a wealthy Jewish family. After the Wehrmacht invaded in 1939, the Nazi persecution of the Jews in Czechoslovakia escalated to such levels that Landsberger was forced into hiding. She was found in February 1942 and taken to the Theresienstadt concentration camp. In December 1943, she was deported to Auschwitz where she survived the initial selection and was helped by fellow prisoners. About six months later she was chosen for work in Hamburg and transported to the Neuengamme subcamp Dessauer Ufer. Here, she was forced to clear rubble in the port area.[4] On 13 September 1944, all women were moved from Dessauer Ufer to other Hamburg subcamps. Anita Landsberger was sent to Hamburg-Neugraben.[5]

In Neugraben, the women continued the work of the Italian POWs building panel houses, making concrete roof tiles, concrete slabs, concrete pipes, fence posts and bricks. They lived in unsanitary conditions, were poorly fed and suffered cruel punishment. Twenty-five women slept in a 6m by 4m room on wooden beds with one, sometimes two, thin blankets. Woken early, they each dressed in underpants, shirt, dress and jacket. No stockings or socks. Coats and woollen stockings were issued towards the end of November, but many were stolen by the female SS guards, so there were never sufficient clothes for each woman to have a full set. On their feet, they wore wooden clogs which often broke leaving a woman to work barefoot even in freezing weather.

For breakfast, the prisoners received a cup of watery coffee. No food was supplied at lunch. For dinner, they got a very thin, poor-quality soup (usually made from rotten cabbage and turnips), about 200g of bread and 2g of margarine. They were constantly famished and the poor diet contributed to disease in the camp. Many women suffered the pain, degradation and humiliation of dysentery. The women were allowed to wash once a day, in cold water, but this small privilege was often taken away as punishment. There were no arrangements for washing clothes.[6]

After morning roll call, the women left the camp to march to various workplaces where they laboured for 12 hours a day with barely a break. At work they were watched over by former customs officers who were no longer needed in the damaged port of Hamburg. Inside the camp, however, they were guarded by the SS. Both types of guard would slap, kick and beat the women. The first camp commandant was SS 2nd Lieutenant Otto Schulz. In October 1944, he was replaced by SS Sergeant Major Friedrich-Wilhelm Kliem who terrorized the women, punishing them during evening roll call or in his room with at least twenty-five blows of a leather strap or a rubber hose.

In February 1945, the SS transferred the women to the Hamburg-Tiefstack satellite camp and Kliem went with them. Here the women worked in a cement factory, dug anti-tank ditches or cleared snow in the winter. The misery of diarrhoea was made worse as the lavatory had no walls or roof. A month later, the Tiefstack camp was hit by Allied bombing and an unknown number of women were killed. On 7 April 1945, the surviving women were taken to Bergen-Belsen.

When the British began investigating war crimes in the Hamburg area, they naturally focussed on the large Neuengamme concentration camp and discovered that its influence was vast. There were over eighty subcamps spread throughout the British Zone. Staff and inmates alike had been moved between them several times and countless prisoners had perished. Some subcamps had been evacuated, but many still contained the dead and dying. War crimes investigators faced a mammoth task in finding and arresting the accused. Some of the more senior staff were able to escape entirely by changing their identities and travelling to faraway towns. For the lower-level guards, particularly the women, this was not an option. Perhaps that is why so many were captured and prosecuted for crimes committed at Neugraben and Tiefstack. Locating witnesses was difficult. Those that survived and were willing to give evidence were presumably found in Bergen-Belsen, since they had been transferred to this camp during the end phase of the war. Remarkably, many agreed to stay in Germany to testify and among them were a handful of 'star' witnesses; Erna Fuchs, Gertrude Karpeles, Eva Donat, Lotte Lange and Gertrude Neumann.

As the ill-treated women were Czech, the JAG sent a copy of a report on the subcamps to the Czechoslovak War Crimes Mission. Captain P L Horetzky inquired of the JAG whether the British intended to try the case or would agree to hand it over for trial in Czechoslovakia. The JAG explained that as the British were trying the staff of Neuengamme, the main concentration camp, he also intended to prosecute the supervisors of the subcamps.[7] The British tried fifteen people in the Curiohaus for their parts in the terror inflicted upon the women in Neugraben and Tiefstack. The proceedings are presented as one trial (the same court sat from 11 June to 3 July 1946), but there were fifteen mini-trials conducted over four weeks.[8] The accused were not prosecuted as a group, but individually. The first fourteen hearings concerned the guards in the camp who were charged with the war crime of ill-treating Allied nationals. The final mini-trial was of Kliem, the last commandant, who was charged with the war crimes of ill-treating and killing Allied nationals in the subcamps.

First to be tried for ill-treating the women was 56-year-old Erich Schulz, second in command at the subcamps and foreman of one of the outside working parties. When his customs job became redundant (the British had bombed the port to pieces and Schulz had lost his house twice), he was directed to guard Neugraben. He had a unique way to describe his membership of the NSDAP. He told the court, 'I was forced to join the Nazi party in 1937 by the bribe of promotion'. Prosecution witness Gertrude Neumann testified that Schulz was a guard at the Möller brick salvage worksite outside the camp. He would beat and kick the women, especially the older ones. He beat them if they went to the lavatory or found a turnip to eat or just didn't move quickly enough. Eva Donat told the court that she had been in a working party digging the wet ground. It was cold, but they were not allowed to wear coats. If they rested for a moment, they were reported to the commandant (whose punishment was feared). Donat told the court that she had seen Frau Lange one evening covered in wounds and that Lange had told her Schulz was responsible. Schulz denied making the women work without coats and beating anyone, saying Neumann and Donat must have mistaken him for someone else. It took 10 minutes for the court to find Schulz guilty and he was sent to prison for one year.[9]

Three days later, on 14 June 1946, the court tried Maria Szaroletta. Neuman testified that inmate Marianne Braun had insulted another prisoner, but guards Szaroletta and Annaliese Kohlmann had thought the insult was aimed at them. They set about beating Braun with tree branches for about ten minutes. The beating around her head caused bruises and a swollen eye. It also made an existing ear problem worse. Neuman told the court this was the only occasion she knew of that Szaroletta, whom she admitted had 'rather a good reputation', had beaten a woman. Defence witness Erna Fuchs went further telling the court, 'She had a very good name and was known to be decent to the prisoners. She did not report us or object to us receiving gifts. She did not make the work harder for us.' Szaroletta admitted striking Braun, but with a twig, not about the head nor for ten minutes. The court stopped the trial and acquitted Szaroletta.[10]

On Monday 17 June 1946, Georg Heidtmann took the stand in the Curiohaus. Neumann told the court Heidtmann was brutal, always shouting and kicking the women. She saw him punch, kick and hit Edith Engel with his rifle for several minutes. His defence witnesses never saw him mistreat a woman and Heidtmann said himself that he had slapped only occasionally. His defence counsel, Dr Gerken, told the court that Heidtmann had a difficult job, that Neumann was a liar and that in any case, beating the women was not a war crime. This approach may not have caused the court to look favourably upon his client. Heidtmann was found guilty and sentenced to two years' imprisonment.[11]

Julius Zederkopf was tried on Wednesday 19 June 1946. There was more persuasive evidence against him. He was one of the guards in the cement factory where some of the women worked and hundreds slept after their quarters were damaged by bombing. The work was arduous, even some of the accused thought it was too heavy for women, especially as they were malnourished. Women had to load a cubic metre of sand into a cart and push it 200m to a cement mixer. Some then had to produce a daily quota each of twenty-eight square 24kg bricks. Others were each forced to make thirty-two 40kg concrete slabs a day. The women had to shovel the building materials into iron forms, stamp each brick or slab, remove the form and carry the wet block to a drying room some distance away.[12] They were given no safety equipment of any kind. After 11 hours of work, sometimes on hot days, the women were physically wrecked and parched. There was no drinking water in the factory, but there were several containers full in a field kitchen when they returned for their evening meal. Eva Donat told the court that Zederkopf beat them with his rifle butt when they tried to get a drink.

Sleeping overnight in the cement factory was uncomfortable, degrading and dangerous. There were three pots for 500 women to use as lavatories, which rapidly filled to overflowing. The women were not allowed to go to the outside facilities by the guards nor were they allowed into air-raid shelters during Allied bombing. Neumann told the court she had seen Zederkopf beat Hilda Löwe and Erna Fuchs said she had been beaten by him. It took the court just five minutes to find him guilty. He was sentenced to 18 months' imprisonment.

On 26 June 1946, the court reconvened to try Albert Runkel. Neumann testified that he had shot at, but missed Frau Tieber who had rested briefly from the exhausting digging work. Runkel said that he had fired a shot to warn Tieber that Gestapo men were approaching. Hertha Kostscheck told Neumann and witness Donat that Runkel had beaten her and knocked two teeth out. He admitted to beating Kostscheck, 'but only on the cheek with my hand'. Two other witnesses also provided hearsay evidence against Runkel accusing him of throwing burning coals at a woman named Pinszovska whose head was burnt. He denied throwing hot coals, but remembered a civilian doing so. The court took five minutes to find him guilty and he was sentenced to three years' imprisonment.[13]

The trials of the remaining accused Josef Müller, Christian Koopmann, Christel Dibbern, Anita Frank and Hertha Sürth all proceeded along the same lines; they were cruel to varying degrees and beat the women into submission. Their defences were also similar; the prosecution witnesses exaggerated, they were compelled to be guards and their conduct was not a war crime. The court found them all to be guilty and sentenced them to between 6 and 18 months' imprisonment.

Last to be tried at the beginning of July 1946 was the camp commandant Friedrich-Wilhelm Kliem. In the opinion of Eva Donat, 'Kliem was not of normal mentality. He would repeatedly give orders and counter-orders. He would tell prisoners to do one thing one minute and shortly afterwards would beat them for doing so.'[14] He was feared above all others by the women in the camp.

Kliem came to Neugraben in October 1944 as the successor to Otto Schulz (himself tried for war crimes in Lübeck).[15] In depositions, Kliem stated, 'living conditions were poor, the clothing was very bad, washing and toilet installations were also bad. The food supplied for the prisoners was by no means sufficient; and I also admit that the work which had to be done at the arbeitskommandos [work sites], was much too heavy for women.' Remarkably, he made no mention of any efforts he made to change these circumstances. He admitted, 'on many occasions at Neugraben and Tiefstack, I beat female prisoners' and he even recalled some of their names.

He remembered beating Gertrude Neumann in December 1944. She had received a parcel of bread against regulations. At the morning parade, in front of all the women, he told Neumann to take off her overall and bend down. He then hit her on the back twenty-five times with a rubber truncheon. He said she was lucky that the truncheon was not fully inflated with compressed air. Neumann spent two months in the camp hospital after this beating and continued to suffer its effects after the war ended. She received treatment from a hospital specialist until January 1946.[16] In his deposition, Professor Dr Gustav Hopf said,

> Her complaint consisted of heavy elongated skin eruptions and gland poisoning lasting an unusually long time, as the result of the complete breakdown of bodily resistance. Moreover she was suffering from severe depression and

> was in an acute state of shock. The overall physical and mental exhaustion can only be the result of heavy suffering and shocks to which Frau Neumann was exposed in the concentration camp.[17]

Kliem also remembered beating Erna Fuchs in March 1945 for receiving a precious parcel of bread, butter and sausage. She refused to reveal the name of the person who had given it to her. Fuchs told the court, 'Accused ordered me to undress and bend over a stool. Accused took off his belt and beat me severely with it. After a few blows I fell to the ground and begged him to stop. He continued to beat and kick me and he said he would beat me until I died. I fainted several times for a few seconds. He continued to beat me without interruption.' She said, 'Accused pulled me to my feet and continued to abuse me. He put his revolver to my head and said he would shoot me if I did not tell him the name of the person who gave me the parcel before he counted to three. He then put his revolver away and ordered me to bend over again. He continued to beat me until he broke his belt. So he got another belt. I must have received 100 blows.' Fuchs crawled out of the room to the infirmary where a female doctor bandaged her bleeding wounds. She had several broken fingers and was blinded in her left eye. The next day, Kliem ordered her to go to the Bilstraße work party where the women sorted bricks from rubble. They were each required to find and stack 400 bricks a day. It was an hour's march to get there and was considered the toughest work site by the women. Fuchs had to be supported by other women that day. She returned to find her food withheld for eight days.[18] Dr Eugen Klewansky examined Fuchs in May 1945 and found that she had fractures of two fingers of her left hand, which had been set badly. Additionally, she had contusions of the head and bruises on her left thigh. In Dr Klewansky's opinion, 'It was clear that this was the result of brutal treatment. It was obvious that Fraulein Fuchs was suffering from shock and she had slight difficulty in speaking and thinking.' He went on, 'Erna Fuchs also complained of pains in her back and ribs so that I thought that she had broken some ribs, which was not confirmed'.[19]

Kliem was the sole member of the camp staff charged with the additional war crime of killing Allied nationals. This related to one incident on 14 September 1944. A group of women were clearing debris from bomb damage when a wall collapsed on two of them. Anna Reichmann and another Czech woman, known only as Rosa, were gravely injured.

After being dug out, a guard named Hoppe drove them to Hamburg Hospital which was full, so he drove them further to Wilhelmsburg Flakturm Hospital. Here Hoppe telephoned Kliem who told him that the Neuengamme camp commandant, Max Pauly, had forbidden non-Aryan prisoners to be taken to German hospitals and he should bring them back to Neugraben at once. Dr Hildegard Cupey examined the women in the Wilhelmsburg hospital. Anna had a fractured skull and was unconscious. Rosa had a fractured neck, but was sufficiently conscious to speak. Both had many other injuries. Dr Cupey testified that she set their broken bones and stitched their smaller wounds. She thought, however, that their condition was hopeless and so did not object when the women were taken on an open truck back to Neugraben the same day. Gertrude Neumann was in the camp hospital when the two women were brought in. She told the court, 'The two women were crying and shouting. They suffered enormously. The doctor had only paper bandages. She tried to do all she could.' One of the women died the same night, the other the next day.[20]

Kleim's trial lasted for two days. He had admitted to ill-treating the women and even his defence counsel told the court, 'I have no easy task to defend this man'. The court deliberated for less than an hour. It was obvious to all that the women who died when the wall collapsed, would have had a better chance of survival in a proper hospital than in Neugraben, but was Kliem personally responsible for their deaths beyond a reasonable doubt? He was found to be guilty of the charge against him except for the words 'and killing' and sentenced to 15 years' imprisonment. He was released in 1955.

Alter Banter Weg

It went by many names, Banter Weg, Banter Lager IV, KZ-Wilhelmshaven, Außenlager Wilhelmshaven and Kriegsmarinewerft, but whatever it was called Alter Banter Weg was a place of brutal hard work, little food and much punishment. In September 1944, barracks built for 500 workers in the Bant district of Wilhelmshaven were repurposed to house 1,000 prisoners from the Neuengamme concentration camp. The prisoners were forced to work 12-hour shifts in the naval shipyards performing heavy dock work or clearing rubble after bombing raids. By January 1945, 1,500 to 2,000 inmates were jammed into the unheated buildings. The men, mainly French and Russian, worked six and a half days, spending the remaining half day on other disagreeable mandatory tasks in the subcamp. Five SS men were in charge and Alter Banter Weg was guarded by 200 German sailors. Punishment was liberally meted out by the notorious Danish SS Deputy Commandant Gustav Jepsen and kapo Heinrich Sürig.[21] Even the civilian shipyard managers, Gottfried Drossen and Hans Horstmann, pummelled the prisoners. Men were beaten to death, drowned and hanged in various ways. At least 226 died there.[22]

On 4 April 1945, the subcamp was partly evacuated. Four hundred prisoners were forced onto a train for Bergen-Belsen. After the men had endured seven days of torture locked in closed cattle wagons without food or water, the train stopped at Lüneburg station. When American bombers flew in to destroy the railway infrastructure and hinder the movement of freight, the prisoners' train too was bombed, killing about 250 of those onboard. The survivors that could still walk were marched 80km to the concentration camp, Jepsen ordered the remaining sixty to eighty to be killed on the spot.

On 5 April, the 700 or so that had not left Alter Banter Weg by train were force-marched for 13 days over 150km to Stalag X-B at Sandbostal, near Zeven. Many perished along the way and more died shortly after arrival. For some, the ordeal did not end there and they were transported by coal freighter to Flensburg before being liberated. Stalag X-B was described by its British Army liberators as a 'mini Belsen'.

The court convened for the first Alter Banter Weg trial in the Curiohaus on 4 February 1947.[23] Nine former guards and kapos were indicted, but only seven were prosecuted in the first trial.[24] Georg Radatz was named, but later tried alone in the second alter Banter Weg trial. The accused Ernst Pingel escaped justice entirely. He was in the Russian Zone where a report suggested he was working for Soviet military intelligence as an informer on the local population.[25]

Gustav Jepsen was on trial by the British for a second time – in August 1946 he had been tried and sentenced to life imprisonment for killing those evacuated from the subcamp in Lüneburg station in April 1945.[26] This time, however, the court was in no mood to be lenient. Witnesses told how he beat prisoners with an ox-hide whip. One told the court he had received fifty blows, been denied medical attention and forced to work the next day. William Carr and others saw Jepsen throw men into a reservoir in the camp compound. A Frenchman died from pneumonia two days after this treatment. A Russian was repeatedly punched and kicked by Jepsen as he tried to climb out – this man died of his injuries. One of the most feared punishments inflicted by Jepsen was hanging on the cross. Harold Le Druillenec and others saw Jepsen tie prisoners' hands behind their backs and lift them onto a cross where they would hang in agony from their bound hands.[27] The court found him guilty, sentenced him to death and he was hanged on 26 June 1947.

SS Captain Otto Thümmel was the first Alter Banter Weg commandant. He joined the NSDAP and the SS in 1932. He opened the subcamp in September 1944 and left at the end of October. He claimed to have no knowledge of any ill-treatment of prisoners, but revealed his callous nature in his deposition. He told the War Crimes Investigation Team that he had sent a Russian accused of sabotaging a drilling bench to the Neuengamme concentration camp. The man had actually fallen asleep as he was exhausted. When the prisoner returned to Alter Banter Weg two weeks later he had 'a slip of paper which said that he was to be executed on the working site'. Incredibly, Thümmel continued, 'I do not know who signed the slip of paper. Thereupon I gave the order to hang the Russian by the boring machine which was carried out by German kapos.' Thümmel was sentenced to five years' imprisonment.

The second commandant, Rudolf Günther, came to the subcamp in November 1944. He joined the NSDAP in 1929 and the SS in 1932. Since 1940, he had worked in the concentration camp regime as a guard at Neuengamme and as security for various outside working parties. He claimed to have worked hard to improve conditions, but his relaxed approach to the German kapos had allowed them to become increasingly violent. He said he did not beat prisoners himself nor allow prisoners to be punished in any way and he never saw any such punishments. But it was during his administration that 'the barrel' penalty was introduced. A prisoner's head was pushed into the barrel, his arms held out and he was flogged. This occurred almost every day after the evening parade in the presence of the whole camp and witnesses had seen Günther watching on many occasions.[28] There were also brutal deaths while he was in charge. Frenchman Jean Boeuf, accused of stealing bread, was killed after being tortured. His hands were crushed in the door of an air raid shelter and he was sexually abused. Witness Henri Payen then saw the Germans put a noose around his neck and hang him from 'a piece of iron which jutted out from the wall'.[29] Günther was sentenced to 15 years' imprisonment.

SS Company Sergeant Major Ernst Hoffmann was largely a clerical worker. His defence was that he never took part in any of the camp atrocities and he did not know of them. Former prisoners told a different story. They said he had seen many beatings and had never tried to stop them. He was sentenced to four years' imprisonment. German kapo Heinrich Sürig stole the rations of his fellow prisoners and helped in the frequent brutalities. He was given 18 months' imprisonment. Hans Horstmann and Gottfried Drossen were in charge of the dockyards where the prisoners worked. Both showed nothing but cruelty to the prisoners whom they considered to be numbers, not men. They worked them to exhaustion, beating and kicking them with impunity. Both were sentenced to 15 years' imprisonment.

The second Alter Banter Weg trial involved Georg Radatz alone. He came to the Curiohaus for trial on 8 July 1948 accused of ill-treating Allied nationals.[30] He was a thief and had been a prisoner himself since 1940 when he was sent to Dachau concentration camp. In January 1941, he was transferred to Neuengamme and came to Alter Banter Weg when it opened in 1944. As a German, he was given nightshift foreman duties and slightly better food.

The Shipyard-West, where the men worked, was on an island and it was here that the prisoners made parts for ships and submarines. It had a welding shop and a smithy (a blacksmith's shop with a forge) where Radatz supervised 120 men. They were marched there to work a day shift (6am to 6pm) or a night shift (6pm to 6am). The men wore a suit of striped wood fibre 'cloth', a light shirt, ragged socks and wooden clogs. Some had undershorts. The insect-infested clothes were changed every three or four months when they had rotted on the body (there were no clothes washing facilities). The night workers were constantly tired as the daytime activities in the camp often made sleeping impossible. For the first few months of the camp operation, there was no food at breakfast. At midday or midnight, the men were fed, but there was only a half-hour break and often not enough food. If there was sufficient, but you were served last, there would be little time to eat before the break ended. Radatz would often knock a prisoner's bowl away from his mouth before the ration could be consumed and beat the unfortunate man back to work with a rubber truncheon. Often there was no food to look forward to after work. Consequently, the men fought to be first to get the meagre turnip soup and they were also beaten for this disorder.

Radatz would beat a prisoner at the shipyard for the slightest reason. The man would be ordered to a separate room and to remove his trousers. Radatz would then set about him with a leather belt. On one occasion, Georges Jenvresse was too exhausted to lift a heavy forge hammer. Radatz punched and kicked him and then beat him with an iron bar.[31] If he could not administer a beating at work, Radatz would make a note of a transgressing prisoner's number and report him to the SS when returning to the camp. Then the favoured punishment was the barrel. After roll call, with all the prisoners still on parade, Radatz would hold the prisoner's head down and his arms were secured. Russian prisoners especially chosen for the job would then whip the man with a length of heavy electrical cable, 60cm long and 2.5cm in diameter. Usually, it was 25 strokes, but up to 250 were given. Prisoner Lloyd Gybels saw Frenchman Fegos beaten so badly that he died afterwards.[32] British agent Michael Tapperell, arrested in Antibes by the Gestapo, also died in Alter Banter Weg, possibly from the beatings he received at the hands of Radatz and others.

Radatz, in his testimony, admitted that he had hit men in the workshop with a rubber tube, but only as they had been thieving from each other and never with any 'physical consequence'. He denied ever reporting a prisoner or being involved with camp beatings. His defence counsel, Dr Meyer-Labastille, said in summing up that the accused was a prisoner himself and not responsible for the camp conditions. Had he not been brutal, his counsel suggested, he may have been killed himself, and anyway his behaviour did not constitute a war crime. The court disagreed and sentenced him to eight years' imprisonment.

Steinbergen Quarry

After the Americans occupied the Hannover region at the end of the war, it became part of the British Zone. During an investigation of the Lahde-Weser Work Education Camp, the British War Crimes Group (NWE) came across a work party assignment for the Steinbergen Quarry. On closer inspection, they realized there was also a case to be answered for the conditions in the quarry. Working with stone, even today, is physically demanding and dangerous. With modern equipment and safety measures it can be fulfilling work, but being forced to quarry by a brutal regime 80 years ago was harrowing. At the Steinbergen Quarry, an outside working party of prisoners from Lahde-Weser were compelled to cut huge blocks of stone from the cliffs, break them into small pieces and load gravel into trucks. The work was repetitive, gruelling and carried out for long days in all weathers. The men were not given adequate rest periods, clothing or food and were constantly beaten.

In 1943, the owner of Schaumberger Steinbrüche AG, Walter Schmidt, was asked by the power company Prussische Elektrizitäts AG if he could supply 30,000 tons of building materials to complete the local power station. Schmidt explained that he could not as his workers had been conscripted and he was short-handed. According to Schmidt, a power company engineer suggested that he should approach the Gestapo who would supply labour from the Lahde-Weser Work Education Camp.[33] Schmidt did just that and signed a contract with the Gestapo for the supply of forty workers. Schmidt had been a member of the NSDAP since 1934 and knew the term 'worker' was used to sanitise the true definition of the men he got. They were slaves: the men were prisoners, had no choice in the work, could not leave and were not paid. Additionally, armed guards would ensure that they worked the required number of hours, produced the daily tonnage needed and did not slack. The first forty men supplied in July 1943 were mostly Polish and Russian. Having been in Nazi custody for some time, they were hardly the physically fit, well-nourished men required for the heavy work and the conditions in the quarry did not improve their capabilities. Fed appallingly thin rations that provided less than a tenth of the daily calories needed and forced to work 11 hours every day, the men could not hope to achieve the output required. Rather than try to increase the rations, improve the working conditions and reduce the number of back-breaking hours of toil, Schmidt asked for a further twenty men.

Walter Schwarz, born in Berlin but arrested in Lithuania for being 'a half-Jew', told the British investigators about conditions in the quarry. He was taken there from Lahde-Weser with twenty-one other men in January 1944. Their billet was an old latticed shed where they were crammed together with forty other men. On arrival they were addressed by Schmidt who told them unless they worked to their utmost, they would not leave the quarry alive. He explained that there was a nearby cemetery 'already overcrowded with such lazy types' as them. Their daily food was a breakfast of thin, watery cabbage soup and a lunch of three slices of bread with a cup of coffee. Dinner, a bowl of turnip soup, was provided only if the men managed to cut and load $8m^3$ of stone per day. To force the men to work hard, foreman Wilhelm Rinne 'beat the prisoners whenever he met them'. He also had men shot. Schwarz said,

> A young Pole, who was very emaciated, was dragged to work, where he soon collapsed completely. Rinne happened to pass. He gave me as well as another guard the order to take the Pole to the rubble-dump, where he would be shot in the back of his neck. I made excuses as I myself was very weak. Thereupon Rinne himself took the Pole, the guard ran beside him, and thus he pulled him along to the rubble-dump. Immediately afterwards a shot was fired. The Pole did not appear again, and in the evening his blood-stained clothing was distributed in the billet.

This distribution of soiled clothing was a common occurrence and a sure sign to Schwarz that the former owners had been killed. It also happened every time that Gestapo guard Friedrich Koch took a man to the rubble-dump. Of the sixty-one prisoners he knew of in the quarry, only eight returned to Lahde-Weser three months later. Some had fallen ill and perhaps returned to Lahde-Weser for treatment (Schwarz did not know, they simply disappeared), but all had been cruelly treated and many had died.[34]

Hermann Kruse, a German civilian foreman in the quarry, resigned in August 1943. He said, 'I left because I would not stand those conditions any longer. It was a simple massacre.' Kruse explained that the maximum sentence for a man committed to Lahde-Weser was 56 days, 'but these people were kept there for at least a quarter year, as the *Betriebsführer* [Chief] Schmidt did not want to change his workers so often'. He added,

> Schmidt would insist on the fixed output, and that every method should be used to obtain it. The prisoners were in a very bad bodily condition. They collapsed every time they had to lift the hammer of 16lbs. Nobody was allowed to report sick. Then they were called malingerers. Most of them had no shoes, they had to walk about on the stones bare-footed, and had to push the specially heavy lorries [trucks]. The chief Schmidt was absolutely responsible for everything that went on in the quarry.

In the few weeks that Kruse had seen the men from Lahde-Weser working in the quarry, he had seen some of the ways the men were treated. He had seen quarry foreman Rinne order a guard 'to administer 10 strokes with a rubber hose to every prisoner'. He had seen men shot too:

> At first these people were beaten terribly, then they were chased away, and, as they called it, shot whilst trying to escape. These six men were not buried, but simply covered with rubbish and screes in the quarry. I know this place well. The guards received from Schmidt a weekly quantity of beer in order to urge these people to beat the prisoners even more and to increase the output by force.[35]

Throughout November 1947, Major F M Warner and Captain P Nielsen both of the Field Investigation Section, War Crimes Group (NWE) took many depositions from prosecution and defence witnesses so that Lieutenant Colonel Gerald Draper could build a case against Walter Schmidt, Wilhelm Rinne, Friedrich Koch and Wilhelm Bruns. In early December 1947, Draper sent his summary to the JAG's office in London. Bruns was removed from the trial as he was already accused in the Lahde-Weser case (also tried by the British). Draper's report included a list of thirty-seven prisoners that had died between 13 August 1943 and 27 March 1945 where 'the cause of death is a sickening and futile repetition of "shot whilst trying to escape" and "shot because of resistance against the state authority" and occasionally "death through general weakness"'. He doubted the list was a complete account of those who died in the quarry. He admitted to weaknesses in the case, that he had only one witness (Schwarz) who had been a prisoner in the camp and that nobody had seen Koch kill a prisoner. Although there were ex-employees who would be prosecution witnesses, many were still under the influence of Schmidt who was described as 'a local tyrant'.[36]

The trial opened in the Curiohaus on 28 April 1948. Schmidt, Rinne and Koch were all accused of the first charge, 'Committing a war crime in that they at Steinbergen Working Camp, Germany, between July 1943 and May 1945, in violation of the laws and usages of war, were concerned in the killing of a number of allied Nationals, internees of the said camp'. Only Schmidt and Rinne were accused of the second charge, 'Committing a war crime in that they at Steinbergen Working Camp, Germany, between July 1943 and May 1945, in violation of the laws and usages of war, were concerned in the ill-treatment of a number of allied Nationals, internees of the said camp'. All pleaded not guilty to all charges.[37]

In addition to evidence from Schwarz and Kruse, the prosecution introduced witness Karl Möller who had worked in the quarry since 1927. In his deposition, he said,

> The foreman Rinne behaved bestially in the quarry. Rinne beat the prisoners all the time. He used a stick to beat with . . . I personally have seen corpses lying near a heap of broken stones . . . I can still remember the case of a prisoner, I think he was a Russian, who meant to commit suicide. I was quite certain of that because I had already watched him all morning. Eventually he put his head on the rails in front of the trucks which carried stones. The truck driver stopped in time. The Russian was alive. When I returned after quarter of an hour later on, after I had emptied my train of trucks, the Russian had been shot in the meantime. I myself have seen the corpse.[38]

In his defence, Schmidt said that he had asked for working hours to be cut from eleven to eight and for the prisoners to be recognized as heavy workers, which would improve their food, clothing, footwear and even provide cigarettes, but there was no evidence that any of this occurred.[39] His defence counsel, Dr Meyer-Labastille suggested that the work for Prussische Elektrizitäts AG, which required the prisoners from Lahde-Weser, could not be refused. Additionally, Meyer-Labastille in his opening statement said, ' . . . the agreement between the Gestapo and my client relative to the furnishing of prisoners was not executed upon his own initiative but upon the urgent request of the Prussische Elektrizitäts Akt.-Ges. and under pressure by the Gestapo'. This is not how Schmidt himself represented the agreement in his deposition and there was little doubt that he, as a long-term NSDAP member, was a willing party. The defence counsellor argued that Schmidt could not alter the conditions of the prisoners which was fully controlled by the Lahde-Weser camp commandant. But Schmidt himself had already suggested that he had improved their conditions (even in a meagre way), so this defence was weak. Meyer-Labastille also spent some time arguing that it was perfectly lawful for Schmidt to use prisoners to work in the quarry. This was, however, immaterial as he was not charged with 'using', but with the war crimes of ill-treatment and killing.[40] The defence of Rinne by Dr Krueger-Nieland was straightforward and clichéd – he was a simple foreman who followed the orders of his superiors. For Koch, defence counsel Dr H Burchard-Motz attempted to discredit Schwarz, the only witness against his client.[41]

Prosecuting barrister Mr A Vollmar carefully considered his closing address delivered on 19 May 1948. For the first charge, in law, Vollmar needed to prove beyond reasonable doubt that the killing in the quarry was unlawful. He knew he had to show that there was the intention to commit an act where the natural and probable result was that a person would die. Further, he wanted to show that the killings were unlawful because the accused had a duty of care to the dead (who were helpless because they were prisoners) and that prisoners had been allowed to die through gross neglect. For the second charge, Vollmar wanted to persuade the court that conditions in the quarry amounted to ill-treatment and that the accused were responsible for the conditions. Using the evidence, Vollmar attempted to show the court three things: prisoners died unnatural deaths, such deaths were the reasonable and probable consequence of overwork and undernourishment, and the accused were responsible.[42]

On 20 May 1948, the court found Schmidt and Rinne not guilty on the first charge of killing, but guilty on the second charge of ill-treating. Schmidt was sentenced to 15 years' imprisonment and Rinne to 10 years. They were both released in September 1951 having served just three years and four months. Koch was found guilty of the first charge (he was not accused of the second) and sentenced to life imprisonment. This was chipped away: seven years were removed for good conduct and a further two and a half years for time he had spent in custody pretrial. He was allowed 12 days leave from prison in 1951 when his wife had been involved in a traffic accident and a further day's leave in June 1954 to visit his sister in hospital. His release date was set as 8 November 1959. The Mixed Consultative Board reviewed his case in mid-1954 and found 'the evidence was inadequate to establish the allegation' that Koch had been concerned in the killings. The United Kingdom High Commissioner in Bonn wrote to Anthony Eden, the British Foreign Secretary, on 1 September 1954 saying 'I support the unanimous recommendation of the board that he should be released'. Consequently, a note from Eden was added to the Queen's red box of official papers in

October 1954 recommending 'that Your Majesty will be pleased to issue instructions that Fredrich Karl Rudolf Koch be released'. The Queen signed her approval and Koch walked free on 21 October 1954 having served just six and a half years.[43]

Andrzej Szablewski

The lives of slave labourers were held in little regard by their captors in the labour camps. But life could be just as dangerous for individuals forced into labouring on German farms.

The racist laws that followed the *Reichsparteitag der Freiheit* (Rally of Freedom) in Nuremberg (10 –16 September 1935) led to the opposite of liberty for millions of people. The 'Law for the Protection of German Blood and German Honour' forbade 'mixed marriages' and extramarital relationships between 'full Jews' and persons of 'German or related blood'.[44] The intense regulation, investigation and control of this aspect of Nazi ideology resulted in thousands of Germans being tried in court for 'race-defilement' (*Rassenschade*). Officially, judicial punishment could be meted out only to the male participant (women could only be witnesses) and ranged between one day and 15 years in prison. In practice, convicted men and women witnesses were handed over to the Gestapo. Most were transported to concentration camps where they faced torture and eventually death.[45] The Polish Decrees of March 1940 supplemented the race laws and included a strict prohibition of sex between Germans and Polish forced labourers.[46]

Hildegard Reiner was a young German domestic servant who helped out on local farms during the harvest in the north-west Hamburg suburb of Poppenbüttel. She lived with adoptive parents, the Carstens,[47] She first met Walter Grimm in 1937 or 1938 when she went to pick potatoes on his farm. He was a Nazi Party local farm leader who managed the Gut Hohenbuchen estate. After about six months of knowing Grimm, she had sex with him several times. It ended for her when she met and later married Heinrich Lütten, but Grimm often pestered her for sex. Heinrich joined the German army in December 1939 and was posted with the medical corps to France.[48]

Hans Frank, head of the General Government in Nazi-occupied Poland, wanted 'The supply and transportation of at least a million male and female agricultural and industrial workers to the Reich'.[49] In April 1940, 27-year-old Andrzej Szablewski, his brother Kazimierz and friend Jan Kardacz were forced under German military guard to come to work in Germany as slave labour. They were held in the 'Hamburg Labour Cage' until they were assigned to work at Gut Hohenbuchen.[50] Hildegard and Andrzej met each other in January 1941 and had a brief sexual affair. Knowing that sex between Germans and Polish people was forbidden, the couple had tried to be discreet. Unfortunately, Grimm suspected the pair and informed local policeman Willi Schmidt. He took his information to the Gestapo who arrested Szablewski on 15 July 1941. Lütten was arrested by the Gestapo a week later when she reported to their headquarters at the Stadthaus in Hamburg.

Lütten was interrogated several times by Alfred Bauer. She admitted nothing, but after a beating said that she had sex with the Pole three times. Szablewski was beaten by Bauer in Lütten's presence, but he would admit nothing, knowing that to do so might cost him dearly. Without a hint of a trial, Lütten was sent to the Fuhlsbüttel Gestapo prison in Hamburg where she languished for almost a year before being transferred to Ravensbrück concentration camp on 9 May 1942. She suffered in Ravensbrück for almost three years. While there her husband divorced her.[51]

Szablewski was also sent to Fuhlsbüttel, but on the 13 March 1942 he was taken back to the Gut Hohenbuchen estate. An oak tree had been chosen and the snow was cleared around it. A rope with a noose tied was thrown over a suitable branch. Two trestles and a plank were brought from a barn and set up beneath the noose. Two hundred Polish slave labourers were brought to the site, but kept some distance away by numerous police, Gestapo, SS officers and NSDAP members. Szablewski was made to stand on the plank and the charge against him, having sexual relations with a German contrary to the race laws, was read. He denied it. At 1.15pm a trestle was kicked away and he was hanged. The slave labourers were gathered around the still hanging body and Gestapo SS Sergeant Major Josef Weiss lectured them. Four of Szablewski's close Polish colleagues were then ordered to cut him down and place his body in a coffin. When they did so, several of them reported that Szablewski was still alive. Nevertheless, the coffin was sealed and sent to the Department of Anatomy at Hamburg University for dissection. The policemen, Gestapo, SS and Nazi party members then went for drinks and lunch at a local inn.

When Hamburg capitulated on 3 May 1945, another of Szablewski's brothers, Kasinin, lobbied the British to investigate the murder.[52] There were two trials of Germans accused of murdering Szablewski: the first in April 1946 and the second in July. The British wanted to try eleven people for the war crime, but they only had seven in custody. SS Captain Albert Adolf Schweim, an eighth suspect, was deemed unfit for trial. A further number of Germans that the British wanted to prosecute for the hanging were either at large or had not been identified in the various prisons, detention centres and displaced persons camps in the British and American occupation zones.[53] The trial of seven accused went ahead, much to the annoyance of the officer in charge of War Crimes Group (NWE), Group Captain A G Somerhough, who complained that the British were rushing into trials without having all the accused available.[54]

The first Poppenbüttel trial against the seven accused in custody began on 4 April 1946 in the Curiohaus.[55] Captain Dromgoole, the prosecutor, charged Willi Schmidt, Walter Grimm, Karl Mumm, Alfred Bauer, Max Stahl, Otto Schulz and Wilhelm Wichmann with, 'Committing a war crime in that they at Poppenbüttel, Germany, on or about 12 Mar 42 in violation of the laws and usages of war were concerned in the killing of Andrzej Szablewski, a Polish national'. All pleaded not guilty. The trial proceeded as usual for a war crimes trial under the Royal Warrant: opening speech for the prosecution and presentation of prosecution evidence (depositions and witness testimony). Opening speeches for the defence and presentation of defence evidence. Closing speeches for the defence, closing speech for the prosecution, summing up and verdict. The trial was completed on 12 April 1946. There is no trial transcript, but the interrogation notes, depositions and some testimonies are in various archives.

The court accepted that Szablewski had been murdered, but needed to assess the degree of active participation by the accused. The main prosecution witnesses were Lütten, her adoptive father, Heinrich Carsten, and Szablewski's Polish colleagues Jan Kardacz, Tadeusz Janiak and Boleslaw Zawidzki. Lütten told the court her story, adding that she could also identify Mumm as being present when Szablewski was beaten in front of her. Critically, she stated that she had never been before any court or given evidence against Szablewski.[56] This was strong evidence that Szablewski had not been given a trial. Carsten told a British interrogator that he had seen Grimm tie a rope over a branch and bring out trestles and a plank. It looked like Grimm had set up the execution.[57]

Kardacz, Janiak and Zawidzki did not see the hanging as they were kept some distance away, possibly in a barn. However, they were paraded around the swinging body and subjected to Weiss's lecture. The three of them together with Jan Wlodarski were ordered to cut Szablewski down. They reported that he was still breathing when they put him into a coffin.[58]

When interrogated by Major Forbes of 2WCIT, Grimm said that he had fetched ropes with Gestapo SS 2nd Lieutenant Karl Mumm and then cleared snow while Mumm fastened a rope to the tree.[59] Mumm, on the other hand, told Forbes that the ropes were arranged before he arrived.[60] In court, Grimm said that Schweim had ordered him to supply the rope, board and trestles, but Schweim had tied the rope to the tree. In short, Grimm, Mumm and SS Major Wilhelm Wichmann said that the leader in the murder was Schweim. Conveniently, Schweim was the suspect unfit for trial and so could not contradict them. Schmidt and SS Major Max Stahl blamed Weiss who was also not present (he may have been dead). All the defendants worked hard to distance themselves from the hanging. The drinks and lunch at Otto Sparr's inn was downplayed from a celebration of a job well done to a mere requirement for sustenance.

The court found all seven defendants guilty. Schmidt, Grimm and Mumm were sentenced to death by judicial hanging. Bauer was sentenced to 15 years' imprisonment, Wichmann to 12, Stahl to 10 and Schulz to 5 years.[61] Schmidt committed suicide in prison. Grimm and Mumm were hanged at Hameln Prison on 8 October 1946 at 10:27am by Albert Pierrepoint. Grimm, at a weight of 158lbs, got a drop of 7ft 1in while Mumm, 15lbs lighter, was given a drop 8in more.[62]

The British wanted to put four more people on trial for the murder of Szablewski, but they were not available by the time of the April trial. SS Captain Albert Schweim, declared unfit for the first trial, had been in custody in March 1946 (there is a record of him being transferred from No.5 Civilian Internment Camp in Paderborn-Staumühle to No.1 CIC).[63] but his health had apparently deteriorated so much by 4 April that he was sent to hospital in Rottenburg. He cannot have been seriously ill, however, as he escaped less than three weeks later.[64] It is a shame that Schweim was not brought to justice at this time because his deposition under oath gives much interesting detail about how Szablewski was judged by the police and the SS rather than tried in court.[65]

According to Schweim, while at Fuhlsbüttel Prison, Szablewski would have been 'subjected to a racial examination by the inspekteur of the security police and SD'.[66] After careful interrogation, six photographs would be sent to a 'race tester' who should also have inspected Szablewski. If mainly 'Germanic racial characteristics' had been found, Szablewski would not have been executed. It seems, however, he failed the racist test. Schweim maintained that *SS-Reichsführer* Heinrich Himmler himself would have issued the order to execute Szablewski and that the order would have passed through the Gestapo to a local member of the security police – in this case Johannes Thiele.

Schweim was ordered to attend the execution by the Gestapo. In his deposition, he said that Thiele 'introduced the execution' and passed the order on to SS Major Wilhelm Wichmann (Schweim's boss). Schweim then read out Himmler's sentence, which was translated into Polish by Gestapo interrogator Alfred Bauer.

Eventually, Johannes Thiele, Johannes Rehmke and Otto Hinze were tracked down and awaited trial in No.6 CIC, Neuengamme. The court for the second Poppenbüttel trial finally convened on 22 July 1946 in the Curiohaus Court Two where they were accused of the same war crime as in the first trial.[67] Again, there is no trial transcript, however, there are some details in the statements of the accused and defence petitions. The three were accused as senior officers for aiding and abetting the murder and for not acting to stop it.

Thiele told Major Forbes he was informed that Szablewski was to hang a day before. He decided to attend in his capacity of inspector of the Sipo and SD as a back-covering exercise, 'in order that he could say he attended the hanging if his HQ in Berlin should ask him'.[68] He considered himself the senior officer at the execution and admitted that he had taken no steps to find out whether Szablewski had been tried or to stop the hanging. He also retired afterwards to the inn for refreshments. He was convicted and sentenced to death by judicial hanging. His defence counsel, Dr Johannes Belfanz, petitioned the court against the finding and sentence claiming that Thiele was not Gestapo and that any objection he had made to the hanging 'undoubtably would have threatened him with brutal annihilation'.[69]

Johannes Rehmke was the NSDAP District Leader for the county that included Poppenbüttel. He told Forbes that he attended the hanging to represent the Nazi Party. He was convicted and sentenced to ten years in prison. His defence counsel argued that the conviction was harsh as Rehmke had no part investigating the so-called crime or ordering the hanging.[70] Rehmke claimed to have deliberately arrived late for the hanging (Szablewski's body had already been cut down) as he felt disgusted by it. As he had no knowledge of the case and was sickened, then surely he left at once? No, he too went for drinks afterwards. Hinze was acquitted as he took no part.

Despite Lord Russell of Liverpool, the Deputy Judge Advocate General, recommending that, 'there should be no interference with the sentences passed in this case', Thiele's death warrant was cancelled and his sentence commuted to 15 years custody.[71] Thiele served just over five years as he died in Werl prison on 22 September 1951.

The Nazi exploitation of forced labour is a stark reminder of the lethal depths to which an ideology of racial supremacy and militarism can lead. It illustrates the devastating consequences of unchecked power and the human capacity for cruelty. The stories of those who endured forced labour, often under unbearable conditions, serve as a testament to their resilience – we must remember their suffering.

4

TRIALS FOR THE DEATHS OF CHILDREN

In WW2, millions of children died in villages, towns and cities throughout Europe, but only Nazi Germany targeted children directly. The Third Reich saw any child not matching the ideal of healthy and 'Aryan' as a burden. The term 'useless eaters' as an excuse to kill them was first applied to disabled German children. From 1939 to 1945 at least 5,000 severely mentally and physically disabled children were methodically put to death by overdose or starvation in the child euthanasia (*Kinder-Euthanasie*) programme. Over 4,000 children in psychiatric institutions were murdered as part of *Aktion T4*, and 1.5 million mostly Jewish, Slav, Sinti and Roma children were deliberately killed by armed special deployment groups (*Einsatzgruppen*) and in concentration camps. Some even died in sites specifically designed for children, such as the Przemysłowa youth concentration camp in Łódź.[1]

Millions of women were taken from their homes in Nazi-occupied countries and forced to work in Germany. Many of them were of child-bearing age and, although slave workers were specifically prohibited from having sex, love and lust inevitably developed between these young women and the men they worked beside. In 1941, the general rule was when a female worker reported to her manager as pregnant, she was returned to her home country to have the baby, thus reducing the Reich's medical costs. This had two opposite and unintended consequences. First, women soon realized pregnancy was their ticket home and the supply of slave labour dropped accordingly. Second, many women did not want to be parted from the father of their child and so resisted reporting their pregnancy for as long as possible making their return home impractical. Germany then shouldered the burden of supporting the birth. Whichever way the Nazis looked at it, with increasing numbers of pregnancies, foreign women and babies were becoming too costly.

Accordingly, Reich Work Minister Robert Ley and Chief of the German Medical System Leonardo Conti implemented a new programme.[2]

The Nazis legalized abortion for Soviet and Polish women. In theory, it was voluntary, but in many cases, it was forced upon them.[3] If women did reach term, their baby would be born in a central maternity hospital set up in each district exclusively for them. The ethnicity of the baby would then determine its fate. German families adopted many babies deemed sufficiently 'Aryan', but those not so fortunate would be segregated into units ordered to be meagre and ill-equipped. Specifically, they were not to be cared for by their mothers (who were needed in the fields and factories) and were not to enter normal German hospitals or healthcare facilities.[4]

Everyone involved in the establishment of the 'non-Aryan' baby units knew their true purpose – to ensure the babies died. To hide this intention from the forced labourers so they would willingly leave their babies and return to work, *Reichsführer-SS* Himmler ordered the units to be called 'children's homes' (*Kinderheim*). Local people, however, called them camps and everyone in Germany knew that meant poor food and accommodation, no medical facilities, cruelty and death. There were hundreds of such places in Germany and over 100,000 children died in them.[5] The British convened three war crimes trials for the ill-treatment of Soviet and Polish babies in children's homes. In March 1946, the first was heard in Braunschweig and became known as 'The Velpke Baby Home Trial'. The second took place between May and June 1946 in Helmstedt and is called 'The Rühen Baby Farm Trial'. 'The Lefitz Children's Hostel Trial' is the least known of the three and was tried in the Curiohaus two years later. Lieutenant Colonel H R Bently of the Cheshire Regiment presided over all three trials.[6]

The Lefitz Children's Hostel Trial

Matron Minna Grönitz was shocked when a stone hit her on the head. The mother who threw it had been waiting outside the Lefitz Children's Hostel to see her baby. It had been days since she was allowed to see the child and waiting for the matron to say she could come into the hostel had tested her patience. When she could stand it no longer, she had picked up a rock and hurled it through the window. Grönitz sent for the Council Chairman – Walter Schulz.[7] She knew he would sort things out; he had broken up crowds of angry parents waiting to see their children before. His trusty pistol usually restored order. But this time, the chairman did not come himself. Instead, he sent the Lefitz milkman, Heinrich Koopmann, to see what was happening.

When Koopmann arrived, he thought the hostel was a disgrace, 'The children looked ill and badly nourished. It was cold in the room with laundry drying out.'[8] He told Grönitz the room was unsuitable for children and he thought they would not live long in such conditions. Taking offence, she told him only two had died so far and to keep his opinions to himself as he had no authority over her. Becoming angry and seeing that he was not making his point forcefully enough, Koopmann pushed her against a wall and told her to improve things quickly. Grönitz's pride was hurt, so she picked up her things and left the home. It was Sunday 27 November 1944 and she would never return. She knew her young assistants had lost faith in her authority and were sometimes lazy. She also knew, as she oversaw catering for the children, that food might become short. But her dignity was damaged and she refused to return until Koopmann apologized.

Wilhelmine Machel was the District Manager of the Farmers' Wives Society in the Lefitz area and a member of the National Socialist Women's League. The Farmers' Union had received an order from the regional government to open children's hostels to house the babies of their forced labourers. The workers from the East were there to work and time could not be spared for them to raise 'non-Aryans'. Some of the farms could not accommodate children and Machel thought hostels were a good idea, so she set up four. The Farmers' Union asked her to find a matron for the Lefitz hostel and she chose Grönitz, a woman who was living with the local midwife after having been bombed out of Hamburg. Grönitz had no specific qualifications and could take the role only part-time as she was the midwife's driver. She did not go to the Lefitz hostel every day and usually stayed less than an hour when she did. She set the visiting times for parents and decided Sundays would be best as that's when the parents had a day off (although they got one Sunday only every two weeks).

In May 1945, the area capitulated and the US Army took over. The US forces, having already taken towns to the south, had experience of what they would find in eastern workers' children's homes. When they discovered the house in Lefitz, they strongly suspected nine children had died from neglect. Grönitz and Machel were arrested. When the area became part of the British-occupied zone, the US Army handed over the case to the British who opened the trial of Machel and Grönitz in the Curiohaus on 16 March 1948.[9] They were charged with:

> Committing a war crime in that they at Lefitz, Germany, between June 1944 and 20 January 1945, in violation of the laws and usages of war, were concerned in the ill-treatment of Russian and Polish child inmates of Lefitz Children's Hostel, in consequence of which nine children, Rosemarie Brylinska, a Polish national, and Peter Fedorinowa, Anni Syrta, Jan Pasternack, Wande Pryzlylowa, Wanda Schyschlo, Franz Wienck, Katja Lewoeka, Katharina Ritnitschenko, Russian nationals, died.[10]

Following the case in the files at the British National Archives is made difficult by many of the witnesses being called Schulz – the Lefitz Council Chairman, schoolmaster, innkeeper and several farmers all had the same surname. Reading the witnesses' testimony, however, it is clear that most of the local farmers were fond of their forced labourers. Despite the conditions, they often became friends, and many would have allowed the babies of their workers to stay on the farm or work premises. One witness, Emma Schulz, helped her husband to run the inn at Sachau. She told prosecutor W P Grieve that while Sofie Pietrowska was working for her in 1943 she had a baby, Richard, which Schulz happily kept in her own house. When an order came in September 1944 that the child had to go into the Lefitz hostel, Schulz went to appeal to Grönitz who insisted Richard be sent to her.[11] The baby went to the home, but a few weeks later his mother took him back to the inn – he was cold and hungry. Pietrowska described the conditions she found in the hostel, 'the children were hungry, dirty and covered with lice . . . the children's beds were very dirty and the children had their feet tied to the beds'. Grönitz went to the inn and insisted Pietrowska return the child to the hostel. When Schulz protested, Grönitz became threatening and said she would get the innkeeper's wife sent to Lüneburg, which Schulz feared although it's not clear why. Pietrowska was fined RM 100 for taking her child and Richard was returned to the hostel.[12]

Russian forced labourers Boleslaw Wiazdzyk and Wera Fedorinowa also had a child, Pietr Fedorinowa (named Peter in the charge), who was taken into the Lefitz hostel in June 1944 aged three months. His father visited as often as he could, sometimes three times a week, but always in the evening when he knew Grönitz would not be there. He told the court, 'The conditions were very bad. The children were tied to the beds, the beds were wet and the children were covered in sores because of this.' He added, 'The home was dirty and cold everywhere. The girls sometimes told me they had no food to give to the children.'[13] Pietr was the first child to die in the Lefitz hostel, on 3 October 1944, he was just seven months old. His death certificate lists teething problems (*Zahnkrampf*) as the cause of death.[14] By this time, however, such a diagnosis for infant mortality was long discredited and was almost certainly used here to cover up that he had died from neglect.[15] Irena Brylinski's six-month-old baby girl, Rosemarie, died from pneumonia a few weeks later on 21 November 1944, the Monday before the incident with the milkman.

It was almost a month before Machel heard about Grönitz leaving the job. By this time, the children were succumbing fast. Anni Syrta died five days before Christmas from nutritional disruption (*Ernährungsstörung*) according to her death certificate. She probably starved to death because the assistants could not get sufficient food. They also failed to call a doctor, but they may not have known whom to call and probably did not speak German. Jan Pasternack and Wande Pryzlylowa died in the week between Christmas and New Year's Day. No cause of death was recorded for Wande, but Jan's diagnosis was lung inflammation (*Lungenentzündung*). In the first half of January, four more babies aged six months or younger died. Machel asked the Lefitz Council Chairman's wife, Alwine Schulz, to be acting matron while she found someone more suitable, but Schulz appeared to be useless and seemed incapable of calling for medical help. Machel finally appointed Johanna Zündt, an evacuee from Cologne, but she did not take over the hostel until 20 January 1945 as the doctors feared spreading an infectious disease. Seven children had died since the piqued Grönitz left.

Zündt described the conditions, 'When I took over the hostel I found it in a very dirty condition. Bed frames were covered with human excreta, palliasses [mattresses] were completely dirty and I had to replace them immediately.' Regarding the children, she said, 'They were all very weak from under-nourishment and insufficient care, some children had eczema and lice'.[16] Conditions improved and there were no more deaths after she arrived.

The doctor responsible for the nursery, Dr Edmund Zimmermann, visited infrequently. He told the court, 'I went only once or twice in

December and January'. Zimmermann could not remember whether there was medicine at the hostel, whether there were proper facilities for bathing the children or anything about the assistants. He testified, 'I thought a lot about these deaths, and we investigated the cause of these deaths. We found that there were an unusual number of deaths in other homes in the Kreis Lüneburg among the foreign children.'[17] But he did nothing about it. He was fortunate not to have been a defendant as, following the 'Rühen Baby Farm Trial', Dr Körbel had been executed for much the same behaviour.

When the prosecution closed, Machel's defence counsel Dr Eissner submitted that his client had no case to answer. He pointed out the prosecution had not proven Machel to be responsible for the hostel or that she knew of any 'irregularities' there. He also reminded the court that several prosecution witnesses said Machel had helped the children with food and clothing. Grieve, the prosecutor, replied that Machel had admitted responsibility for setting up the home and she visited often enough to 'have known sufficient of what was going on'. The court asked Machel to testify. She claimed not to be responsible for the home, that she could not give orders to the matron and added she had helped supply some food. The court found her not guilty.

Grönitz's defence was more complex – she considered herself a caring matron. Evidence from Hermann Thomann of the Criminal Investigation Department, who had investigated the case for the German police after the war, was used to defend Grönitz in three ways. First, to discredit Hermann Schulz, a local schoolmaster who had testified for the prosecution. The defence revealed him to be an ardent Nazi who had political quarrels with Grönitz and had perhaps used the trial as an act of vengeance. Second, to discredit the Polish prosecution witnesses, who Thomann suspected had been unduly influenced by the milkman Koopmann. Third, to show the 33 per cent death rate at the Lefitz hostel was normal and the rate at which all children in the area died.

Thomann's figures, however, were deceptive. For the Lüchow-Dannenberg area, he gave the death rate as 33 per cent (eighty-two births and twenty-seven deaths), but forgot to mention there were at least two other homes for foreign children in this region; Seerau in der Lucie and Liepehöfen. The conditions in these places were likely no better than in Lefitz and children probably died from neglect there too, thus falsely inflating the figures in his favour. He claimed the rate in Clenze was also 33 per cent, but his figures (thirty-seven births and thirteen deaths) included the children from the Lefitz home. Take these away and the rate is 24 per cent (seventeen births and four deaths). Thomann further tried to reduce the death rate in the Lefitz home by saying he thought it possible forty children had passed through the home rather than twenty, but this was speculation and not mentioned by any other witness. Thomann's figures did not add up.

After three more defence witnesses for Grönitz, Dr Meissner closed his case and the Judge Advocate, John Aubrey-Fletcher, summarised for the court. He clarified why the charge was a war crime and how the constitution and authority of the military court were valid. He further explained, 'If you find that there was ill-treatment or neglect but that such ill-treatment and neglect merely accelerated the death of the children or lowered their resistance to natural illness from outside causes then the charge would not be proved in full, but it would open you to bring in a special finding omitting the words: "in consequence of which nine children died".'[18] This is exactly what the court did. On 1 April 1948, it found Grönitz guilty of the charge, but omitting all words from 'in consequence of which . . .'. The court sentenced her to six months' imprisonment. Just over three weeks later, DJAG Brigadier Robert Halse sent a review of the case to the Hamburg District Commander. He concluded the part of the charge which stated the children had died from ill-treatment was not sufficiently proven in court, ' . . . because no medical evidence was called to show how the children died'.[19] Exhumations and autopsies were not routine – if they had been then some medical evidence may have been obtained (as it had been in the Rühen case). Two babies had probably died from neglect and seven as the consequences of an argument between an unqualified part-time matron and a milkman. The person convicted of ill-treating them served just 20 days in prison for each life.

Deaths of Babies in Ravensbrück

The huge NSDAP propaganda machine urged women to follow a traditional female role focused on the household. Many German women supported the family values of the past wrapped up in the phrase, 'children, kitchen and church' (*Kinder, Küche und Kirche*). In truth, the Nazis wanted to keep women subservient to men – they should support their husbands, bear many children and care for the home. Nazi Germany did not integrate girls into the Hitler Youth (*Hitlerjugend*), rather they had their own organization, the League of German Girls (*Bund Deutscher Mädel*). The League encouraged girls to become good wives, mothers and homemakers. They were specially instructed to avoid racial defilement (sex with 'non-Aryans'). In adulthood, they joined the National Socialist Women's League (*Nationalsozialistische Frauenschaft*) where they were urged to marry 'Aryans' and start a family. While 'Aryan' women were encouraged to bear children, the opposite was true for women considered subhuman by the Nazis in Germany and occupied countries. They were to be used as slaves or killed by the million in concentration camps. The Germans even built one specifically for women.

Construction of Ravensbrück by men of the Sachsenhausen concentration camp began in November 1938 on the bank of Lake Schwedt about 100km north of Berlin. The first 900 women inmates who arrived in May 1939 were transferred from the Lichtenburg concentration camp where they had been held after relocation from women's prisons throughout Germany and Austria. As the war progressed and the Germans occupied more countries, the population of Ravensbrück increased to a maximum of 45,000. The women toiled hard outdoors digging sand or in construction. Factories were built where they worked long shifts as slaves producing textiles and electrical components. Food was in short supply and of abysmal quality, clothing inadequate and living quarters intolerable. Of some 132,000 mostly women who passed through the camp between 1939 and 1945, between 90,000 and 117,000 died.[20] They suffered malnourishment, overcrowding, overwork, exposure, poor sanitation, medical experimentation, constant brutality and execution by injection, bullet or gas.

Naturally, wherever there are large groups of young women, babies follow. When the Germans opened Ravensbrück, however, this seemed to come as a surprise. They dealt with it in their usual deadly way: either they gave the mothers drugs to kill the unborn child *in utero* or they murdered the child soon after birth. In 1944, when the Germans brought many pregnant Polish women to the camp, the SS permitted some live births. But the women had to return to work within seven days of giving birth and were allowed to nurse their babies only twice daily. Since the SS did not feed the mothers sufficiently to enable them to produce milk, most of the babies starved and died. The exact number of infant deaths is unknown as the SS had the records burnt.

Soviet troops liberated Ravensbrück between 30 April and 1 May 1945. They found about 3,000 sick women there who had not been forcibly marched out of the camp a month earlier. As a result of the post-war partitioning of Germany, the camp remained in Soviet hands and Moscow was expected to convene any war crimes trials. But there was little Soviet interest in the case, probably because they held few potential defendants, most having escaped to the West. Along with other former camp staff, the British had seven doctors and an operating theatre nurse in custody whom they were investigating for performing human experiments in concentration camps. This group became known as the 'Hohenlychen Group'.[21] The Polish and French petitioned the British for the extradition of members of the Hohenlychen Group to their countries for the Ravensbrück trials they were preparing. The British, however, resisted as their trial preparations were progressing rapidly.

The British War Crimes Investigation Unit deposed camp survivors in 1946 in preparation for the main Ravensbrück trials. Dr Zdenka Nedvedova-Nedjedla arrived in the camp in August 1943 with a group of prisoners transferred from Auschwitz, where she had been sent after being arrested for anti-fascist activity. Nedvedova-Nedjedla, a Czech paediatrician, told the British investigator, 'The almost 100 per cent death-rate for children born in the camps was according to my opinion as a specialist doctor for children caused by an absolutely unhygienic nursing of these children, by their mass-accommodation in big blocks, which led to mass-infections, and for the majority of them by starvation.' Furthermore, she said, ' . . . mothers lost their milk soon after labour and artificial nutrition was not arranged, although during this time matron Elisabeth Marschall [accused] had in her store an immense quantity of dried milk'. According to Nedvedova-Nedjedla, 'She also energetically used her influence to prevent any improvement in nutrition of feeding mothers'.[22]

Sylvia Salvesen, the wife of prominent Norwegian doctor Harald Salvesen, gave a deposition to Royal Army Medical Corps doctor Major Keith Mant in Oslo on 15 September 1946. She told him, 'When I just arrived [in 1943] a large number of abortions were carried out in the camps. These took place at night and were carried out by the camp doctors. There were no children allowed to be born in the camp for about the first year of my stay there.'[23]

Anna Seidemann, a Danish woman, was arrested in German-occupied Riga in January 1942. She was accused of illegal correspondence with the Danish and Swiss Legation and sent to the Majdanek concentration camp. The Germans transferred her to Ravensbrück in April 1944 where she was made a block leader. It was her job to ensure prisoners followed camp rules in her barracks. Between November 1944 and April 1945, Seidemann was the block leader for Block 11 where SS doctor Percival Treite and matron Elisabeth Marschall were in charge. In her deposition she said:

> Between November and January 1944 to 1945 all children (newborn) were kept in a special room in Block 11, they were placed in two-tier bunks, ten to a bunk, there were about 50 in this room. About 1 or 2 died every day. There was no extra food for the children or the mothers. Between November and January about 150 passed through this room, about 30 survived to be transferred to Block 5.[24]

Treite was a skilled gynaecological surgeon, a member of the NSDAP and the SS. By 1943, he seemed close to becoming a professor of medicine in Berlin. Before that could happen, however, the authorities moved him to Oranienburg concentration camp, making him a camp doctor. Having passed a field medicine course in Austria, he had expected a transfer to the front. His superiors, however, saw his future in the concentration camps, perhaps Auschwitz or Mauthausen. As he was a gynaecologist, he logically matched to Ravensbrück and he was transferred there to be the medical supervisor of Block 5.

The British handed over four of the Hohenlychen Group to the Americans for the first of their subsequent Nuremberg trials, 'The Doctors' Trial' (officially United States of America vs. Karl Brandt, *et al.*).[25] They kept Dr Rolf Rosenthal and Dr Percival Treite and eventually held seven trials in the Curiohaus for crimes committed at Ravensbrück.

The main British Ravensbrück trial began in December 1946, just a few days before the US trial, and lasted two months (with a few days off for Christmas). As a token acceptance of the interest Poland and France had in the case, the court included a Polish and French member.[26] Sixteen defendants appeared charged with, 'Committing a war crime in that they at Ravensbrück in the years 1939 to 1945, when members of the staff of Ravensbrück concentration camp, in violation of the laws and usages of war, were concerned in the ill-treatment and killing of Allied Nationals interned therein'. The charge included the mistreatment and killing of children.

Prosecution Counsel Stephen Stewart had the unenviable task of describing the crimes against women and children committed in Ravensbrück which included the usual starving, beating and murder. In addition, there was appalling experimentation, forced sterilisation, forced abortion, inhumane treatment of the insane, and the killing of infants. His junior counsel, John da Cunha, vomited when he first read the depositions preparing for the trial.[27] Prosecution witness Dr Nedvedova-Nedjedla told da Cunha in court that not only were the babies starved by the accused matron Elisabeth Marschall, when there was plenty of food available, but they were crammed together in bunks with insufficient nappies or clean laundry. Marschall also appointed two untrained German prisoners, accused of being anti-social, to look after the babies when there were qualified children's nurses available. She said Treite regarded the first few babies as a novelty, but 'later when their number was increasing, he lost all interest in their life'.[28] Anna Seidemann told the court that Marschall had forbidden anyone to stay with the babies at night, resulting in some dying of suffocation. On average, two or three children died each night of starvation or suffocation. She estimated that 80 to 90 per cent of children died during the six-month period she worked in Block 11.[29]

Treite denied mistreating the babies and told the court the death rate of between 50 per cent and 80 per cent was also true of newborns in German cities. This was nonsense. Essentially, he told the court he was a model doctor and if he had done anything wrong, it was under orders from Berlin. Marschall also claimed to be a humanitarian in her defence testimony, saying she had tried to get extra food for the mothers and babies. If she had not been nice, she told the court, it was because the prisoners had misbehaved.[30]

All sixteen of those tried pleaded not guilty, but all sixteen were convicted. Treite, Marschall and nine others were sentenced to death by hanging. Pierrepoint hanged Marschall in Hameln Prison on 2 May 1947. At 60 years old, she was the oldest female Nazi war criminal executed by the British. Treite cheated the noose by committing suicide on 8 April 1947. His post-mortem examination by Lieutenant Colonel F E Buckland (Royal Army Medical Corps) revealed he had died from cyanide poisoning.[31]

Murder at the Bullenhuser Damm

The Germans did not limit involuntary human experimentation to women in Ravensbrück. Other cases occurred in men, women and children in many other concentration camps. Perhaps the best known are Dr Josef Mengele's hideous twins experiments in Auschwitz.[32] In contrast, some of the least known are the experiments on children in the Neuengamme concentration camp.

It began with an assassination attempt on SS Lieutenant General Reinhard Heydrich in Prague, which left him severely injured. Himmler sent SS Major General Dr Karl Franz Gebhardt, Director of the Hohenlychen Sanatorium, the main SS medical facility, to assume Heydrich's medical care. Gebhardt was also the Chief Physician of the Reich and Himmler's personal physician. Although Gebhardt arrived too late to operate on Heydrich, he took over the post-operative care. Gebhardt did not believe in the effectiveness of the most common antibiotic then in use in Germany and refused to treat Heydrich with sulphonamides.[33] Dr Theodor Morell, Hitler's physician, however, was strongly in favour of sulphonamides.

When Heydrich died of sepsis on 4 June 1942, Gebhardt's decision came under scrutiny. Himmler and Hitler were both great admirers of Heydrich and questioned whether the doctor had been negligent. Himmler told Gebhardt he might find a way out of the hole he had dug himself if he could prove experimentally that sulphonamides could not have prevented the death.[34] Gebhardt began inhumane experiments into the progress and prevention of gas gangrene almost immediately on women in Ravensbrück, the closest concentration camp to Hohenlychen.[35]

Gebhardt's Assistant Director at the Hohenlychen Sanatorium was SS Captain Dr Kurt Herman Otto Heißmeyer. He believed the Nazi principle that there were inferior and superior races and medical treatment should be determined by a patient's racial group. To further his career, he wanted to confirm by experiment the theory of two Austrian physicians, Adolf and Hans Kutschera-Aichbergen. They thought a sub-cutaneous injection of tuberculosis bacteria might improve the immunity of a patient with tuberculosis of the lungs.[36] The theory was, however, ridiculed by the scientific community. Heißmeyer was not a research scientist and had no specific training in immunology or bacteriology. Emboldened by the widespread use of unwilling people from concentration camps in research by his boss, however, he wanted to begin his own unethical human experiments as soon as possible.

Gebhardt had been less than subtle about his activities and Allied intelligence knew German doctors were forcing prisoners to be subjects in terrible experiments. After the invasion of Normandy in June 1944, Himmler began to be more careful about how Germany was perceived by the Western Allies and he needed to be convinced to allow Heißmeyer's human testing. Unfortunately, Heißmeyer had good Nazi connections. His uncle, SS Lieutenant General August Heißmeyer, had deep Nazi credentials. His aunt, Gertrud Scholtz-Klink (married to Uncle August), was the leader of the National Socialist Women's League and nicknamed 'The Female Führer'.[37] In addition, Heißmeyer was friends with SS Lieutenant General Oswald Pohl, head of the SS Main Economic and Administrative Office and the lead administrator of the concentration camps. They added their support for Heißmeyer and Himmler eventually agreed to the experiments. Pohl passed a message to Heißmeyer that experiments were not, however, to be done in Ravensbrück. Together, Pohl and Heißmeyer instead chose the Neuengamme concentration camp near Hamburg.

Heißmeyer began his deadly work with live tuberculosis bacteria in the summer of 1944 by experimenting on Polish and Russian adults in Neuengamme. Most of these people were in a pitiful state having been in concentration camps for years. Many were already ill with tuberculosis, but those who were not were deliberately infected by Heißmeyer using the painful process of passing a tube into the trachea and injecting a bacteria-laden solution. Some medical records from these unfortunate people survive showing that Heißmeyer experimented on at least fifty-two prisoners. After four weeks of observation, the prisoners were hanged and Heißmeyer dissected their corpses in the Neuengamme morgue. Under interrogation after the war, Heißmeyer admitted that far from improving tuberculosis in any of the people he had experimented on, he had made all their cases more severe. He realized inoculation with live tuberculosis bacteria did not cure the disease, it made it worse.[38] Despite his lack of success, he ordered the transfer of twenty Jewish children from Auschwitz to his facility in Neuengamme. His rationale for continuing the experiments was to see whether the Jewish children were less immune to tuberculosis and if he could immunise them. In one of his research papers, he explained that, in his opinion, 'racially inferior people' (by that he meant Jews, Slavs and anyone whom he considered should be in a concentration camp) had naturally lower resistance to illness.[39]

Ten boys and ten girls between the ages of 5 and 12 left Auschwitz by train on 27 November 1944. The Germans had already killed most of their parents or moved them to other camps. The children left behind whatever hope they had of seeing their families again when they arrived at the Neuengamme concentration camp on 29 November 1944. The camp covered a huge area about 30km to the south-east of Hamburg. It had a large brickworks onsite with associated clay pits and loading docks. Prisoners were badly housed, brutally treated, starved and worked to death here and in its many subcamps. One hundred thousand people passed through Neuengamme between 1938 and 1945. Lord Russell estimated 40,000 had died: the Germans had executed 3,000 and the other 37,000 had died slower deaths in the terrible conditions.[40] At its height, half the camp inmates were Russians and Poles. French, Dutch, German and Scandinavians made up the rest in roughly equal proportions.

The children entered Revier 4, a special hut cleared of adult patients, which was heated and had sufficient bedding. They were reasonably fed, at least compared to the other inmates, and looked after by four kindly prisoners. Two Dutch orderlies, Dirk Deutekom and Anton Hölzel, treated the children like their own. Two French doctors, René Quenouille (Professor of Radiology from Villeneuve-Saint-Georges) and Gabriel Florence (Professor of Biology from Lyon), kept the children's medical records and nursed the children the best they could as each child became sick with tuberculosis from Heißmeyer's repellent methods. Each child had an incision on a breast or arm into which tuberculosis bacteria was rubbed.[41] In the sixth week after being infected, the children suffered yet more unnecessary pain. In a deposition under oath, medical orderly Franciszek Czekala told the 2WCIT,

> . . . the orderlies brought the children in singly from Revier 4 to Revier 1. I was in the first-aid room of Revier 1 and was present during all the operations. The children were stripped to the waist and laid on the operating table. The skin under

> their arms was painted with iodine, and they were then injected with 10cc 25 Novocain. Dr Dozlik Bogumil, the operating doctor, then felt the glands under the arm, made an incision about 5cms long and took thc gland out. Thcn hc stitched the wound with cotton.[42]

Heißmeyer took the surgically removed lymph nodes back to Berlin and sent them for microscopic examination by pathologist Dr Hans Klein in Hohenlychen.[43]

By March 1945, all the children had become so ill they were bedridden. The British Army was getting closer to Hamburg and the camp staff and local businesses, which had used the slave labour supplied by the Neuengamme camp, worried how they might be treated if the British found out what had happened there. In April 1945, an order to evacuate the main camp meant over 12,000 prisoners left Neuengamme. A rapidly assembled ragtag of vehicles evacuated the luckier ones, the Scandinavians, to Denmark. The Germans transferred the unlucky to other camps, including the notorious Bergen-Belsen, or onto ships in Lübeck Bay such as the *Cap Arcona.*[44] What was to be done with the children? Commandant SS Colonel Max Pauly claimed to intercept an order from Berlin to the camp doctor ordering their execution.

On the evening of 20 April 1945, with the British Army just a few miles away, a truck driven by SS Sergeant Hans Friedrich Petersen arrived at the camp. Inside were six unknown Russian POWs. The children climbed in with their Dutch and French guardians. SS Sergeant Major Wilhelm Dreimann, SS Platoon Sergeant Major Peter Wiehagen, SS Sergeant Adolf Speck and SS Captain Dr Alfred Trzebinski (the senior camp physician) also boarded the truck. Dreimann was especially dangerous. Phillip Jackson testified that he,

> was a sadist in every respect. He always attended all the hangings. On these occasions the prisoners were made to take their clothes off before they were hanged, and he used to shout, 'Get a move on — the quicker you are, the quicker you will be dead' or words to that effect. I heard that sometimes these people were not killed outright, and afterwards Dreimann would go to the mortuary and strangle the bodies with his own hands.[45]

None of the thousands of prisoners who came into contact with him would have doubted that in the slightest.

Some of the SS guards claimed to believe the prisoners and children on the truck were to be transferred to another facility. But this was a lie, the SS *knew* the men and children on the truck were to be executed. It was policy for an SS camp leader to be present at executions. In Neuengamme, this would usually have been SS Lieutenant Anton Thumann, but he was not available that day, having gone to inspect the concentration camp at Wöbblin. So first they drove to the Hamburg-Hammerbrook subcamp on Spaldingstraße to liaise with the next senior officer, SS Lieutenant Arnold Strippel. If the children were merely to be transferred (and not executed) they would not have needed him.

Strippel had run the Hamburg-Hammerbrook subcamp since December 1944. It was a former tobacco warehouse containing over 2,000 prisoners whose daily task was to clear war damage and defuse unexploded bombs. Since Strippel also oversaw all the other Neuengamme subcamps, it was his responsibility to choose where to kill the children. He got into his car and ordered the truck driver to follow him to an empty subcamp. Once a school, Bullenhuser Damm had been another Neuengamme subcamp and housed several hundred rubble-clearing inmates. It had been recently abandoned and cleared of prisoners. A janitor, Wilhelm Wede, and two SS men, Sergeant Johann Frahm and Company Sergeant Major Ewald Jauch, guarded the building.

The SS guards led the Russians into a boiler room, the children into an air raid shelter and their guardians into an adjoining room. Trzebinski stayed with the frightened children while Frahm, Jauch and Dreimann hanged all the adults. They attached ropes around their necks, threw the ropes over a pipe and hauled them into the air leaving them to strangulate for about 30 minutes. Trzebinski learnt from Frahm the children were also to be hanged. He told the court he 'wanted to ease their final hours'. Rather than offer them his protection, he called each into a small room where he gave them a morphine injection to sedate them. Some needed two injections. Frahm then hanged the children two at a time from hooks on the wall. The guards burnt the children's clothes in a coal stove and locked their bodies in the Bullenhuser Damm cellar. Strippel took the bodies back to Neuengamme the following night where SS Sergeant Wilhelm Brake cremated them.

Hamburg formally surrendered to the British less than two weeks later on 3 May 1945. The British Army liberated the Neuengamme concentration camp on 5 May 1945. It had been hastily cleaned up and evacuated, and to their surprise they found hardly anyone there. Max Pauly, the camp commandant, was discovered hiding in Flensburg and taken to No.1 CIC in Neumünster. Frahm, Dreimann and Speck rapidly joined him there. The British unearthed Jauch hundreds of miles away in Schwenningen where they arrested him and took him to No.7 CIC in Eselheide. They finally caught Trzebinski in February 1946. He was working as a doctor in the Hesedorf camp where the British Army was sorting and discharging German POWs. They took him to No.8 CIC at Westertimke.

Speck was the first to tell the story of what happened to the children. He told his interrogator, Captain H P Kinsleigh, he had travelled in the back of the truck and stayed there with Petersen and Wiehagen when they got to Bullenhuser Damm. He confessed to transporting Russian prisoners to the former school where twelve were murdered – the six transported with the children and a further six later in the night.[46]

Frahm told Kinsleigh about murdering the children, but put the blame squarely on Trzebinski who he said had given the children 'an injection into the heart'.[47] Frahm was further interrogated by Major Anton Walter Freud. He gave a full description of the children's murder. He told Freud that Trzebinski had sedated the children and he and Jauch, '. . . carried the children into another room. A rope was put around their necks and they were hung up on hooks like pictures on a wall.' He said Trzebinski, Dreimann and Strippel were sometimes present. He also confessed to hanging the Russian prisoners.[48]

There were several Neuengamme trials. The first began in the Curiohaus on 18 March 1946.[49] Among the fourteen men accused were Pauly, Thumann, Dreimann, Speck and Trzebinski charged partly in connection with the murders at the Bullenhuser Damm. None appeared to feel any shame. All tried to shift blame away from themselves and relied on the defence of superior orders. Prosecutor Major Stewart, however, had an ace up his sleeve. He had discovered Fritz Bringmann, a German anti-fascist whom the Germans sent twice to Neuengamme between 1940 and 1945. He was a medical orderly in a Russian ward in the camp. His superior was SS Sergeant Willi Bahr who was also in the dock. Bringmann told Stewart, 'In the middle of February 1942 Bahr came to me and gave me the order to give these Russians injections [of phenol] and through these injections to liquidate them, to finish them off'.[50] Bringmann flatly refused and obviously survived, demonstrating to the court that even *prisoners* could refuse murderous superior orders without major consequences.

Camp commandant Pauly admitted he knew the experiments on the children were injurious. Asked by his defence counsel, Dr Wessig, 'Were you under the impression that these experiments would be beneficial to the children, or did you think they might be harmful?' Pauly answered, 'Everybody knew that they would not be beneficial'.[51] But he desperately tried to wriggle out of responsibility for the deaths of the children. Wessig asked, 'Who issued this order of execution?' Pauly answered, 'General Pohl'.[52] Wessig asked how Pauly had learnt of the execution order and Pauly said, 'It was addressed to the Standartz, and I read it at that time'. Pauly was adamant Pohl's order was addressed directly to the senior doctor (*Standartz* or *Standortartz* – there is some confusion in the record) who was Trzebinski and could not be interpreted as his own order. Trzebinski, however, doubted Pohl would send an order to him and thought Pohl had ordered Pauly who then passed it on as his own. Pauly may have distanced himself from killing children, but the conditions in Neuengamme were his responsibility and provided ample evidence on which to find him guilty of a war crime. Pauly, however, denied knowing about the conditions in the camp, the poor food and cruel punishments. He did this so often in testimony that the incredulous prosecutor repeatedly asked whether or not he was the commandant.

Thumann, a trained carpenter, joined the NSDAP in the 1930s and worked in Dachau from 1933 to 1940 as a clerk. The authorities then posted him to Gross-Rosen concentration camp where he worked until 1943. From February 1943 to April 1944 he was the camp leader of Majdanek concentration camp where he earned the nickname of 'Hangman'. Thousands were shot, hanged and gassed while he was in authority there. He spent a few weeks in Auschwitz before coming to Neuengamme as camp leader. Thumann was greatly feared for his seemingly random beatings and for setting his dog onto defenceless prisoners. He admitted being present at all executions in Neuengamme, but when asked by his defence counsellor Dr Koenig, 'During your activities of one year at Neuengamme did you ever take a life?' he answered 'No'.[53] Perhaps he believed it as he had made prisoners perform the hangings. His part in the deaths of the children was ordering Dreimann to transport the children. Thumann claimed he was not further involved as he was away from Hamburg.

Speck and Wiehagen had watched over the children, their guardians and the Russian POWs in the back of the lorry which took them to Bullenhuser Damm. Speck, who had been a member of the SA, joined the Hamburg police in 1940 and then an SS police division where he served in France, Russia and the Netherlands. He came to Neuengamme in 1943 as a block leader. He kept order in the prisoner barracks using a cane.

Dreimann, to whom all block leaders reported, admitted beating prisoners with a whip and seemed to relish his unofficial title of 'camp executioner'. He had form for hanging people. In March 1945 he had helped to execute between sixty and eighty Dutch prisoners in this way. French Professor Eugene Prenant told war crimes investigators, 'The hanging went on all day . . . We had to unhang the corpses hastily and carry them one after another to the mortuary.'[54] Dreimann told the court how he had hanged the Russian prisoners (but not the children) in the basement of the Bullenhuser Damm. He had hoisted them up, in batches of four, on ropes slung across a pipe and then left them for half an hour. This did not break the necks of the men, they were strangulated. It's easy to imagine how the sounds of this brutality, shouting, crying, choking, kicking and banging would have terrified the children in the adjoining room.

Frahm, one of the Bullenhuser Damm guards, was a prosecution witness at this trial. Stewart asked him about hanging the Russian POWs, 'When you say they were being hanged, where were they being hanged and by whom?' He answered, 'We all were present, Jauch, Dreimann, Trzebinski and myself were in the cellar.' To clarify, Stewart asked, 'When you say they were hanged, who hanged them?' He answered, 'We all.' Trzebinski's defence counsellor Dr Lappenberg, in cross-examination asked, 'Did the children die as a result of those injections [from Trzebinski] or did they die because of anything else?' Frahm told him, 'They died as a cause of the injections. Some of the children were hanged on top of that . . . Dr Trzebinski and I myself helped.' Lappenberg asked him, 'Who put the rope around the neck of the children?' and got the answer, 'I'. Finally, Frahm revealed he and Jauch had received cigarettes and liquor as a reward for what they had done that night.[55]

On the 30th day of the trial, Lappenberg opened the defence of his client Trzebinski. Although Trzebinski was Polish by birth, he would have difficulty claiming to be anything but a committed Nazi. He had joined the SS in 1932 and the NSDAP a year later. He had spent three months in Auschwitz as a camp physician and almost a year in Majdanek before coming to Neuengamme in September 1943. He claimed to have done everything to help prisoners and knew nothing of lethal injections. And yet, somebody had ordered Bahr the medical orderly to kill dozens of sick Russians and thousands of people had died while he was the camp doctor. Trzebinski told his lawyer he had heard about the order to kill the children from Thumann who had said to him, 'Hold on, I have got some bad news for you. Pauly wants me to tell you that he had received an execution order from Berlin for the medical orderlies and the children and that you are to carry out these executions either by injections or by gas.'[56] Trzebinski claimed never to have seen the order and to have tried to think of a way to save the children. He did not try too hard. He was the most senior SS officer that night – he could have diverted the truck on the way to Strippel and surrendered to the British forces. This would have been dicey, but surely it was a better choice than the mass murder of children. The possibility never seems to have occurred to him.

When the children arrived at Bullenhuser Damm, Trzebinski told the court, Frahm ordered them to undress – he could not conceive of killing people with their clothes on. The doctor made an excuse telling the children their nakedness was necessary for vaccination. Trzebinski claimed to have decided to 'make their last hours as easy as I could' by injecting them with a solution of morphia. After the injections, the children got dressed, but Frahm returned to tell them, 'You must undress again as you are going to have a bath.' According to Trzebinski, Frahm then took a 12-year-old boy into another room, ' . . . and there I saw a noose hanging on a hook. He then put the sleeping boy into this noose and hung himself onto the body of the boy with all his weight to cause the noose to contract.' Even this horror did not incite Trzebinski to do something to save the remaining children. Instead, to compose himself, he left the building and walked around the block a few times. When he returned, he saw hanging the bodies of three children and the bodies of about ten adults, which included the children's guardians. A few of the stronger children were awake and so Trzebinski injected them again before leaving for Spaldingstraße where he thought working on patient files might take his mind off the night's murders.[57]

The court announced the verdicts of the first Neuengamme trial on 3 May 1946. It sentenced Pauly, Thumann, Trzebinski, Dreimann, Speck and six others to death. Lord Russell of Liverpool rejected clemency and on 26 August 1946, the GOC-in-C BAOR signed eleven death sentences. Pierrepoint hanged them all at Hameln Prison on 8 October 1946.

The evidence uncovered in the first trial resulted in a further trial (the third Neuengamme trial) for the murders in the Bullenhuser Damm which ran from 24 to 31 July 1946 in the Curiohaus. Johann Frahm, Ewald Jauch and Gustav Wilhelm Brake were tried for their involvement. The cover of file WO 309/396 in The National Archives suggests five others were considered for trial, but were not charged.[58]

Frahm was a factory worker. He joined the SS in 1933, the NSDAP in 1937 and trained as a guard in the Sachsenhausen concentration camp. He served in Neuengamme from November 1942 and, from 1944, reported to Dreimann. Frahm was arrested by British investigators in October 1945 at home in Kleve.[59]

Major Anton Walter Freud was the lead investigator for the 2WCIT. For months in 1946, he gathered the evidence prosecutor Captain Cleaver would need to prove the guilt of the three accused. He took depositions from former Neuengamme prisoners, illustrating the brutality of Frahm. Willi Eggebrecht told him Frahm would beat prisoners to the ground and continue striking them with a truncheon. He took great delight in throwing prisoners into the water-filled fire ditches surrounding the camp from which they struggled to escape. At almost any time of the year, this would have meant a dunking in cold water. If it happened on a winter morning, it meant breaking through the ice in the ditch and working thereafter in temperatures below zero wearing thin, wet clothing.[60] Karl Hoevelborn said Frahm beat two Russian prisoners with a square fence post causing appalling injuries. He also saw him break a prisoner's arm one morning with a stick. Frahm ordered the man to continue work for the day and he was not treated until the evening.[61] On 2 May 1946, Freud took a sworn deposition from Frahm who told him the children were killed, 'like pictures, they were hanged on hooks on the wall. This was done by Jauch, myself, Trzebinski and Dreimann.'[62]

Jauch was a former salesman from Schwenningen. He joined the NSDAP in 1934 and the SS two years later. He was a guard in the Neuengamme camp from 1940. For a short period in 1944, he was commandant of the Schandelah subcamp where prisoners toiled in an open-cast mine quarrying oil shale for processing into petroleum products by Steinöl GmbH. In November 1944 he transferred to the Bullenhuser Damm. His subordinate, Frahm, had already given testimony in the first Neuengamme trial regarding Jauch's involvement in the hanging of the children. In his deposition, however, Jauch was careful to downplay his role. He said he stayed in the room where the children had undressed and saw only one child injected by Trzebinski. He continued, 'I am not aware that the children were subsequently hanged'.[63] Jauch knew the adults were hanged, however; he went into the room several times and helped to take the bodies down. He had seen all the corpses in the evening, when they were collected for transport back to Neuengamme, and it is unlikely that he did not notice rope marks on the children's necks too.

Albin Lüdke made a sworn deposition to Freud about Brake who, he explained, was head of the camp registry. This meant he was also responsible for the busy crematorium. Lüdke was the kapo in charge of selecting prisoners to transport bodies from wherever they had died in the vast camp to the crematorium. On more than one occasion, when the horse-drawn cart got stuck in mud, Brake would snatch the horsewhip and, ' . . . with the thick end of the whip beat the prisoners madly not caring where he hit them'. In February 1945, Lüdke remembered the cart getting stuck in mud up to the axle.

> On this occasion, he [Brake] got hold of the handle of a shovel and beat the prisoners with it until they had carried the cart to a new place approximately 30 metres from the new crematorium. As from there the cart could not be moved any further and all beating was in vain, the prisoners had to carry the bodies singly to the crematorium.[64]

Brake himself admitted striking prisoners with a whip. His statement about the bodies from Bullenhuser Damm was phrased to distance himself from being an accessory after the fact. He said a transport arrived of forty or fifty corpses and he was told they were not to be burned. He cycled quickly to the crematorium, however, when he got there cremation had begun. Riding back, he reported this to Thumann who then spoke to Trzebinski, and he was told the cremations could go ahead. Once more, he cycled to the crematorium and told the prisoners they could proceed with the burning. He was at the crematorium and saw the bodies on two occasions, but would only state, 'The prisoners told me that there were about 20 children amongst these corpses'.[65] It's difficult to believe he had not noticed himself half the dead were children nor that he had missed the rope marks on the bodies.

The trial opened in the Curiohaus on 24 July 1946 accusing Frahm, Jauch and Brake of the war crime of being concerned in the killing of Allied nationals.[66] Brake was additionally charged with the war crime of ill-treating Allied nationals. After a week of hearing evidence, the court found Frahm and Jauch guilty of the first charge and sentenced them to death by hanging. The court found Brake not guilty of the first charge, but guilty of the second and sentenced him to five years' imprisonment.

Defence counsellor Dr Eugen Schöndienst petitioned for a reduction in Frahm's sentence, arguing Frahm was 'mentally slow' and unable to consider not following the order to kill the children. Schöndienst seemed to think the court should take into account that Frahm had 'not committed any war crimes before this disastrous night – in spite of existing temptation in the concentration camp'.[67] Defence counsellor Dr Eberhard Cappelle petitioned for his client Jauch, who he said was in the Bullenhuser Damm basement but took no active part in the killing. Unfortunately, Dreimann and Frahm had said the opposite. Cappelle also made a plea for mitigation of sentence asking the court to consider the fact that, 'shortly later he helped about 30 prisoners whom he had to transport in a bus to the Baltic Sea make good their escape and to gain their liberty'.[68] Cappelle must have known helping any number of people could not excuse killing others. Pierrepoint executed Frahm and Jauch on 11 October 1946 in Hameln Prison. Dr Georg Beermann's application for reduction of Brake's sentence amounted to nothing more than an attempt to discredit Lüdke, but the court preferred to believe the witness.

After the case, prosecutor Cleaver wrote a report to Lieutenant Colonel J Leicester-Warren in which he scorned the administration of the trial. He claimed to have received no help from the British Army HQ Hamburg District, 'until requested, entreated or threatened'. The addresses they gave him for the witnesses could not be understood as the spelling was incorrect. Two witnesses were in the Fuhlsbüttel Prison, but when he went there, the officials would not let him in without a pass from the Penal Administration. When he had been admitted and seen the witnesses, the staff would not let him out, seeming to confuse his identity with the men he wanted to interview. At the trial, he found HQ Hamburg District had not extended the correct assistance to the defence counsellors. One of them had heard only by accident the trial was to be held in the Curiohaus. Moreover, Cleaver had to '. . . initiate proceedings for securing the attendance of defence witnesses. I also had to arrange for a medical examination when a plea involving sanity was suggested.' None of these things should have been the prosecutor's responsibility and he was angry that it was '. . . unfair to counsel and unjust to the accused'.[69]

Four men involved with the murders at the Bullenhuser Damm escaped trial at the Curiohaus. Wiehagen escorted some 7,000 former Neuengamme prisoners up to Lübeck Bay where they were forced onto two ships, the *Thielbek* and *Cap Arcona*. On 3 May 1945, as a result of poor communications, the RAF attacked the vessels.[70] Some prisoners dived off the ships, only to be shot at in the water by the guards. Infuriated, the prisoners turned on those shooting. One shooter was Wiehagen and the prisoners beat him to death. Just a few hundred prisoners survived to be liberated by the British. Truck driver Petersen fled to Denmark where he served a short prison sentence in 1946 for his SS membership. He died in Sønderborg in December 1967.

Heißmeyer eventually settled in Magdeburg where he opened a private tuberculosis clinic using his real name. In 1964, it was revealed that the lung specialist had carried out criminal experiments. The East German General Prosecutor's Office arrested him and he was charged with crimes against humanity. At first, he denied the accusations but eventually led investigators to a box he had buried after the war in the garden of his house in Hohenlychen. The box contained documents and photographs relating to his experiments. The Magdeburg District Court opened a trial against Heißmeyer on 21 June 1966. Nine days later, they sentenced him to life imprisonment at Bautzen (one of the Stasi prisons). He died just over a year later in 1967.

Strippel joined the SS in 1935 and entered the concentration camp system. He tortured and murdered in Buchenwald, Natzweiler, Majdanek, Peenemünde, Vught (in the Netherlands) and Neuengamme. At the end of the war, Strippel went into hiding, but in 1948, a former Buchenwald prisoner recognized him. The German police arrested him and he was tried in Frankfurt. In June 1949, the court sentenced him to 21 life imprisonment terms plus 10 years. After serving almost 20 years in Butzbach Prison, he petitioned for a revision of the judgment. In 1970 the court quashed the sentence. They re-sentenced him to six years as an accessory to murder, but immediately released him for time already served. For the other 14 years he had spent in prison, he received compensation of almost DM 121,500 (about $46,000). He bought a house in Frankfurt-Kalbach. Strippel's luck held out in 1981 when a court sentenced him to three and a half years' imprisonment as an accessory to murder in Majdanek. Regarded as unfit to serve a prison sentence, he remained at liberty.[71]

In 1964, the Hamburg public prosecutor's office investigated Strippel for his probable involvement in the Bullenhuser Damm murders. After a long investigation, the Chief Prosecutor of Hamburg, Helmut Münzberg, decided not to proceed with a prosecution. Under German law, a murder conviction required proof a person acted with a 'base motive' such as to satisfy sexual desires, out of greed, insidiousness or cruelty. Münzberg made the decision that Strippel had not acted in any of these ways. He stated:

> The investigations did not prove with the certainty that is demanded of them that the children suffered unduly before they died. On the contrary, much can be said for the fact that all the children became unconscious as soon as they received the first injection [of morphine from Trzebinski] and were therefore not aware of all that happened to them thereafter. And so, beyond the destruction of their lives no further harm was done to them; and in particular, they did not have to suffer especially long, either in body or soul.[72]

It fell to the relatives of the victims of Bullenhuser Damm to file criminal charges against Strippel. Finally, in 1983, the Hamburg public prosecutor accused him of forty-two murders – the twenty children, their four attendants and the Soviet POWs. It looked like justice might be done, but the court suspended the trial because Strippel was regarded as unfit to stand. He died a free man in 1994.

5

TRIALS FOR MURDER IN WORK EDUCATION CAMPS

The concentration camp system spread from Germany, infecting the occupied countries until it was a massive murderous machine. The camps had started as a means of locking away enemies of the NSDAP, particularly communists, to protect the party's fragile hold on German politics. During the 1930s and 1940s, they evolved into a complex hierarchy of misery. There were, broadly, four types of camps: extermination camps, slave labour camps, hybrid camps which were a mix of both the former two types, and transit camps. There were also many varieties of police camps, prisons and interrogation centres. Other than a handful of Nazi-era scholars, however, few people have any knowledge regarding 'work education camps'. They have been overlooked, even in German literature, and there is virtually nothing in English to enlighten the interested reader.

A work education camp (*Arbeitserziehungslager* or AEL) was a Gestapo camp where anyone could be sent by the secret police for breach of labour contract or disobedience of service obligations. In reality, this meant for almost any reason. AELs were designed to teach a lesson: you must toil industriously for the Third Reich. Nothing less than total commitment would be tolerated. For the Nazis, brutality was the key to this lesson. Nobody incarcerated there, if they survived, would ever want to go back and would spread the message to all colleagues that no effort was to be spared in the workplace. At first, the punishment was applied to German workers alone, but as the proportion of slave workers in Germany increased, they also found themselves being sentenced, without trial, to eight weeks in an AEL. In practice, many were kept imprisoned far longer, especially when the Gestapo gained an income from prisoner labour assigned to local companies.

Release usually meant being sent back to work, but if the Gestapo considered the 'education goal' had not been achieved, the worker could be put into the 'protective custody' of a concentration camp. In 1940, there were a handful of work education camps, but by 1945 there were up to 200 and about 500,000 people passed through them. Most camps were set up near industrialized areas, some were even on factory grounds. In addition, there were work education camps *inside* other types of concentration camps.[1]

Called 'punishment camps' by the British, they were deliberately harsh. Inmates carried out especially heavy and dirty forced labour under cruel penalty regimes with dreadful living conditions. Clothing was inadequate and included nothing for protection. Food was meagre, of pitiful nutritional value and could be withheld for days as punishment. Prisoners were beaten with sticks, rifles, belts, rubber hoses and truncheons, sometimes to death. Medical facilities were either poor or non-existent. The type of work depended on the site. It included clearing rubble and unexploded bombs, excavation, producing cement for building bunkers and laying rails.[2] Many became debilitated within days and thousands died from ill-treatment, starvation and disease.

AEL Bremen-Farge

Bremen-Farge was a huge shipyard on the River Weser and vital to the German navy. The Germans needed slave workers there by the thousand to build docks, transport facilities and submarine bases. Established in 1943, the Neuengamme subcamp Bremen-Farge provided labour for the construction of a subterranean U-boat shipyard codenamed 'Valentin'. Initially, all the prisoners lived in appalling conditions underground in a former fuel tank, but as their numbers increased, they took over several naval barracks. Between 1943 and the summer of 1944, when the foundations were laid, hundreds died and more prisoners had to be brought in from Neuengamme. By March 1945, the subcamp housed over 2,000 prisoners. Five hundred and fifty-three victims, mostly Frenchmen, have been identified, but the total number of deaths may be as high as 6,000 as nobody recorded the names of the Polish and Russian dead who vastly outnumbered the French. Work there was punishing. But the subcamp was not the AEL.

A rudimentary AEL had been part of the other Bremen-Farge subcamps since 1940, but in the autumn of 1942, four barracks were fenced off between a workers living camp called 'Tesch' and a navy camp to house forty or fifty work education prisoners (this number grew to over 600 by the end of the war). Unusually, thirty or forty British and Irish seamen were among the prisoners. Most of what we know about the hellish conditions at AEL Bremen-Farge comes from their testimony. They had previously been held in various POW camps, but were eventually transferred to the AEL in February 1943 when they refused to work for Germany. Believing they were being taken back to a POW camp, they arrived smoking cigarettes and chatting to each other. As they entered the gates, the cigarettes were knocked from their mouths and the beating began. All their possessions were taken, their heads shaved and a large number sewn to their uniforms. Worst of all, their overcoats were confiscated. When their clothes later turned to rags, many took their blankets to work as protection against the weather. Shoes soon fell apart and were replaced by wooden clogs. Socks were a rare luxury.

Prisoners were turned out of bed at 4am and given three or four minutes to drink half a litre of watery swede soup. Each was handed two slices of bread to last the whole day. Then they were paraded outside whatever the weather, which often meant they were soaked before work. They stood at attention for up to two hours while being counted and beaten. Work parties were organized and the men marched to their allotted workplace where they toiled from 6am to noon. They were given half an hour to drink another bowl of soup or a cup of ersatz coffee and then worked until 6 or 7pm. After marching back to the camp there was another roll call. The prisoners were then made to exercise until 7 or 8pm while being beaten with lengths of hosepipe or wire. Next was another parade and a long wait in strict silence for more soup. If it had been raining, they slept in damp clothes and blankets – there was no drying room. The British and Irish men couldn't believe the conditions and had to harden themselves rapidly. Their overriding emotion was hopelessness.[3] The Field Investigation Section of the War Crimes Group (NWE) estimated that between March 1942 and the evacuation of the camp in April 1944 well over 400 prisoners lost their lives there.[4]

Thirteen men were accused of the war crimes committed at AEL Bremen-Farge. All were charged with ill-treating Allied nationals and five were additionally charged with killing Allied nationals. A court convened in the Curiohaus on 19 December 1947 led by Lieutenant Colonel B G Melsom of the East Lancashire Regiment.[5] The court heard how the British and Irish men had seen floggings every day when three or four guards and kapos would beat a man unconscious and then revive him with cold water to endure further beating. Dogs would be set on men to rip their clothing to pieces and cause horrific bite wounds. The 'hospital' contained living corpses lying in faeces and suffering many diseases. Some were dragged from their beds to be beaten. Those who tried to escape and were shot dead would be brought back to the camp, their bodies thrown onto the parade ground, coal shed, washroom or refuse pile and left for several days as a warning to the others. The men witnessed terrible atrocities and wrote, 'The mental torture endured by us all nearly reached breaking point'.[6] Five of them died.

The accused all gave testimony in court. Hans Hasse, the first defence witness, was prosecuted on the first charge only. He joined the NSDAP in 1929, the SS in 1931, the Kripo in 1933 and the Gestapo in 1938. He admitted sending men to the AEL, but claimed that was where his duty ended. The conditions in the camp were the responsibility of his superiors. He knew nothing about 'inadequate clothing or terribly hard work' and thought deaths occurred only due to typhus. He was found guilty and sentenced to five years' imprisonment.[7]

Franz Sauer was an Austrian piano maker who joined the frontier police and then the Kripo. He was a guard in the camp from March 1942 to May 1943. He contradicted himself in testimony saying, 'I never struck them', but later 'And whenever I have clouted a prisoner it has never been brutal or violent, just the kind of clout I used to get myself when young'.[8] Prosecution witness Issac Ryan, however, told another story. He had heard terrible screaming from the punishment bunker where prisoners were beaten with rubber hoses. He had seen Sauer coming out of the bunker afterwards with two others. Prosecution witness George Knott also accused Sauer of brutality towards the prisoners. Sauer was found guilty of ill-treatment and sentenced to three years' imprisonment.

Karl Walhorn was a German window-dresser. He had previously worked in youth camps, but eventually joined the Gestapo. He was the commandant until early 1944 and claimed the camp was humane. He had two favourite sports: one was to set his dogs onto prisoners, the other was to put small pieces of potato onto a manure heap. When the prisoners tried to get the food, he would shoot them with his sporting rifle. He said, 'I realize it was wrong, but I thought then it was justified'.[9]

The court found him guilty of the first charge and he was sent to prison for four years.

Ludwig Zehntner was a Polish bricklayer and forced labourer. He was sent to the camp in 1944 where he became a foreman. Zehntner was regularly beaten by the camp commandants, but would admit only to slapping the prisoners himself. Ryan, however, told the court Zehntner was 'Another brutal man in every respect'. Prosecution witness Willi Schramm said Zehntner slapped, punched and hit prisoners with a stick. He said, 'Once he beat a Russian with this stick on the bare backside . . . The Russian was screaming with pain. I saw him get 20 to 25 strokes.'[10] Zehntner was sentenced to three years' imprisonment.

Johannes Meyer, a conscripted policeman, was a camp guard. He admitted to shooting dead a prisoner he claimed was trying to escape and to beating others with a rubber hose. Ryan said such beatings might last as long as 20 minutes. Knott accused him of force-feeding raw potatoes to a prisoner, but Meyer denied this. Prosecution witness Friedrich Niemeyer said he saw Meyer together with two others beat a Polish man. He said they 'put the prisoner across a chair and all three beat him up. They took turns . . . They beat him for 10 minutes. He was screaming.'[11] Meyer was also sentenced to three years' imprisonment.

Günther Velke was a salesman. He came to the AEL in November 1944 and admitted to slapping prisoners. Knott said the prisoners called Velke 'The Madman' and that he would greet arriving prisoners with blows from 'the gummy' (rubber hose).[12] Knott, however, was the sole witness to give evidence against Velke and he was given just six months' imprisonment.

Wilhelm Plothe, a former German Navy ships pilot was discharged as unfit for work in 1942 and became a guard at AEL Bremen-Farge in January 1945. He was accused of both charges. He had admitted to shooting at a man in his testimony and was found guilty of the second charge (that of killing Allied nationals).[13] He was given the lenient sentence of seven years' imprisonment, perhaps because it was unclear to the court whether his admitted single shot had struck any prisoner, let alone killed him.

The Judge Advocate, Guy Sixsmith, prepared a careful summary consisting of 345 points, which he patiently read to the court. He explained some witness testimony was uncorroborated and it would be unsafe to accept it as a basis for conviction. He told the court, regarding Hasse, that it must decide how far the policy of sending foreigners to an AEL was a war crime. Furthermore, it must decide whether there was a deliberate intention to mistreat and what degree of violence was allowable as punishment before it became a war crime. He explained that as the Irish men came from a neutral nation they were not Allied nationals and, therefore, did not form part of the charges against the accused.

The Monday after Sixsmith's summary, there was a closed-court discussion in which he, surprisingly, was not involved. When the court voted on who would be convicted, he thought it was provisional. He expected further discussion in which he would take part. He wrote, 'However, all that happened on Tuesday was that the court reassembled and when I tried to start a discussion I was told that everything I said had been considered, and Monday's voting was confirmed.' Sixsmith's misgivings increased when he learnt about the attitudes of the Irish witnesses adding, 'I have been wondering since if the key to whatever pattern there is behind the convictions and acquittals is the personal likes and dislikes of the Irishmen'.

Despite his meticulous guidance, Sixsmith thought the court had acted inappropriately. He wrote, 'I came away from this trial profoundly disturbed at the outcome . . . it has been my experience that an exchange of conflicting views is an asset as tending to establish those which are founded upon rational considerations. When it was too late I realized that it was just in that very respect that this trial may have gone wrong.' He blamed himself for not emphasizing where there was and was not sufficient evidence to convict the accused.[14] Of the thirteen prosecuted, six were acquitted even though there was similar evidence against them. Mentally exhausted by his diligent counselling of the court during the two-month trial and agonizing over the fairness of its verdicts, Sixsmith was ordered to rest by his doctor.

AEL Hamburg-Wilhelmsburg

AEL Hamburg-Wilhelmsburg was also known as 'Camp Langer Morgen' as it was situated on the long-gone Langer Morgen Strasse in the northern part of an island in the Elbe. Founded in April 1943, it was originally intended for 800 men mostly from Western Europe and Poland. As the camp grew, however, the largest group of prisoners came from the Soviet Union and included women (they arrived in the summer of

1944 and were separately housed). In May 1944, all the Chinese people living in Hamburg were also interned there on suspicion of sabotage and opium trafficking.[15] Seventeen of them died in the camp. The average population size of the AEL was 500 and, by the time it was destroyed by bombing in March 1945, 5,000 people had passed through its gates.

Prisoners were used after Allied air raids as clean-up squads to clear rubble, salvage unexploded bombs, patch roads and repair railway lines. Among other oil companies, Deutsche Shell AG, Deutsche Erdöl AG and Ölwerke Julius Schindler were happy to use the prisoners from the AEL to clear up following the bombing. Shipyards too, such as Blohm & Voss KG and Howaldtswerke AG, benefitted from their services.[16]

On 21 May 1948, a Curiohaus court tried thirteen men and two women on up to three charges.[17] All faced the first charge of committing the war crime of ill-treating Allied nationals. SS Colonel Dr Josef Kreuzer (head of the Hamburg Gestapo) and Erich Oehmke (the Gestapo AEL commandant from May to October 1944) were further charged with killing a Polish national. Josef Sommerfeld (commandant from October 1944 to March 1945) was further charged with killing an Italian national. All pleaded not guilty, as the accused did in every Curiohaus trial.

The prosecution called several former guards to give evidence. Hermann Scherler, aged 56, told the court the prisoners worked from 7am to 5:30pm unloading bricks, digging ditches, laying cables and other tough physical work. Their clothes were inadequate in the winter, but they were forbidden to use their blankets, so many wrapped themselves in empty cement sacks. Their shoes fell to bits and many worked barefoot through the winter. The guards would kick and punch the prisoners or beat them with sticks and rubber truncheons while they worked. The food was inadequate, for breakfast a mug of ersatz coffee and a slice of bread (if it was available). Lunch would be oat and potato soup, but it was rare that a prisoner found a piece of potato in their meal. Dinner was 400 to 500g of bread.

Kurt Rössler told the court how the prisoners were treated after a punishing day's work. Camp commandant Oehmke had marked out a rudimentary track around the washroom and named it the 'Horner Rennbahn' after the Hamburg racecourse. The prisoners were made to run around it for half an hour while the guards punched and kicked them. One blew a whistle at intervals indicating the prisoners should drop to the ground before getting up to run again. It was utterly exhausting for people who were in pitiful physical condition and had worked all day.

Rössler also gave evidence about the feared 'intensified interrogations'. He said with the whole camp on parade, a man would be stretched out over a table, his buttocks bared and a wet towel placed across them. Oehmke would then beat him with ten strokes of a wooden club. Karl Koopmann (the camp deputy commandant) would then do the same, followed by a block leader. The court heard many other instances of cruelty including teeth being knocked out, whippings and vicious poundings with rifle butts from 'Cossak' guards.[18] Koopmann, particularly, dished out savage beatings usually aiming for a prisoner's genitals. Friedrich Behnke whipped and beat the prisoners liberally. He had kicked a Polish woman in the stomach and boasted of taking part in mass executions in Poland. Martin Klimkeit was merciless, especially to Polish people. He injured prisoners in his working party so often that he was removed from its charge. Koopmann, Behnke and Klimkeit, were each sentenced to 12 years' imprisonment, but served about six.

Women gave evidence of brutal treatment by the female guards Kätchen Obernhuber and Else Weinhert. German housewife Ludowika Nikolic spent eight weeks in the AEL and her deposition illustrated its harshness. She explained how the women all suffered from diarrhoea, but were not allowed to use the toilets at night, 'therefore the huts were completely filthy'. She saw one seriously ill woman scrubbed with hard brushes after complaining she could not go on. The woman was carried from the bathhouse dead. She saw guards beating women with boards and other objects.[19] Obernhuber and Weinhert, however, were acquitted along with male guard Hermann Schmidt.

One serious incident involved the guards Hans Paudert and Fritz Ohlmeyer. A working party, known as the 'River and Port Commando', were marched from the camp to a landing stage by the Rethe Bridge. Here they boarded a barge to take them onwards to their worksite. A Frenchman jumped from the barge as it left the bank and ran into the grounds of an oil company. He was pursued by Ohlmeyer, but seeing the man could not escape, Ohlmeyer asked the company's security guards to capture the escapee and return him to the camp, which they did. Paudert was later sent back to the camp to collect the prisoners' midday meal and he returned with the recaptured Frenchman. Fellow guard Wilhelm Hügelmann told the court how Ohlmeyer and Paudert made the man run up and down an embankment carrying water or cement, pouring buckets of water on him until, exhausted, he collapsed. They then stood on his wrists. When he was revived, while the others ate their lunch, they forced him to stand at attention with his arms raised. Following this, they chased him around at gunpoint. Finally tiring of it themselves, Paudert shot the prisoner in the back.[20] Ohlmeyer and Paudert were sentenced to death. On review, however, it was pointed out they had not been charged with killing but with ill-treatment and their sentences were reduced to 15 years and 10 years, respectively. Ohlmeyer served less than half his sentence and walked free on 20 September 1955. Paudert was freed on 16 December 1953.

Accused of killing a Polish national, camp commandant Erich Oehmke told the court how the death had come about. He said some prisoners had told him they heard a Polish man touting for accomplices to help murder him. Oehmke claimed to have reported this to Kreuzer who had ordered the man to be executed. Kreuzer denied this and blamed his superior. Oehmke believed the RSHA in Berlin had issued an order signed by the chief Ernst Kaltenbrunner himself authorizing the man to be shot.

Oehmke paraded the whole camp who he claimed were outraged and had shouted, 'He must be shot dead'. This is stretching credulity to breaking point. It is hard to believe that prisoners had acted in any way to support Oehmke – he had invented the 'Horner Rennbahn', which so tortured the inmates, and beaten men in 'intensified interrogations'. Whatever the truth, a three-man firing squad shot the Polish man and Oehmke stepped forward to give him the *coup de grâce*.[21] The Judge Advocate advised the court that, as there had been no trial of the Polish man, the killing was unlawful. If the court believed, however, that there was an order from the RSHA, this could mitigate the sentence. This appears to be what happened as Oehmke and Kreuzer were sentenced to life imprisonment. Both were released in the autumn of 1954 after serving just over six years.

Josef Sommerfeld, the camp commandant from October 1944 until the AEL was destroyed in March 1945, was found guilty of killing an inmate of undetermined nationality. As the court did not know whether the prisoner had been an Allied national, they sentenced him to 20 years' imprisonment of which Sommerfeld served under six years.

Unusually in a British war crimes trial, the prosecution called a German doctor of forensic medicine, Professor Hans-Heinrich Koopmann, to give evidence regarding the dates and causes of death of forty-nine inmates of AEL Hamburg-Wilhelmsburg between May 1943 and March 1945. He read into the record evidence of the autopsies he had performed. First on the list was Myroslav Sasacki who died from a gunshot wound to the head on 18 September 1943. This was probably the Polish man executed by Oehmke. The other people had died from various illnesses including pneumonia, chest fracture, peritonitis and tuberculosis, but most had starved to death. The bodies had come to his morgue naked and 'covered with a layer of lice'. He said, 'We were all incensed and disgusted'.[22] From the beginning of March 1945, Professor Koopmann refused to take any more corpses from the AEL as his mortuary was overcrowded. Four bodies from the camp were instead taken to Dr Erich Fritz, a professor of forensic medicine at the Hamburg Institute of Forensic Medicine. He performed an autopsy on each finding that three of the bodies were malnourished and all had died from lung infections.

Of the fifteen defendants accused of punching, kicking, whipping, clubbing, beating, starving and shooting thousands, three were acquitted. The others faced prison terms of up to life, but none served more than eight years.

AEL Nordmark

Early in 1944, running out of space in local prisons, head of the Schleswig-Holstein Gestapo, SS Major Fritz Schmidt,[23] applied to the RSHA for the construction of a new work education camp. Building by prisoners from the nearby Drachensee police detention camp began in May 1944. AEL Nordmark in Kiel-Hassee, on the north-western shore of the Russee, opened in September 1944 and was in operation for just nine months. In this relatively short period, 5,000 mostly Eastern European men and women passed through the camp.

Camp prisoner accommodation consisted of five full-sized huts measuring 40m by 9m each with a small room in the middle for 'orderlies' who acted as kapos. One was exclusively for women. Plank beds were arranged in two tiers on each side of the hut, enough for 150 people. A further two huts were divided in half. One housed seventy-five men and the rudimentary camp 'hospital'. The other housed seventy-five women and their female guards. There were three huts for male guards, a command centre, a stable, a canteen, a workshop, two washrooms (eventually) and, astonishingly, a guest house.

When a man or woman arrived in the camp, all their possessions were taken and put in a sack. Anything valuable was rarely seen again.

They disrobed and put on camp clothes; a shirt, underpants, cap, trousers and jacket (made from blankets). Foot rags were issued instead of socks and each received a pair of shoes with wooden soles or clogs. There were no overcoats. When they entered a hut to find a bed, they were given one blanket. No mattresses were issued, so they slept on bare boards. There were no washrooms until March 1945, so inmates washed in the lake, although there was no soap or towel. Toilets were a plank over a pit, but at night, the prisoners used buckets. These had no lids, often overflowed and added to the atrocious conditions.

Prisoners were woken at about 4:30am and paraded for about an hour while they were counted and assigned to work parties. They worked from 6am until 6pm when there was another parade. Work parties assigned to the inside of the camp received two slices of bread with a little margarine and a cup of ersatz coffee for breakfast, a bowl of thin swede soup for lunch (a half-hour break at noon) and a few slices of bread for dinner. The men and women worked until they dropped, building more barracks or shovelling in the gravel pit. Outside working parties fared even worse. They had to march to and from work and received food at lunch only if the local population took pity and gave them something – the camp supplied nothing. In the evening they had the thin swede soup. They cleared rubble, built bunkers and worked in local companies. At all times, prisoners were punched, slapped, kicked and beaten with sticks, plaited electrical cable and rifle butts.

In April 1945, the usual camp population of about 900 doubled in two days as prisoners arrived from the Fuhlsbüttel Gestapo prison in Hamburg and the Riga ghetto. As the Allies approached, hundreds were executed, many in mass shootings. At least 578 prisoners died before the British liberated AEL Nordmark on 4 May. When they arrived, the British soldiers found terrible conditions and many graves scattered around the camp. Dr Keith Mant, the forensic pathologist from the Special Medical Section of the War Crimes Group (I), gave details of how some had died. He wrote, 'The ages of the bodies exhumed varied from about 16 years to extreme old age. Most of the bodies were reduced completely to skeletons, this being due to the fact that they must have died in a state of extreme emaciation.' Five of the bodies he examined had died from being shot in the back of the head. One probably died from being beaten to death – there were multiple fractures including of the left eye-socket, five ribs and a pelvic fracture.[24]

Unusually for an AEL, this camp had a dual purpose. In addition to the 'work education' aspect, AEL Nordmark was an interrogation centre for those suspected of subversive activities in the area. The most feared place in the camp was called the 'bunker', a complex of forty-eight small isolation cells. They were partly underground, made of porous concrete and often had 2cm of water on the floor. Each had a plank for a bed balanced on a bucket and a stool. They were unlit and unheated. Prisoners were locked away here for many days as punishment or to weaken them during interrogation. Kiel resident Annmargret Hölzel spent three weeks in one of these cells. In her statement, she said, 'We only got one woollen blanket at night time and this was withdrawn at any petty occasion . . . Only towards the end of my internment in the bunker were buckets put into the cells. Before that, the prisoners were taken to the lavatory once in the morning and once at night.' She explained that since the roof leaked everything became wet, 'if one laid down, one lay literally in the water and all this at an outside temperature below freezing point'.[25]

There were four Curiohaus trials for the crimes committed at what the British called 'Kiel-Hasse' consistently misspelling the area of Kiel where AEL Nordmark was located (Kiel-Hassee). Evidence was relatively easy to gather: the crimes had been committed towards the end of the war, some of the witnesses still lived in the Kiel area and many of the camp staff were in custody. The first trial began on 10 October 1947 where eight Germans and one Dane were charged with the war crime of ill-treating Allied nationals. Five also faced a second charge of killing Allied nationals. Gustav Klostermann alone was further charged with beating an Allied national to death, but was acquitted on this charge.[26] As usual, all pleaded not guilty. SS Major Johannes Post, the AEL Nordmark commandant, had just been convicted and sentenced to death in the first Stalag Luft III trial in the Curiohaus. He was not charged or called to give evidence, but was executed on 26 February 1948 for his part in killing Allied airmen POWs.

Josef Braitmann was the prosecution's key witness and gave evidence against many of the accused.[27] He told the court that Willy Stender, a detective sergeant in the Gestapo who led the camp guards, had beaten him with a walking stick. The attack was so ferocious that Braitmann lost two teeth. When the stick broke, Stender picked up a chair and continued the beating. Braitmann had also seen Stender interrogating a Russian prisoner who he hit twenty-five times with a bamboo stick.

During the trial, many harrowing details of cruelty and abuse were revealed. Two interrogators, in their depositions, gave illustrative examples. Gustav Klostermann said, 'He [the prisoner] had to lie down on a block and received 5 to 8 strokes . . . The strokes were obviously painful, and many prisoners had screamed.' Heinrich Unruh, a Ukrainian of German descent, had beaten hundreds of prisoners. He admitted, 'I would beat prisoners with a stick at his orders. Normally Staeglich ordered 10 strokes, if the prisoners would still not speak he was given another 10. If they still would not talk, they would possibly get another 10, and if that were no use they were locked up again in the detention cells, and interrogated again on the following day or the day after.'[28] Klostermann was sentenced to 12 years and Unruh to five, but both walked free in 1951.

Of the hundreds of murders committed in AEL Nordmark, four occasions particularly stood out in the trial: the shooting of people in a gravel pit, the execution of thirty amputees, the killing of two Russian women and the mass execution of sixty prisoners just before liberation.

German clerk Bernhard Scoor was a prisoner in AEL Nordmark for about six months from October 1944 to March 1945. One day in February 1945, he was ordered with seven other prisoners to wait behind a hut near a gravel pit. He heard Post read an order and shots fired. Scoor and the others then retrieved six naked bodies from the pit and put them against a hut. This happened with another group of six and a group of five. Some of the shot men were not dead and 'They received a *coup de grâce* fired by Jensen'. Eventually, there were seventeen dead bodies.[29]

SS Staff Sergeant Otto Baumann had been a farmer until 1939 when he was conscripted into the Gestapo where he worked as a driver and mechanic. After many postings, he was arrested in 1943 for allegedly helping in the escape of a French prisoner. He was sentenced to a year imprisonment, but after seven months was released on probation to work in AEL Nordmark. Here he took the rank of SS Sergeant and became the camp leader (*Lagerführer*) in October 1944. In testimony, he said he had tried to improve conditions, but there was no evidence of this. Baumann explained his part in the execution described by Scoor. He had just unloaded his truck when Commandant Post,

> waved a machine pistol and called me over. He shouted at me and said that I should come down into a hole to administer *coups de grâce*. In the hole I saw an SS man

Above: **1.** Curiohaus Court One as it looks today. (Author)

Below: **2.** Curiohaus Court Five as it looks today. (Author)

Above: **3.** Vemork hydroelectric power plant close to the town of Rjukan in Norway. (Public domain – out of copyright)

Below: **4.** Bullenhuser Damm – the open door leads to a basement room where twenty Jewish children were hanged. (Author)

5. SS Sergeant Major Friedrich-Wilhelm Kliem, second camp commandant of Neugraben. (The National Archives)

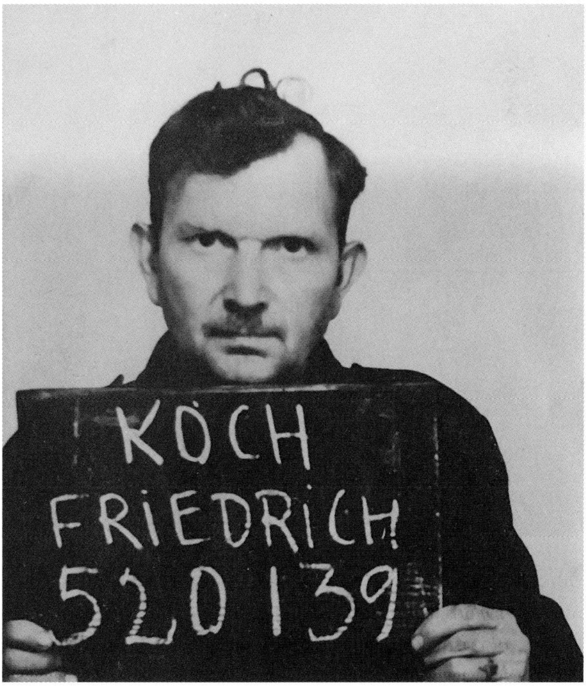

6. Gestapo Steinbergen Quarry guard Friedrich Koch. (The National Archives)

7. Düsseldorf criminal police Detective Superintendent Dr Victor Harnischfeger. (The National Archives)

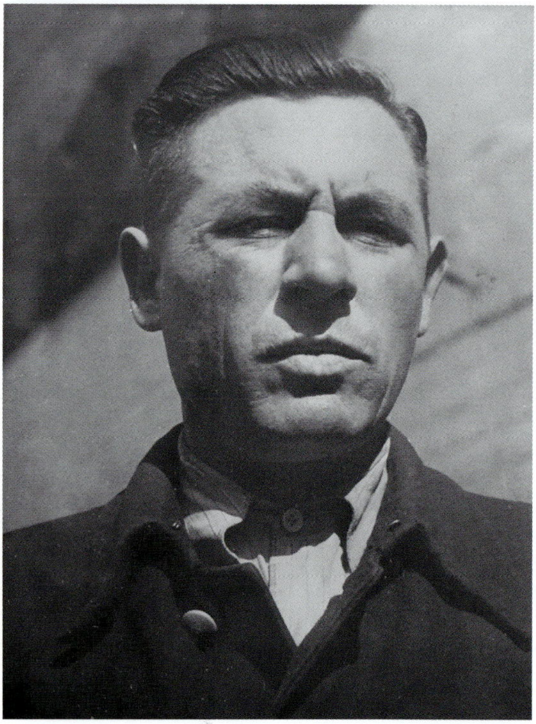

8. AEL Nordmark camp leader Otto Baumann. (The National Archives)

9. Pyotr Palnikov (centre, in uniform) – Seelhorst Cemetery exhumations. (Pen and Sword)

Above: **10.** Cromwell tank of 7th Armoured Division British Army by the Elbe Bridge in Hamburg 3 May 1945. (Wikicommons – public domain)

Below: **11.** Horsa Mark 1 glider as used by the men of Operation FRESHMAN. (Wikicommons – public domain)

Above: **12.** The accused in the Zyklon B Trial, Tesch, Weinbacher and Drosihn. (Wikicommons – public domain)

Right: **13.** Le Paradis Memorial, outside Norwich Cathedral. (Creative Commons)

14. The stumbling stone (*stolperstein*) for Andrzej Szablewski in Hamburg-Poppenbüttel. (Wikicommons – copyright free)

15. Erich von Manstein, the last man tried in the Curiohaus. (Creative Commons)

> armed with a machine pistol and one prisoner. I also saw some people down there lying on the ground. I do not know how many there were, but they had been shot. As Post was threatening me with his machine pistol, I had to obey his order, and I jumped into the pit.[30]

His account then became improbable. He told the court, 'Thereupon Post fired three shots into the pit. He fired at dead prisoners. I told him to stop firing as otherwise I would fire at him.' He continued, 'I did not fire any shots at all on this occasion'. In his handwritten notes, prosecutor Vollmar had underlined this statement as it implied Baumann *had* shot on other occasions.[31] In his closing statement on behalf of Baumann, Dr Hensel said, 'If the court judges about the legal character of an execution by the question, whether, or not, there was a sentence by a Court or an order by 'Reichsführer SS' in hand, one must take into account that Baumann lacks, or at any rate, lacked, the necessary intelligence to be able to understand such difference'.[32] But in his own testimony, Baumann never claimed to have heard a sentence read to the prisoners – he arrived after the shooting began.

Orla Jensen was still in his early twenties when tried in the Curiohaus. He had trained as a medical orderly and been sent to work in Kiel by a Danish company. After about five months, he got a job as a medical orderly in the 'free labour camps'. In July 1944, he transferred to AEL Nordmark where he set up the infirmary while the camp was being built. He admitted to watching the execution in the gravel pit. He explained, 'I went along the line of bodies with Post and the corporal. As the camp doctor had not yet arrived, I pointed out to Post that two or three men were not yet dead. Then I turned back in the direction of the gravel pit. Then two or three shots rang out . . . I could not see who fired the shots.'[33]

Stender also remembered the execution of the seventeen. He said the men to be shot had all arrived in the camp an hour before being killed on, he thought, 1 March 1945. In a hut by the gravel pit, they had their sentences for looting read. He added the sentences were reinforced by order of head of the RSHA Ernst Kaltenbrunner. Stender emphasised the sentences had come from courts martial in Neumünster and Lübeck. He led the firing squad of twenty men and the prisoners were shot in three batches.[34]

Company Sergeant Major of the AEL Nordmark guard, Hans Forck, admitted to taking part in the execution, but details were insufficient to find him guilty. He was convicted on the first charge only and sentenced to ten years' imprisonment. He was released in December 1951 having served four years.

April 1945 was a particularly perilous period for those in AEL Nordmark and the surrounding detention centres. One evening early in the month, witness Braitmann saw Danish medical orderly Jensen lead thirty Russian and Polish prisoners, some of whom had missing hands or feet, to a pit dug a few days before. The camp doctor and Kiel GP Dr Dietrich Freehse explained men had lost hands, feet and sometimes legs due to the frostbite they had suffered in the freezing bunker detention cells. Their limbs were amputated in the local surgical hospital and they were then returned to the AEL infirmary. Through a narrow gap in the window of his hut, Braitmann saw the men shot. He could not see who fired, but Jensen, Baumann and one other guard were present.

On 22 or 23 April 1945 Braitmann had also seen two Russian women, known to him as Raya and Tamara, led into a cement storage hut by Post and Baumann. He heard two shots. Later he saw the decomposing bodies of the women in a waste water ditch. Baumann admitted his part in the killing of the Russian women. He explained,

> I went with him [Post], and we went to the bunker. There he ordered the sentry to open cell number three. In this cell there were Raya and Tamara. Post had a piece of paper in his hand and read out to them that they had been sentenced to death. Post went in front, I went with him, and Raya and Tamara came with us. About 30 metres further on there was a cement hut. Post led Raya and Tamara into that hut. He said to them that they would be shot. He then told them to kneel down. To me he gave the order to shoot. But I did not want to shoot. Post already had his pistol in his hand. When I said that I would not shoot, Post asked me for my pistol. I gave it to him, and Post shot the two women.[35]

When Dr Mant exhumed their bodies, one of the women was dressed in a nightdress and had died from a shot in the back of the neck. The second wore a pair of socks and was shot twice in the neck. Importantly, her wounds showed powder burns indicating that she was shot at point-blank range.[36] By the time Baumann's counsel, Dr Hensel, got to commenting on this killing in his closing statement, he appeared to be grasping at straws in defence of his client. He said, 'The heroic way in which the two Russians died surely also can be regarded as one more proof that the execution had legal foundation'.[37]

At the end of April 1945, Braitmann saw Jensen lead about sixty prisoners out of the hospital hut to the washhouse in groups of four. He said, 'The prisoners, on arrival at the washhouse, had to undress completely. Then they had to lie down on the ground outside the washhouse completely naked.' Those who refused to lie down had their legs kicked away by Jensen. Baumann then 'put one foot on their buttocks and shot them in the back of the neck'.[38] Baumann, again claimed that his action was only administering *coups de grâce* (this appears to have been his speciality) and said, 'I must emphasise that these people were already dead'.[39] Baumann's ridiculous assertions that he hadn't shot anyone who wasn't dead already was exposed by Vollmar in cross-examination. Vollmar reminded Baumann that point nine of his sworn deposition read, 'I believed I have killed approximately 20 – 25 men with my own hand'.[40] Baumann said, 'What I meant to say was that these people were already dead'.[41] His accounts were simply not believable. The court found him guilty of the first and second charges and sentenced him to death. He was hanged in Hameln Prison on 9 June 1948.

Jensen said he had examined the pile of shot bodies and found no signs of life. He made no mention of taking part in the killing described by Braitmann and Baumann as having occurred on this day. Instead, he said, 'In order not to give the prisoners the impression that we were going to bury a man alive, I fired one shot . . . But I am sure that he was dead before I fired.'[42]

The files in The National Archives contain many other examples of killing in the AEL. The orderly Jensen told the court of another occasion that he had given a *coup de grâce*. He said he had found a man 'lying inside a cell door in the detention hut'. He had several severe head wounds and a fractured skull. Jensen had him brought to the infirmary and asked permission to send him to a hospital, which was refused. Jensen said,

> I returned to the infirmary and on arrival found that the man was about to die. I examined him thoroughly and found that at the most he would live for another two or three hours. He was suffering terribly. I had the man carried to the mortuary, and there I relieved him of his pain by a shot fired from my revolver. I was convinced that I could not save his life.[43]

Jensen was found guilty on charges one and two and sentenced to death. Three months later, his sentence was commuted to 20 years' imprisonment.

Stender, leader of the camp guard, explained to his defence counsel, Dr Erich Brügmann, his part in an execution at the AEL which occurred before prisoners had been accommodated in the camp in August or September 1944. He said Post had ordered him to train ten men as a firing squad and they were to shoot two Eastern workers. On the evening of the execution, he said two men had been read their death sentence in translation. It had been handed down by the SS and Police Court in Hamburg and confirmed by Himmler. The men had been found guilty of sabotaging tools and instruments belonging to the Air Raid Patrol and fire brigade which had resulted in the loss of lives and property. The men were lined up in front of a turf wall, Post gave an order and Stender gave the command to fire whereupon both were shot dead. Stender was sentenced to 15 years' imprisonment, but was released in 1953.

If a constitutionally valid court had decided the fate of those executed in AEL Nordmark by a proper, legally valid, trial then those accused by the British may have had a valid defence. So, the court spent some time debating and taking advice about courts martial (*Standgerichte*), special courts (*Sondergerichte*), SS and police courts. Eventually, however, it seems to have decided that, besides some vague defence testimony, there was little evidence to suggest any of the victims had been lawfully tried and sentenced.[44]

There were three trials of so-called 'minor accused' after the main trial. The first took place in the Curiohaus between 10 March and 4 April 1948. Twelve men faced the charge of committing a war crime for ill-treating Allied nationals in AEL Nordmark. Eight were found guilty and sentenced to between one and eight years' imprisonment. Hans Diederichs was further charged with killing Allied nationals, but found not guilty. Cornelius Hans was further charged with ill-treating and killing a Polish national called Kukolinsky. Dowe de Jong was further charged with killing an unknown Allied national in the camp. Both were found not guilty. On 6 April 1948, the second minor accused trial opened in the Curiohaus. Three men were charged with war crimes for killing Allied nationals in the AEL, but all were acquitted after four days.[45]

The third minor accused trial in the Curiohaus was of Ukrainian Emil Dier.[46] He was accused of two war crimes: ill-treatment of Allied nationals and ill-treatment of an Allied national which led to their death.

Dier was used by the Germans as an interpreter during the 'intensified interrogation' of Russian prisoners, but he admitted to beating them himself with a length of rubber hose. Prosecution witness, Annmargret Hölzel told the court, 'I saw the accused beating a prisoner who was screaming terribly. Dier was beating with a cable . . . About five to ten minutes later I saw the door of this interrogation room opened . . . I saw accused dragging a body out of the room.'[47] Other witnesses saw Dier commit similar acts. After two days, he was found guilty on the first charge, but not guilty on the second and sent to prison for five years.

6

TRIALS FOR KILLING DURING THE 'END PHASE'

The Industrial Revolution in Germany led to the establishment of hundreds of mines, coke works, iron and steel plants in the Ruhr area. By the 1930s, it had become the largest urban region in Germany. It included several big cities bordered by the rivers Ruhr to the south, Rhine to the west and Lippe to the north. Millions of people lived and worked there. During WW1, the Ruhr supplied Germany's weapons, highlighting the strategic as well as the economic importance of the area. When Germany defaulted on reparations at the end of 1922, the region was seized by French and Belgian troops hoping to force Germany to reopen its purse. The occupiers did not withdraw until 1925, leaving behind much resentment and feeding German political radicalism.

Throughout the Nazi era, the area remained key to the German ability to wage war. In addition to manufacturing armaments, the extensive network of rivers, canals and railways allowed the district to supply raw materials to factories in many parts of the Reich. Hundreds of thousands of German men worked there, but as the war progressed, the Wehrmacht devoured them. To fill the labour gap, the Nazis forced POWs and deported people from all over Europe to work in the Ruhr mines, mills and factories.

There are various dates for the beginning of the end of WW2: the unsuccessful attempt by Colonel Claus von Stauffenberg to assassinate Hitler on 20 July 1944, the western Allied armies reaching the west bank of the Rhine in March 1945 or the death of the Führer in his Berlin bunker on 30 April 1945. Whichever date is chosen, the spring of 1945 was a treacherous time for the millions of slave workers taken to Germany and living in labour camps close to the heavy industry where they were forced to work. The Gestapo policed them rigorously throughout the war, but as the fighting reached German soil, slave workers began to look less like an asset and more like a liability – they had to be fed and guarded otherwise they might rebel, threatening the lives of German women and children.

In the early months of 1945, the Allied forces made significant progress across Europe, advancing towards the German heartland. The Ruhr represented a formidable obstacle on their path to victory as the area had been transformed into a fortress, with German troops and resources concentrated within its confines. Undeterred, the American forces launched a daring operation. Through a meticulously planned series of manoeuvres, they encircled the region, cutting off crucial supply lines and trapping the German army within an area known as the 'Ruhr Pocket'.

As the siege unfolded, the flow of battle gradually shifted in favour of the Allies. With the German defenders finding themselves increasingly isolated and overwhelmed, they adopted ever more desperate measures to recruit the remaining male population to fight at the fronts and to police the slave workers. The Hitler Youth were armed and a ragtag bunch of men, formerly too old or medically unfit for combat, were formed into a militia called the People's Storm (*Volkssturm*).[1]

As the land forces pushed hard, so too the British and Americans launched the largest air raids of the war on the Ruhr cities practically unopposed by the Luftwaffe. Often air defence batteries had been moved to support ground-based operations, leaving cities further undefended. The Allies were aware the area was densely populated and any bombing would cause civilian casualties. This consideration, however, was secondary to the basic need to destroy the German ability to wage war and bring the conflict to an end. Thousands of people abandoned their homes, moving in with more rural friends and family or simply becoming refugees. In some cities, where fewer and fewer buildings were left standing, the exodus resulted in slave workers becoming a large proportion of the population. As their daily ration grew smaller, getting something to eat became an overwhelming preoccupation. Under cover of the air raids, some escaped the work camps holding them close to the bombers' targets to scavenge in the rubble. Most often individual slave workers would take the opportunity to enter an abandoned home looking for food (or valuables to trade for food) before returning to their camp. Others formed groups convinced their best chance of survival was to stay out of the camps and forage amongst the ruins until the Allied victory.

The German population became frightened of reprisals from the slave workers they had so badly treated and often acted without pity to report any foreigner outside the camps to the authorities. The Gestapo were concerned on several levels. Operationally, if groups of escaped slave workers became armed and organized, they could be a threat as partisans. Politically, the Gestapo saw the slave workers as rabid communists who might persuade a despairing German population to give up their support for the Nazis or go further and help the Soviet army to conquer Germany. Ideologically, the majority of slave workers were classed by them as Slavs whose lives, the Gestapo believed, were far less valuable than German lives. Many thought it would be better to rid themselves of the problem now while they still could.

As communications deteriorated in Germany, the decisions on who could kill and who would die became decentralized. In November 1944, Himmler issued a decree empowering regional offices of the Gestapo to take 'measures of atonement' as 'reprisal for grave acts of terror and sabotage'. The Gestapo saw this as a licence to kill just about anyone they could claim to be looting. In February 1945, Ernst Kaltenbrunner, (Chief of the RSHA) authorized the police to shoot foreign workers without judicial review.[2]

Life for a slave worker during the end phase of WW2 became a gamble. If he stayed in the camp, where he was badly housed, fed and treated, he could be killed by an Allied bomb (he was not allowed to be in a shelter). If the Germans decided to evacuate the camp, he could be compelled to join a 'death march' and be moved deeper into Germany further away from liberation. He might be 'liquidated' – it was known for the Germans to kill all the inmates of a camp and to raze the infrastructure. If he left the camp, he had to decide: would it be temporary perhaps to raid abandoned buildings for food before returning? If he intended to abscond permanently, could he hold out against the violence of the ordinary people, the *Volkssturm*, Hitler Youth, German armed forces and the many types of police?

In the Ruhr, where the demand for slave labourers had been especially high, many factories had their own camps to house them. As the social fabric of Germany collapsed, it was here that the killing of foreign workers was particularly prolific and shooting them became commonplace. In January or February 1945, the Ratingen Gestapo hanged eight men in the drying room of Rheinmetall-Borsig's forced labour camp in Düsseldorf-Grafenberg.[3] Between 7 March and 12 April

1945, the Dortmund Gestapo took forced labourers in batches of twenty to a forest clearing in the Rombergpark and shot them. Three hundred people met their death this way.[4] On 13 April 1945, the Ratingen Gestapo shot seventy-one inmates of the Lüttringhausen Prison in a gorge near Wenzelnberg. They were mostly German communists and social democrats, but also some Russian forced labourers.[5] The end phase atrocities were reported to the US Army when the region capitulated and thousands of slave workers were freed. Some cases were handed over to the British when the Allies divided Germany into zones of occupation and a few reached trial.

Hannover

In 1942, a group of armament firms in Hannover registered a company that would oversee the forced labour camps needed to run their factories. Two of these companies, Machinenfabrik Niedersachsen Hannover (MNH) and Continental AG, set up a plant in a mine beneath Hannover-Ahlem. Here they manufactured components for tanks, aircraft and field guns. From November 1944, hundreds of forced labourers, including some transferred from Auschwitz, toiled in frightful conditions to expand the tunnels. By December, at least 250 exhausted prisoners were taken to 'recover' in the Neuengamme concentration camp and were replaced with Russian POWs. By the spring of 1945, half the camp population (about 750) had died.[6] As the Americans approached, it was decided the prisoners in the feared work education camp at Lahde-Weser should be transferred 60km further east to the Ahlem camp. At the beginning of April 1945, 850 prisoners were crammed into the camp under the control of Gestapo SS Lieutenant Heinrich Joost.

A large group of prisoners in Ahlem had been accused of looting and other crimes, so the head of the regional Gestapo, SS Lieutenant Colonel Johannes Rentsch, decided they should be executed. While the majority of prisoners were force-marched to Bergen-Belsen, 155 were taken to the Seelhorst Cemetery, shot and buried in a mass grave. One Russian, Pjotr Palnikov, survived by killing a guard with a shovel and escaping into a wood.

When the US 8th Infantry captured Hannover on 10 April 1945, they discovered 100 prisoners still in Ahlem who were too sick to be moved and Palnikov told them about the massacre in the cemetery. Outraged, the Americans ordered an exhumation to be carried out by senior Nazis and witnessed by the population of Hannover. On 5 May 1945, 153 men and a woman were exhumed. Some wore civilian clothes, but most were wearing a mixture of POW clothes (dyed German uniforms) or Russian military uniforms.

No autopsies were performed, but it was clear they had all been shot in the head at close range.[7] The bodies were wrapped in clean sheets and loaded onto fifteen trucks, driven in a slow procession through Hannover and buried individually in a cemetery beside the Maschsee in the centre of the city.

When the area was handed over to the British, War Crimes Group (NWE) began an investigation of the case. Rentsch escaped into the Russian zone and was never tried, but many others were eventually rounded up by the British and the case was heard in three different trials. The first Hannover Gestapo trial was held in Braunschweig between 9 and 14 April 1947 and developed most of the evidence used in the subsequent Curiohaus trials.[8] For this first trial, Reinhold Plünnecke, Kurt Rasche, Adolf Methfessel, Felix Ziese, Karl Wolters and Alfred Peek of the Hannover Gestapo were accused of killing Allied nationals, internees and prisoners at Seelhorst together with Wilhelm Heidorn, Heinrich Joost and three others.

Wolters told the British Field Investigating Team he had attended a conference called by Joost for his unit of about twenty-five men. Joost told the unit various foreigners should be shot as they had been sentenced to death. Wolters said, ‘Joost did not tell us who had sentenced them to death or who had ordered the execution’.[9] A day or so later, Wolters, Heidorn and some guards from Ahlem were ordered by Joost to take a group of about twenty prisoners to Seelhorst Cemetery where they were to dig a large grave for those to be executed. As they could not finish that evening, they returned early in the morning to finish the job. When the other members of the Gestapo unit arrived, Wolters reported to Plünnecke (his superior) that the work was complete and he went home, he said he had not seen any shooting.

Others told a slightly different story. Peek said he had supervised the digging of the mass grave in the morning of 6 April 1945. When it was finished the thirty prisoners who had dug the grave were made to lie face down in it while SS men shot them with automatic weapons. He said this was his only involvement in the killings and after these people had been shot, he returned to his Gestapo department.[10] Methfessel said he escorted a group of about sixty to the cemetery. When he got there the first detail was still digging. When they had finished, the prisoners were shot in groups of about fifteen. After two or three batches, he went home.[11] Rasche said he had been ordered by Joost to transport 150 prisoners to the Seelhorst Cemetery and deliver them to Plünnecke. When the shooting started, he was fetched by Plünnecke and ordered to join in. He told the war crimes investigator he had no weapon and was leant a defective pistol by a guard. He fired two shots into the bodies in the grave, his gun jammed and he was reprimanded by Plünnecke. He returned the gun to the guard, got on his bicycle and rode away.[12] All the Gestapo officers tried hard to limit their involvement in the shooting, but only Plünnecke mentioned an air raid causing panic among the guards.

Plünnecke had joined the NSDAP in 1937 and the Hannover Kripo in July 1939. Later that year, he was transferred to the Gestapo, spending time on active service before returning to Hannover in September 1943. He may have been a member of one of the murderous execution squads in the east (*Einsatzgruppen*) because it was their methods used in Seelhorst Cemetery where Plünnecke was the senior officer.[13] When another 125 prisoners were delivered to the cemetery, he claimed an air-raid alert sounded. 'Panic broke out', he said, and it was increased (among the SS and Gestapo men) 'by a number of prisoners trying to escape.' He continued to explain, 'Wild shooting started and as I was the most senior official present, I took charge. In order to speed up the matter, I ordered all Gestapo officials to take part in the shooting. The first 25 men were driven into the grave where they had to lie face down. We then shot them in the head. I admit firing altogether 25 shots, including those during the escape attempt.'[14]

At the trial, all pleaded not guilty. Apart from Ziese (who was not present at the Joost conference or the killing), all the accused had admitted in deposition some part in the massacre and relied on the familiar plea of following superior orders. They also tried to make the court believe they had considered the executions to be lawful as the prisoners had been tried. The Deputy Judge Advocate General in his summary, however, said, 'All the circumstances surrounding the previous conference and the scene at the cemetery must, in my opinion, negative any suggestion that these men for a moment thought they might be doing something that was lawful'.[15]

Rasche and Peek were sentenced to death and hanged by Pierrepoint in Hameln Prison on 26 June 1947. Wolters was sentenced to 13 years' imprisonment and Methfessel to eight years. Both had their sentences reduced to five years and were released in August 1950. Plünnecke's post-trial story was remarkable. He too was sentenced to death, but on 23 May 1947, while counting down the days in Hameln Prison with Rasche and Peek, GOC-in-C BAOR Lieutenant-General Sir Richard McCreery stayed his execution on request of War Crimes Group (NWE). Plünnecke was required as a witness in two further trials for the murders in Seelhorst Cemetery.

The second Hannover Gestapo case was tried in the Curiohaus between 7 and 13 January 1948.[16] SS Lieutenant Hans Heinrich Joost, head of the Gestapo Eastern Workers Unit (*Ostarbeiter-Referat*) in Hannover-Ahlem, was charged with committing a war crime by being involved in the killings of Allied nationals, internees and POWs, at the Seelhorst Cemetery on 6 April 1945.

The first prosecution witness was Plünnecke. He told the court about the conference held by Joost to inform his unit that 150 prisoners were to be executed. He said ten officers had been detailed with the task and each had been handed a carton of cigarettes as an incentive by Joost. He then told the story of reporting to the Seelhorst Cemetery, overseeing the prisoners digging a pit and shooting them all. This time there was no mention of an air raid. Plünnecke said he had reported to Joost the next day in Braunschweig (the Hannover Gestapo had moved there due to the approach of the US Army) and told him 150 prisoners had been shot and one had escaped.[17] Wolters and Methfessel also gave testimony for the prosecution continuing to downplay their involvement.

The main defence witness was Joost himself. In an earlier deposition, he said he had saved three kapos from Lahde-Weser from being shot. He also claimed that while he had ordered Rasche to march the men from Ahlem to the Seelhorst Cemetery, he had given no other instructions. Much to his dismay, Plünnecke, who was 'quite unsuited for that', had taken charge and this had led to the shooting.[18] Rasche's deposition, unfortunately for Joost, did not support this. Rasche said he had been ordered (by Joost) to take the prisoners to the cemetery and 'report to Plünnecke and I should help until everything was finished'.[19]

In court, Joost said the regional Gestapo head Johannes Rentsch had given instructions to Commandant Winkler of the Lahde-Weser work education camp to have the most dangerous criminals in the camp shot dead. This hardly sounds like a trial had taken place. He then said he had been ordered to drive to the Seelhorst Cemetery to see whether an execution could take place there – the cemetery administrators were only too willing. Joost then tried to make the court believe he did not want the executions to occur and was trying to play for time so the Allies might take Hannover before he had to carry out the order. He claimed to be 'quite shaken' when Wolters told him, 'there had been some shooting at Seelhorst Cemetery' and said 'Plünnecke was not entitled to assume power of command'.[20]

Joost's defence was that his unit had acted on their own initiative and not under his order when they shot 150 people. His defence counsel, Dr Meyer-Labastille, in summing up, explained that Joost thought *nothing* would happen when he had ordered a mass grave to be dug and prisoners to be marched to it under armed escort. Dr Meyer-Labastille said, 'He thought that nothing would happen with the prisoners as long as he, as the chief of the Dienststelle, did not appear at the cemetery and give orders for the shooting . . . No matter what happened, Joost had hoped, that the day would develop in a way that no shooting would be necessary.' It must have taken some nerve to suggest to the court that Joost had expected the prisoners to stand on the edge of the grave under armed Gestapo guard until they were liberated.

Earlier in his summing up, Dr Meyer-Labastille had described the situation in Hannover as 'nerve-racking, demoralising and horrible. One cannot suppose that there were many people left in Hannover then who were in full possession of their normal power of judgement.'[21] The court seemed to accept this version rather than Plünnecke's. Joost was found guilty except for the words 'internees and prisoners of war' and sentenced, more as an accessory to murder than the person who had ordered it, to two years' imprisonment.[22]

When the trial was finished, Brigadier Robert Halse from the DJAG wrote to McCreery who then lifted the stay of execution on Plünnecke. Shortly after this, however, Halse received a plea from Frau Plünnecke pointing out a disparity. Her husband had been sentenced to death, but Joost, who had ordered the killings, had been sentenced to just two years' imprisonment. McCreery again stayed the execution so that all involved could review the case. After consideration, Halse again contacted McCreery saying the trial of Joost 'made no difference to the accused Plünnecke's case. Therefore in my opinion, the stay should be removed.'[23] McCreery did so on 4 February 1948.

McCreery expected Plünnecke to be executed when Pierrepoint flew over to Hameln Prison to execute the next batch of convicted war criminals and he was aghast when his order was not carried out. In a letter to Army Commander Lieutenant-General Sir Brian H Robertson, he wrote, 'The executioner arrived in this theatre at the end of February 1948 and carried out the instructions contained in a number of warrants which I had issued. Plünnecke was not executed on that date despite the orders which I had given . . . I am still awaiting an explanation as to why I was not informed earlier that my orders had not been carried out.' Further, McCreery wrote, 'In my opinion, having regard to the part played by Plünnecke in the crime and the fact that two of his fellow-accused, who took a lesser part in the crime, have already suffered the death penalty, it would be inequitable in this case to commute the sentence of death to one of imprisonment.'[24]

The reason that Plünnecke had not been executed on 26 February 1948 was that the British authorities had waivered and only decided to check with McCreery after the executioner had returned to the UK.[25] Robertson agreed the original death sentence was just, but felt the public might not find such a delayed execution fair. For the best part of a year, Plünnecke had lived with the threat of imminent execution. Robertson accepted there had been an error, but wrote he had 'decided to exercise my powers of clemency and to commute the sentence to imprisonment for life' as Plünnecke had 'suffered considerable anguish of mind'.[26] Little thought appears to have given to the anguish of the people murdered in the cemetery.

Having escaped the noose and had his sentence reduced to 15 years by the Wade Review Board, Plünnecke must have been delighted to have another year knocked off by the Queen herself. In May 1954, following further sentence reviews, British Foreign Secretary Anthony Eden asked Queen Elizabeth II to 'issue instructions that the sentence of Reinhold Plünnecke be reduced to fourteen years' imprisonment', which she did.[27] In the same year, the Mixed Consultative Board recommended his immediate release. One hundred and fifty-four people were dead, but the senior Gestapo officer directly responsible stepped free from Werl Prison on 10 October 1954.

William Friedrich Heidorn was the sole person accused in the third Hannover Gestapo trial also heard in the Curiohaus and known as the 'Seelhorst Cemetery Trial' (16 to 18 June 1948). Heidorn had joined the NSDAP at the end of 1931 and the SS in January 1933. He served with the Hannover Gestapo from February 1942, dealing with Dutch civilian workers, which brought him under the command of Joost. At the end of the war, the Dutch had taken him to an internment camp in Vught where he awaited trial for crimes committed against Dutch nationals.

He was not included in the first trial in April 1947 as at that time the War Crimes Group (NWE) had not found him. Once he was located in Vucht, however, the Dutch wrote a note to the British, 'the Netherlands authorities have no objection that a/n [above named, Heidorn] is returned to you for interrogation and trial'.[28]

The Curiohaus trial of Heidorn proceeded in much the same way as the first Hannover Gestapo trial.[29] Three witnesses gave evidence, Plünnecke (who had been permanently saved from the hangman earlier in the year), Joost and Wolters, but the only new evidence was that Heidorn had assisted when a Russian prisoner had tried to escape from the graveside. Heidorn had returned the man to Wolters. It must have been obvious the man would be shot, but Heidorn pleaded he was ignorant of this. The case against him was admittedly weak, but in his summing up, prosecutor Nicolson explained that Heidorn could not have been unaware of the impending executions of the prisoners. He said, 'Do you really think it is possible that the accused walked about in an office for more than two days where everybody else knew about this impending mass execution, even for a Gestapo office an extraordinary event, and he did not? He witnesses the digging of a mass grave in the evening and never asked.'[30] The court agreed and found him guilty sentencing him to two years' imprisonment, the same term as Joost.

Most of the twenty Gestapo and SS men involved in the Seelhorst Cemetery murders were never charged. Of the few tried, two were executed. Those mass murderers given prison terms were all free within ten years to live with their families and to resume their careers.

Düsseldorf

April 6th 1945, when 154 people were shot in Hannover, was an especially dangerous day to be a forced labourer in the Ruhr. With Allied troops approaching from the south and east, the head of the Düsseldorf criminal police, SS Major Friedrich Class, ordered Kripo Detective Superintendents Dr Victor Harnischfeger and Dr Josef Ochs to execute a group of slave workers described as 'looters'. The group consisted of ten men and a woman, Russian and Dutch nationals, thought to have come from the forced labour camp of Schieß AG, a machine tool factory in Düsseldorf. They were taken by truck with their luggage from the cells in the Fürstenwall police station to the Kalkum Wood near Tiefenbroich (part of Ratingen). In the truck were several Kripo officers, two SS men, two customs officials and the eleven prisoners. Harnischfeger and Ochs followed on motorcycles. It may seem odd for the prisoners to have luggage with them, but they were probably arrested at the camp where they lived and ordered to bring their belongings, perhaps to fool them into believing they were to be transferred. There was quite some discussion in the trial whether anyone, except the two detective superintendents, knew the workers were to be executed or merely transferred to Wuppertal. The large number of guards, however, and the fact that the workers were not going by foot (they would normally have been marched) would have been a clear signal to the Kripo and SS of the true intent of the journey.

On arrival at the woods, they were forced to walk a short distance along a path and were shot. After stripping them of all identifying documents, their bodies were thrown into two bomb craters and covered with branches and earth. One man was spared as he had offered to give valuable information to the police. He was taken back to Düsseldorf where Harnischfeger interrogated him for information about Russians hiding in the harbour area.

Rudolf Ribbert, a 16-year-old forestry apprentice, discovered the bodies on 10 May 1945 and reported the finding to the German police. The police in turn informed the occupying US forces who began an investigation. The US Signals Corps located the burial site and forced local former high-ranking Nazis to exhume the bodies. On 13 May 1945, the US Army ordered thousands of Ratingen citizens to walk past the open coffins of the victims and to attend a funeral for them. The bodies were reburied in the churchyard of St Peter and Paul in the centre of Ratingen with the new mayor, Franz-Josef Gemmert, delivering a eulogy. In part, he said, 'If the victorious powers treat us harshly today, then these are little paws compared to the claws our representatives showed in the occupied territories'.[31]

When Düsseldorf became part of the British Zone, the Americans handed the investigation over to the War Crimes Group (NWE). Initially, several Düsseldorf cases were investigated, but only cases that involved Harnischfeger (the first and second cases) came to trial.[32] Perhaps to allow the development of evidence against Harnischfeger, the second Düsseldorf case was the first to go to trial and concerned the killings in the Kalkum Wood. Originally, seven men were accused; Harnischfeger and Ochs (the senior Kripo officers) and five more junior officers: Fritz Neuss, Friedrich Reinarz, Josef Daniels, Paul Rohde and Franz Scholten.[33]

The German police had already amassed some evidence as they had interviewed many of those involved before transferring the case to the Americans. Neuss, the driver of the truck containing the eleven prisoners, told the German investigators the original transport order was for the prisoners to be taken to a work camp near Wuppertal. He had driven towards the *autobahn*, but before joining the motorway, Neuss had waited for the senior officers on motorcycles to catch up. When Harnischfeger drew alongside, he reprimanded Neuss for driving so far ahead and then told him to divert to the Ratingen dog training ground. Neuss said he refused the instruction as he knew this to be where 'plunderers and burglars' were shot. He argued with Harnischfeger that his written movement order was for transfer to Wuppertal. Neuss kept the original order as proof he had not known about the pending executions when he had climbed into the driver's seat that day. Harnischfeger then ordered him to drive towards Kalkum and into the woods. Once there the prisoners were taken out of the truck and led about 200m into a clearing. Neuss saw Harnischfeger leading a woman by the arm. Immediately before the shooting began, he heard Harnischfeger shout, 'First rob and plunder and then make excuses'. There was considerable panic with prisoners running to escape automatic gunfire and police officers themselves diving for cover. When it was over, Harnischfeger and an SS man shot dead all those who had been injured. Nuess said the junior Kripo officers were 'unwilling witnesses . . . only under armed threat did they assist in putting the executed bodies into a bomb crater filled with water'. He believed they were unaware of Class's execution order.[34]

Reinarz told the German police that Rohde and he sat in the front of the truck with driver Neuss and they had guessed the transport was for execution rather than transfer. Not wanting to be part of it, they had shrunk to the back of the cabin, but Harnischfeger had reacted angrily and ordered them each to escort a prisoner into the woods. When the shooting began, Reinarz said he drew his pistol, but did not fire. He was ordered back to the truck to fetch shovels and to help bury the dead.[35]

Rohde gave a slightly different account. He said the Russian he escorted indicated he had useful information about others hiding in the Dusseldorf harbour area. Harnischfeger took him aside and he survived the shooting in the woods. Harnischfeger then shot the Russian woman, panicking the male prisoners who began to run in all directions only to be cut down by submachine guns. Rohde had not drawn his pistol (neither had Daniels according to his statement) and Rohde believed Harnischfeger, Scholten and the two SS men had done all the shooting.[36]

The British began their investigations in January 1947.[37] Towards the end of the month, two of the graves in the churchyard of St Peter and Paul were opened and the bodies were transported to the Institute of Forensic Medicine in Düsseldorf where Dr Kurt Böhmer performed an autopsy on each. He found the first was probably a man, judging by the clothing and shoes. He had been shot in the back of the head, the bullet exiting through one of the eyes – the pathologist could not be sure which. The second body, also most likely a man, appeared to have been shot three times, in the chest, arm and back of the head.[38] Later, Dr Böhmer produced a second report based on the samples and bones he had preserved during the first autopsy. Regarding the first body, he noted the shot to the back of the head had hit the frontal bone of the skull, fracturing the roof of the left eye socket and remaining in the brain. He found the 9mm bullet inside the skull. He also discovered a shot had hit this victim's pelvis. Böhmer found a bullet in the skull of the second body and this victim had been shot across the mouth, in the neck into his vertebra and twice in the right upper arm (one of these shots perforated the victim's chest). The British investigators almost certainly thought this was sufficient evidence to prove the victims had been executed.

Captain William Ellery Anderson of the War Crimes Group (NWE) took many depositions.[39] Police Inspector Reinarz expanded on the account he had given to the German police. He told Ellery Anderson,

> I walked in about the centre of the line and had to escort a tall Russian. When we had walked about 200m, I heard that the woman started crying. I turned round, heard Dr Harnischfeger shout, 'first looting and thieving and then lamenting' and saw how he hit her in the face. Immediately after I heard one single pistol shot. One or two seconds later

> a machine-pistol started firing from behind me. I jumped to my left in order not to get hit.[40]

Detective Police Inspector Rohde said, that after the woman had been shot, 'two or three prisoners attempted to run into the wood' and were shot with submachine guns. He said, 'The other prisoners were already lying on the ground. Then I saw how Dr Harnischfeger and the SS men went to the prisoners laying on the ground, stood over them and shot them.'[41] Criminal Investigator Secretary-in-Chief Neuss and Ochs (who had been arrested in the French Zone in February 1947) added little to the account.

Harnischfeger gave an initial deposition in Saint-Gilles Prison, Brussels, where he was being held to give evidence against Belgian collaborators. He blamed Neuss for choosing the place of execution and denied telling him to drive to the Kalkum Wood. His account of the atrocity was very matter of fact, 'I escorted the woman, who was amongst the prisoners; I was the last in line. When we arrived at the clearing, the woman hesitated to walk on. I then gripped her arm and shot her. At about the same time the others too shot the prisoners whom they had escorted.' When he was brought back to Germany by the British, he expanded on how the executions had come about. He told Ellery Anderson there had been a conference of Kripo officials in February 1945 where Class informed them 'on the express order of Inspector Albath, the Kripo would now have to undertake the duties of the Gestapo, because the latter had left'. He explained this meant the Kripo would have to deal with all crimes committed by foreign workers, including crimes which the Gestapo would have 'punished with special treatment'. Everyone knew this meant summary execution. Harnischfeger had revealed too much and rapidly tried to row back saying, 'The case of the Kalkumerwald was not a case of "special treatment", but the execution of sentence by a Standgericht'. This was the first time any of the accused had alluded to a court martial (*Standgericht*) and seemed to have been mentioned by Harnischfeger simply to cover himself. [42]

In May 1947, Major J W da Cunha, Field Investigation Section, War Crimes Group (NWE), wrote a report on progress in the case. In the course of the investigation, he discovered Scholten (who was originally also indicted, but could not be found) was probably dead.[43] He explained how Albath had issued authority in 1945 for the Gestapo and Kripo to carry out the euphemistic 'special treatment' (*Sonderbehandlung*) without prior permission from the RSHA. Major da Cunha outlined the events in the Kalkum Wood and then made a series of recommendations. First, Albath should not be tried in connection with the case. He was involved in many war crimes and da Cunha hoped he might be better connected with another case more likely to secure his conviction. Second, Harnischfeger and Ochs should be charged as principals in the first degree with the murders. Third, Rohde, Reinarz, Daniels and Neuss should be charged as principals in the second degree as they aided and abetted the murders at the very time they were committed. Major da Cunha suggested that if a prosecution witness were needed, Rohde would be the best candidate and, in that case, he should not be arrested. Before the trial started, however, it was decided to use the principals in the second degree as witnesses instead.

A British Military Court, convened under the Royal Warrant, assembled in the Curiohaus Court Three between 19 November and 1 December 1947 to try Harnischfeger and Ochs with killing ten Allied nationals. Unusually, there was no Judge Advocate appointed.[44] Each morning, the accused men had a medical inspection and handed a certificate of fitness to the Royal Military Police (RMP) who transported them from Altona Court Prison to the court. The RMP also searched all German civilian spectators for concealed weapons. British Military HQ for Hamburg provided court guards who checked the identity of all service and Allied civilian personnel entering the court, made sure no unauthorized person entered the courtroom when the court was not sitting and regularly patrolled passages beneath the court. The guards also acted as a mobile reserve force in case the Court Orderly Officer had trouble with German spectators. German civil police checked the identities of all German spectators entering the court and ensured bags and articles which might be used as weapons were deposited in the cloakroom. The German police were also asked to prevent spectators from communicating with the accused or witnesses and to keep order in the German spectators' gallery.[45]

The prosecuting barrister R D L Kelly and each of the defence counsellors, Dr Wilhelm Burchard-Motz for Harnischfeger and Dr Meyer-Labastille for Ochs, gave opening speeches. Reinarz, Neuss and Rohde testified for the prosecution while Harnischfeger and Ochs testified in their own defence. Unfortunately, there are no transcripts of the trial. The evidence admitted, however, followed the pattern of the depositions taken earlier in the year.

In his closing address for Harnischfeger, Dr Burchard-Motz did not contest that his client was concerned in the shooting of the Allied nationals, but did dispute it violated the laws and usages of war. The defence submission was that there had been a court martial and the death sentence was lawful.[46] Dr Meyer-Labastille in his closing address said Ochs was told that Class had confirmed a court martial had occurred and sentenced the '11 looters' to death. He said Ochs had no reason to doubt this was true. The lawyer then quoted from a judgement in English law by Justice Cave, 'At common law an honest and reasonable belief in the existence of circumstances, which if true, would make the act for which the prisoner is indicted an innocent (i.e. morally innocent) act, has always been held to be a good defence'.[47] This, he argued, meant Ochs did not have the essential *mens rea* (guilty intention of mind) required for the court to find he acted criminally. Meyer-Labastille told the court Ochs had not shot (nobody saw him do so) and later, when his pistol was checked, it had not been fired. The element of *actus reus* (guilty act) required for criminal liability was, therefore, also missing.[48]

Barrister Kelly, in his closing speech for the prosecution, explained Harnischfeger and Ochs had been charged with being 'concerned in the killing' which meant 'either they did it themselves or aided and abetted it or encouraged it'. In Kelly's opinion, there should be no doubt the two men were 'concerned'. Kelly thought there should have been a Judge Advocate to aid the court and so made every effort himself to be objective with the evidence and pointed out they should only convict Harnischfeger and Ochs if convinced beyond reasonable doubt of their guilt. He explained, very fairly,

> You may come to the conclusion that these people [those shot] were never in fact tried by court martial. You may come to the conclusion that they never appeared before Class at all, or if they did so appear, they were not given a fair trial. But if you think that the accused nevertheless honestly believed that the victims had been lawfully tried and sentenced then it is still your duty to acquit.[49]

Given this level of guidance from the prosecution it is perhaps not surprising both Harnischfeger and Ochs were acquitted. A report from the officer in charge of War Crimes Group (NWE), Captain A W H Nicolson, regarding the putative court martial had concluded,

'According to the information available, no such Special Court-Martial was ever convened or functioned.' Nicolson believed everyone in all branches of the German police had known 'that the execution of an "Ostarbeiter" after 30 June 43 was the carrying-out of an administrative order and not the execution of a sentence by a Court of Justice'.[50] Ochs, who had been on loan from the French, was returned to them. Harnischfeger, however, faced a second Curiohaus trial for killing Russians in Düsseldorf.[51]

Between 4 and 6 February 1948, Harnischfeger was further tried for war crimes. The first charge accused him of killing a male Russian national between 1 March and 30 April 1945. In his deposition, Kripo Detective Inspector Arthur Brillo told the War Crimes Group investigator he had been detailed to help Detective Superintendent Sachs at a raid in Düsseldorf-Hafen, the harbour area. The neighbourhood was surrounded and searched. A Russian, thought to be a leader, came out of a cellar and was sent to the corner of a yard. Sachs drew his pistol and shot the man in the back of his neck.[52] Detective Emil Hake took part in the same raid and saw Sachs shoot the Russian. He had also seen Harnischfeger wave his pistol in the face of the young man dying on the ground before shooting him in the head.[53]

Predictably, perhaps, Harnischfeger gave a different account in his deposition. He said he had heard a shot and seen a Russian collapsing in the corner of a yard. Seeing Sachs with a pistol in his hand, he asked him why he had shot. Sachs told him the prisoner 'was the leader of the looters who had been previously executed in the Kalkumer wood'. Harnischfeger then said, 'We then approached the Russian who was dying; Sachs fired a shot at him and I did the same'. He considered his shot to be the *coup de grâce* to spare further suffering, but he said, 'As far as I know the prisoner in question had neither been given a trial, nor was there any evidence, that he was personally in possession of stolen goods. I was not in agreement with this killing, as in my opinion the slain should have been confronted with the informer [from the Kalkum Wood].'[54]

In his defence testimony, however, Harnischfeger told a slightly amended story. He said Sachs had fired twice at the Russian and he told Sachs, 'This man must be put before a court or interrogated – you cannot just shoot him'. He thought the Russian was dead, but in case he was still suffering, he gave him the *coup de grâce.*[55] Harnischfeger was acquitted of this charge. The court expressed reasonable doubt about whether the Russian was already dead when Harnischfeger shot him. If the man had been dead, then Harnischfeger had not killed him.

In the second charge, Harnischfeger was accused of killing two male Russian nationals between 1 February and 31 March 1945. Sometime in April or May 1945, two bodies, which had been in the water for some time, were recovered from the harbour by the 1st Section of the Düsseldorf Criminal Investigation Department and buried without autopsy in the South Cemetery. In December 1946, both bodies were disinterred and the skulls were sent to Dr Kurt Böhmer at the Düsseldorf Medical School. He found both had been shot.[56] The timescales matched with the killings of which Harnischfeger was accused.

In deposition, Brillo said he had taken part, together with Sachs and others, in a raid in Düsseldorf-Hafen led by Harnischfeger. Two Russians, under arrest for looting, were to show the police the hiding places of other Russians. With so few police officers, however, the raid merely resulted in spooking the hiding men who ran off before the police could catch them. Frustrated, Harnischfeger offered his pistol to Sachs and, indicating the Russians they had brought along said, 'Here, Richard, you shoot them'. Sachs rejected the offer. Apparently irritated, Harnischfeger led the Russians away from the group to the side of the quay and shot each man in the head. The bodies fell into the water.[57] Detective Inspector Heinrich Schaefer corroborated this account adding that the second Russian had thrown himself at Harnischfeger's feet, apparently begging for his life, before he was shot in the head and thrown into the harbour.[58] Again, Harnischfeger told a different story. In his deposition, he said Class had ordered Sachs and himself to execute the two Russians. His straightforward explanation was, 'We went with the plunderers to the harbour where I shot them on the edge of quay C'. He thought he and Sachs would each shoot one, but explained after shooting the first Russian, the second had run away 'and made as if to jump into the water. I shot him before he could do so'.[59] Harnischfeger could not produce any evidence that the Russians had been tried before their execution and none of the other police officers knew anything about a court martial. Harnischfeger was convicted of the second charge and sentenced to death.

Colonel Robert Halse from the DJAG advised Lieutenant-General Sir Richard McCreery (GOC-in-C BAOR) that the sentence should be confirmed and he duly did so. But there was a grave error in Halse's advice which read in part, 'the accused was convicted of both charges and was sentenced to death'. This was wrong – Harnischfeger had been convicted only of the second charge and all petitions were solely against the conviction and sentence resulting from the second charge. GOC-in-C BAOR dismissed them all as he thought Harnischfeger had also been convicted and sentenced for the first charge, so acquitting him on the second charge would not affect the death sentence.

On 8 June 1948, Lieutenant-Colonel Burnett, acting on behalf of Halse during his absence, received a further appeal against the sentence of death. He passed the appeal, together with his advice to dismiss it (based on Halse's earlier dismissals), to the GOC-in-C BAOR who then confirmed the dismissal of the appeal.

Early in the morning of 9 June 1948, idly reviewing the case, Burnett spotted the error. He had to act quickly as Harnischfeger was due to be hanged that very day. He obtained a stay of execution and rushed to Hameln Prison, arriving just minutes before Pierrepoint was due to put the rope around Harnischfeger's neck. 'On account of the nervous strain which this man has suffered by the last-minute stay of execution', Harnischfeger's sentence was commuted to life imprisonment.[60] By this time, life imprisonment meant 21 years, but Harnischfeger only served a fraction of that and was freed from prison in 1952.

The War Crimes Group (NWE) No.3 Field Investigation Team had tried to develop a third Düsseldorf case. In the autumn of 1943, the arms manufacturer Rheinmetall-Borsig had started to use slave labourers. They housed about 700 prisoners of all nationalities in appalling conditions within the factory area in the so-called 'Camp Berta' (actually a sub-camp of the notorious Buchenwald concentration camp).[61]

The case against SS Company Sergeant Major Walter Knauff the camp commandant, Ratingen Gestapo officer Wilhelm Heiduck, foreman Max Schönwald (a prisoner himself) and German civilian foreman Albert Retz, who were the four men who had run the camp, was based on depositions. Knauff had two bosses: the managers at Buchenwald for the custody of the prisoners and the directors of Rheinmetall-Borsig for their output. He was squarely blamed by the others accused and witnesses alike for the horrible living conditions in Camp Berta and the sadistic beatings in both the camp and factory. There was evidence he had committed at least three murders.

Heiduck was responsible for the general policies adopted in the treatment of slave workers. About once a month, he assembled the German civilian employees of Rheinmetall-Borsig and told them to look upon the prisoners as subhuman.[62] He told the German workers to watch the prisoners closely, to beat them at the slightest provocation and to keep them working without breaks. No German, he promised, would face retribution for following these instructions even if a prisoner were fatally injured by ill-treatment. He led the way and was accused of killing several prisoners.

The prisoner and foreman, Schönwald inflicted most beatings with a rubber truncheon or lead pipe 'using it adroitly, unhesitatingly, unreasonably, and with the severity that invariably resulted in grievous bodily harm'.[63] He had almost certainly beat prisoners to death. Retz, the civilian foreman, also beat the prisoners, but at least appeared to be remorseful.

Lieutenant Colonel R A Nightingale, commanding the Field Investigation Section, recommended Knauff and Heiduck be charged with killing and ill-treatment of Allied nationals. Schönwald and Retz should be charged with severe ill-treatment of Allied nationals. In February 1948, however, the officer in charge of War Crimes Group (NWE), Lieutenant Colonel Gerald Draper, wrote there was a question about the status of the foreign workers in Camp Berta, 'insofar as approximately 80 per cent of the prisoners were Russian, it may be that they are probably to be considered as "stateless". Further, some of the serious incidents of mal-treatment relate to German victims.' Also, he thought the accusations were crimes against humanity rather than war crimes. For these reasons, Draper thought it best that the case was tried before a Control Commission Court rather than a British military court.[64] The case was dropped and the focus of British military justice shifted elsewhere.

Rheinhausen

Showing how ubiquitous the policy to shoot foreign workers was, in Rheinhausen about 30km north of Düsseldorf, the Germans also shot Russian POWS and slave labourers they suspected of looting under the 'cover' of air raids. It is shameful how much latitude soldiers, policemen and ordinary civilians gave themselves to shoot unarmed slave labourers at this time.

Rheinhausen had long been an industrial area, with coal mines, metal works and all the associated urban infrastructure. A huge steel plant on the west bank of the Rhine was owned by Krupp, a company that maintained its manufacturing capability only by using forced labour from a slave labour camp. When the area became part of the British Zone after being taken by the Americans, evidence of the shooting of several Russians buried in the Trompet Cemetery across the Rhine in Duisburg came to the attention of the War Crimes Group (NWE).

In the early hours of 22 May 1944, after an air raid on Rheinhausen, the nearby Moers *Schutzpolizei* were called out. The *Schutzpolizei* (Schipo) were the state protection police in Nazi Germany, a branch of the ordinary police force. They were told some Russians had escaped from the East Labour Camp. A car and a truck full of policemen immediately drove to the camp where SS Captain Wilhelm Brinkmann informed the assembled group, 'Now some Russians will have to be shot'. Everyone in the camp, men, women and children were assembled on the parade ground. Three men, Pawel Pristawko, Alex Kalinin and Peter Spirin were put up against a wall.

Policeman Josef Pohlmann was told to interrogate two civilians who had apparently caught the Russian men 'plundering'. When the Russians had been searched, little of value was found, but the civilians insisted the men had also stolen more valuable articles and both had signed confirmation statements.[65]

Brinkmann had heard enough. He walked onto the parade ground, dismissed the women and children, and explained through an interpreter why the three were to be shot. He told the crowd of men they should take it as a warning not to act in the same way. He asked for volunteer policemen, but nobody stepped forward. Brinkmann became enraged, calling them all cowards, and ordered Johann Broux, Wilhelm Balters and Heinrich Göntgen to form a firing squad. They took a position 30m from the men against the wall and Brinkmann gave the order to fire. Two volleys were fired, but the Russians were still writhing and screaming on the ground – Brinkmann delivered a *coup de grâce* to each.[66]

The next day, Gotthard Spaethe, the Trompet Cemetery administrator, buried their bodies. He told the War Crimes Group Field Investigator he had been informed the Russians were shot while trying to escape and a doctor had determined the cause of death as brain injury.[67]

A British Military Court tried the first Rheinhausen case in the Curiohaus between 30 December 1947 and 5 January 1948. Brinkmann was charged with the war crime of being 'concerned in the shooting without trial of three unknown Russian nationals' to which he pleaded not guilty.[68] The court had to decide whether the instructions to police at the time, not necessarily actual laws, were that looters should be tried in a special court or could be summarily executed. Brinkmann's defence counsel, Dr Matthiessen, argued the 1939 Public Enemy Decree,[69] which stated either military courts or special courts would hold proceedings to establish guilt, had been superseded in 1943 when the head of the German police issued orders looters should be shot (without trial). A second legal argument concerned whether the Russians should have had the protections offered by the Geneva Conventions to POWs.[70] It was agreed the Russians were not POWs, they were housed in labour camps with their whole families and were not guarded by soldiers, but the DJAG thought 'persons brought to Germany for the purpose of forced labour should be treated in the same way as prisoners of war'.[71] The court found Brinkmann guilty, but appears to have ignored the DJAG and been persuaded by Matthiessen's mitigation pleadings. He was sentenced to just two years' imprisonment. The firing squad were originally named as accused in the case, but not tried. In a brief to the DJAG, Major S M Stewart of the War Crimes Group (NWE) wrote, ' . . . it speaks in their favour, that when Capt Brinkmann asked for volunteers, nobody stepped forward' and 'it seems doubtful whether it is desirable to charge members of the firing squad in view of the general state of affairs in Germany at the time'.[72]

The second Rheinhausen case concerned a member of the SA. Wasil Kriwego, a 21-year-old Russian from Kirowograd, had stumbled out of the East Workers Camp when it was hit by British bombs. He ran into some German civilians who detained him and later handed him over to Anton Hohs who intended to take him back to the camp. On the way, however, he met Hugo Schubert and Fritz Dikty who was wearing his SA uniform. Recognizing the uniform, Hohs handed the Russian over saying he had been accused of looting, to which Dikty said, 'Then I will shoot him'. Schubert, however, was a guard at the East Labour Camp and recognized Kriwego as a Russian POW. He intervened telling Dikty he could not shoot him without evidence he had looted. The two took Kriwego to an air-raid shelter where they searched him finding a piece of bread and cheese, which Schubert thought were part of his ration. Dikty disagreed, punching the Russian and still expressing a desire to shoot him. Schubert somehow convinced Dikty to take Kriwego back to the camp and hand him over to the military authorities. Unfortunately, when they did this, camp commandant Becker told them his cells were full and so they decided to try the nearby Italian camp. On the way, seemingly desperate to shoot his prisoner, Dikty drew his 7.65mm pistol and shot Kriwego twice in the face. Schubert noticed Kriwego was still alive, so Dikty stepped forward and shot him a third time in the back of the head.[73]

Dikty, of course, told a slightly different story. He said Schubert was not with him when the shooting occurred. He said Kriwego had jumped to one side, picked up a stone and thrown it hitting his chest. With the Russian one and a half metres away, Dikty said, 'I took my pistol out of my pistol-holster and fired a shot at the Russian in order to prevent a further attack and to prevent escape . . . I felt that I acted in self-defence.'[74] Perhaps Dikty thought he might persuade a British military court it was his word against Schubert's, but there was also hard physical evidence against him. Gotthard Spaethe, the Rheinhausen Trompet cemetery attendant, led investigators to the graves of several Russian POWs. The body in grave 60 was exhumed and autopsied by pathologist Dr Alinero Kok, a captain in the Royal Army Medical Corps. This was Kriwego's grave.[75] Dr Kok's detailed report concluded there were injuries in two places: the left side of the jaw and the back of the skull. He found a 7.65mm bullet lying inside the skull.[76] The injuries were more indicative of an execution than a lucky shot fired when the Russian was trying to escape.

The case was heard in Court One of the Curiohaus between 4 and 9 August 1948.[77] Dikty pleaded not guilty, but was found guilty and sentenced to be hanged. Dr E Stoltenhoff (General Superintendent of the Rhine Province) and Dikty's defence counsel, Dr Wolfgang Graener, petitioned the court to delay the execution as proceedings for lying under oath had begun in the German courts against the witness Schubert. Lord Russell of Liverpool (from the DJAG), however, wrote to the GOC-in-C BAOR, stating even if Schubert's prosecution for perjury was successful, Dikty's sentence should stand. Lord Russell explained:

> The accused, on his own admission, shot the Russian for no better reason than that he threw a stone at the accused. In law a man is justified in using against an assailant a proportional amount of force in defence of himself. Hence, if he has reasonable apprehension of danger, and adopts none but proportionate means of warding it off, he will be innocent even though the wrongdoer be killed by the means

> thus adopted. But the means must be proportionate. The person assaulted is not justified in using firearms against his assailant unless the assault is so violent as to make him consider his life to be actually in danger. In this case the throwing of a stone by an unarmed man at a man with a loaded rifle cannot, in law, justify the armed man shooting and killing his assailant.[78]

We can excuse Lord Russell for confusing a rifle with a pistol as the legal principle still applies.

There were other appeals for Dikty's life. His wife Margarete felt that his sentence was out of all proportion when compared to 'the thousands of other cruelties and atrocities' committed by people in superior positions. The British military did not find her appeal that others committed far worse actions sufficiently persuasive to change the verdict or sentence. Otto Albrecht von Oppen who was interned with Dikty in Braunschweig-Querum was threatening, '. . . your deed [executing Dikty] will start violent nationalistic sentiments and engage much new followers for the communists'. Neither happened after Dikty was hanged in Hameln Prison on 29 October 1948.

A third Rheinhausen case never came to trial. Russian POWs Boris Solowei and Peter Pawelko made statements that three of their comrades had been shot by the SA on the night of 21 May 1944. Based on Solowei's statement, investigator Captain F N Potts outlined the case in his brief for preliminary investigation. He wrote that during a night air raid, three Russians had escaped a camp to get something to eat. They were caught by Paul Steffens who ordered ten SA men to shoot them. Two were given *coups de grâce* by Otto Becker, the third was shot by Johannes Hagemann.[79] Steffens, Becker and Hagemann refuted any involvement in the killings.

Major J A McKee, a field investigator for War Crimes Group (NWE), began a detailed investigation in June 1948. Unfortunately, by this time Solowei and Pawelko had moved to the Soviet Zone where they could not be found. McKee had to get creative to gather evidence. He had a translation of a bill for an autopsy of four bodies carried out on 25 May 1944 by pathologist Dr Bowin. Bowin stated the men had been shot for looting and gave their names as Vasil Kriwego, Ivan Tschernichkow, Roman Kotowski and Gregori Karawaew. They were buried at Trompet Cemetery. When McKee interviewed Bowin, he denied all knowledge of the autopsies, but McKee thought this was because the doctor feared for his professional reputation if he became involved in a war crimes trial.[80]

When Dr Alinero Kok had autopsied Kriwego in the second Rheinhausen case, he had also autopsied the exhumed bodies from graves 62, 64 and 66 recorded by Spaethe as belonging to Tschernichkow, Kotowski and Karawaew, respectively. The pathologist, however, found no evidence of gunshot wounds to these bodies. McKee thought there were two possibilities: either the Russians in these three graves had not been shot but died in the air raid or the bodies in the graves were not the shot Russians. He concluded the only way to clear the matter up would be to exhume all forty-eight bodies buried by Spaethe that day in May 1944, but nobody wanted to do that. Everywhere McKee turned he was thwarted; he could find no other witnesses and no documentation. With only Bowin's bill as evidence, he doubted a trial could prove the men accused by the Russians were guilty. On 9 July 1948, missing the original complainants and with a short time left to investigate, the case was closed.[81]

7

THE END OF BRITISH MILITARY TRIALS IN GERMANY

When the war ended, the British became alarmed by the sheer number of people they had promised to bring to justice. The Belsen trial took two months from September to November 1945 to try forty-four people. At that rate, they realized it would take decades to prosecute the estimated 20,000 accused in the British Zone. Furthermore, there just was not sufficient staff to investigate, prepare the trial papers and set up the number of courts necessary. The pool of military lawyers to prosecute or defend was shrinking and the number of officers to make up judging panels was dwindling as demobilization continued.

As the Soviets morphed from allies into enemies, the West began to see the advantage of using Germany as a physical buffer against them. It became essential to encourage Germany to join the democratic countries so that they would be on the right side of any future conflict. Prosecuting tens of thousands of German citizens ran counter to this aim, becoming an embarrassing prospect, and there began a gradual reduction in the legal aims of the British. At a meeting on 12 October 1945, Attorney General Sir Hartley Shawcross told the DJAG and the War Office he intended to prosecute at least 10 per cent of those criminals in the British zone – about 2,000 people. As an irreducible minimum, he wanted to try 500 cases by 30 April 1946.[1]

In internal communications, the government became hopelessly mixed up with three different figures that should have indicated the progress of British justice: the number of cases (the smallest number), the number of trials (some cases led to more than one trial – the next highest number) and the number of individuals (the highest number as some trials involved many people). These figures are not interchangeable, but were used as if they were and it became difficult to know what had been achieved. In November 1945, a secret cipher telegram from the War Office to BAOR HQ appeared to show some exasperation: 'Target for BAOR is minimum repeat minimum of 500 repeat 500 individuals to be tried for war crimes by 30 Apr 46.'[2] Five hundred *cases* had already been downgraded to 500 *individuals*.

By January 1946, as the Attorney General's deadline approached, it was clear British justice had fallen well short of the target. A mere 20 cases had been tried involving far fewer than 500 individuals. Shawcross despaired, writing to Prime Minister Clement Attlee, 'At the present rate the trial of war criminals will go on until the crack of doom'.[3] By the end of 1946, the number of crimes revealed to the British had escalated dramatically (over 3,000 had been recorded and hundreds were still being investigated). It was becoming overwhelming. As Shawcross feared, it looked like the trials would continue for many years, a fact that was becoming politically unpalatable.

If the politicians were finding war crimes trials distasteful, British public interest had all but disappeared. The dry approach of trial by documentation, championed by the IMT, rather than eyewitness testimony had bored British journalists and readers alike. By the summer of 1946, only German newspapers were reporting on the trials and British attention was focused on the problems of the empire, particularly Indian independence, and local murders. A year later in the autumn of 1947, Group Captain A G Somerhough, the officer in charge of War Crimes Group (NWE), reported to the DJAG on the progress of British war crimes trials. The trials of 669 individuals had been finished while trials of 36 were still in progress. Fifty-four cases were being investigated, but new crimes were still being uncovered. Somerhough had also concluded that unless there was an artificial ending of the process, it would go on and on.[4] The DJAG sent a memo to the British government recommending the current staff take as many cases as possible through the British military courts by 31 March 1948 and thereafter maintain a skeleton staff to investigate and prosecute only very grave cases. Eventually, the Cabinet's Overseas Reconstruction Committee decided all war crimes trials (except for four Wehrmacht commanders in custody) should begin by 1 September 1948. By this time, thirteen cases were proceeding against forty-one accused. While the British trials continued, there was another enormous task to accomplish – 'denazification'.

Having defeated the Germans militarily and removed the government, the Allies had to reverse the commitment of millions of people who had been resolute National Socialists. Plans were made at the Potsdam Conference (17 July to 2 August 1945) to disarm and demilitarize Germany in preparation for its eventual democratization. Within the four Occupied Zones, the Allies declared their resolve to remake German society by demolishing the NSDAP, dissolving all its institutions and repealing all discriminatory German laws. Nazi and militaristic doctrines were to be removed from German education. The judicial system was to be reorganized under the principles of democracy, justice under the law and equal rights for all citizens without distinction of race, nationality or religion.

Denazification was initially pursued in all sectors with gusto. Nazi leaders, influential supporters and high officials of Nazi organizations and institutions were arrested and interned. Others considered sufficiently 'Nazi' were removed from their positions of influence and allowed to assume only more menial positions. Assessment of a German adult's Nazi credentials and leanings was based on completion of a questionnaire called the *Fragebogen*. The estimated total of 45 million people to be processed was daunting and the Allies quickly became fatigued. In many places, the stripping of people from the medical, educational and legal professions was so damaging to those institutions that former Nazi sympathisers simply had to be rehired. It began to look futile and as the victors tired, the vanquished became resentful. At a time when the Western Allies increasingly felt the German population needed to be kept sweet on democracy so they did not turn to communism, denazification appeared to some to be counter-productive.

To regain control, the British began a more pragmatic approach to denazification in their zone. They were fervent about bringing to justice anyone who had committed war crimes against POWs and particularly captured Allied aircrew. But rebuilding German economic power was more important than finding how much of a Nazi each person in the north-west had been. Things were tough at home with their ruined economy and the British could not contemplate the added burden of bankrolling a large part of another country – Germany had to be allowed to help itself. First, the hated *Fragebogen* was dispensed with unless the person was applying for an official or responsible position. Then in January 1946, the British washed their hands of the whole process and handed it over to the Germans who, predictably, allowed it to wither and die.

After the huge British military legal effort to try the concentration camps cases (Bergen-Belsen, Ravensbrück and Neuengamme), there was a shift to pursuing cases involving British soldiers that could be quickly concluded. How the British chose which cases would come to trial is difficult to uncover. The files in The National Archives largely cover investigations, trial processes, petitions and the prison reports of those found guilty. The current Office of the Judge Advocate General has no records about why specific trials were pursued, who chose the court members and officers or why cases were heard in specific locations. What is clear, however, is that the Western Allies increasingly wanted to escape the duty of trying all the accused war criminals in Germany.

The British people seemed to support this. They certainly wanted justice for the crimes committed against their 'boys', but were less informed about the outrages in Eastern Europe and, therefore, less enthusiastic about prosecuting the people accused of them. The British public felt particularly conflicted about just how far the process should penetrate the regular German armed forces, especially regarding potential trials of senior German soldiers. Surely the German generals had simply done their duty just as their British counterparts? Many were increasingly uncomfortable with the accusation of 'victors' justice'.

Although the British still held three former German field marshals (Walter von Brauchitsch, Gerd von Rundstedt and Erich von Manstein) and a senior general (Adolf Strauss) in custody, they were looking less and less likely to try them. The myth of an untainted Wehrmacht was strong and perpetuated by the actions, pronouncements and memoirs of former German soldiers. Jürgen Förster, a prominent German historian, wrote, 'From Nuremberg onwards, the notion has existed of separating the Führer from his followers, the generals from their supreme commander, and the Wehrmacht from the crimes of the SS'.[5] In the minds of many, the ordinary German soldier's duties were disassociated from atrocities, particularly in the occupied countries. The opposite, however, was true – the Wehrmacht had supported, enabled and committed countless war crimes and crimes against humanity.

The Americans ground through twelve further Nuremberg Military Tribunals, one of which was 'The High Command Trial'.[6] The US Chief of Counsel for War Crimes, Telford Taylor, had originally suggested Brauchitsch, Rundstedt and Manstein be transferred to Nuremberg to be indicted in this case.[7] The British, however, still wanted to hedge their bets, retaining the senior men in case it became politically expedient to hold their own trial to show the world it was not just the Americans that could hold the former German high command to account. Evidence from the American trial that appeared to incriminate the field marshals was shared with the British authorities.

Poland and the Soviet Union also petitioned for the men to be handed over to their jurisdiction. Fearing they would not get fair trials, however, the British refused. Having discarded two options, the British appeared to have two left: release the officers or prosecute them. Worried that evidence from 'The High Command Trial' showing the men in custody had given orders leading to mass murder might get into the press, the British were forced to choose the latter. Not everybody agreed with the decision. General Brian Hubert Robertson, Deputy Military Governor of the British Occupation Zone of Germany, tried every argument he could to prevent it, including warning the aged officers might 'collapse either before or during the trial'.[8] Officers of the War Crimes Group (NWE), declined almost to a man to assist the trial of the field marshals.[9] A notable exception was Colonel Gerald Draper who joined the team to prosecute Manstein.

The depth of opposition to the trial of the four formerly high-ranking Germans was typified by a surprising source – Churchill. By 1948 he had turned against war crimes trials saying, 'Revenge is, of all satisfactions, the most costly and long drawn out; retributive persecution is, of all policies, the most pernicious. Our policy, subject to the exceptional cases I have mentioned, should henceforward be to draw the sponge across the crimes and horrors of the past—hard as that may be—and look, for the sake of all our salvation, towards the future.'[10] Churchill wanted an easy route for Germany to become part of a free, democratic Europe on the western side of the 'Iron Curtain.' Critics of the British trials to date, however, pointed out that the killers themselves had faced justice while the 'higher ups' had largely escaped punishment. For this and other political reasons, the British announced their final military war crimes trial would be of Brauchitsch, Rundstedt, Strauss and Manstein.

Manstein had been Rundstedt's Chief of Staff for the invasion of Poland. They and other commanders had been briefed by Hitler in August 1939 on the forthcoming campaign. Hitler had demanded annihilation of the enemy with brutal and merciless action against Polish men, women and children. Keen not to disappoint the Führer, the invasion of Poland was terrifyingly violent and pitiless. The German invasion of the Soviet Union, Operation BARBAROSSA, was equally bloody and ruthless. When the campaign began in June 1941, Manstein commanded a Panzer corps in Army Group North. Later that summer, he took control of the 11th Army campaign in Ukraine. After victories in Crimea, he was promoted to field marshal and assumed command of Army Group Don, renamed in 1943 as Army Group South. He was succeeded by Walter Model in April 1944 and never held command again.

Manstein was arrested by the British in August 1945 and imprisoned in a POW camp near Lüneburg. On 19 October, he was taken to the Nuremberg Palace of Justice where he was held for a year. Here he was tasked with providing a document describing the development of the German Army from the end of WW1 to the end of WW2. Together with General of the Cavalry Siegfried Westphal, Manstein produced a 132-page document, *The German Army 1920 – 1945*.[11]

Between 9 and 12 August 1946, Manstein appeared at the IMT as a defence witness. He was called by Dr Hans Laternser, counsel for the German general staff and high command, to give evidence about the command hierarchy, the Commissar Order and the treatment of Soviet POWs. Afterwards, Manstein was sent to Special Camp No.11 near Bridgend in Wales (known as 'Island Farm') where he lived with the other former field marshals, Brauchitsch and Rundstedt, for almost two years. In July 1948, Manstein returned to custody in Nuremberg where the Americans were hoping he and Rundstedt would be defence witnesses in their 'High Command Trial'. Having been informed they were themselves to be tried later by the British and without the benefit of adequate legal advice, both declined to give evidence fearing they might implicate themselves in war crimes. Manstein and Rundstedt were not returned to the relative comfort of Island Farm, however, but to Munsterlager on Lüneburg Heath where they joined Brauchitsch and Strauss and were held in solitary confinement. Manstein complained to British military historian Sir Basil Liddell Hart who became the centre of a press campaign for better treatment and, towards the end of September 1948, conditions were eased. After a few weeks, the four were moved to the 94th (Hamburg) British Military Hospital in Hamburg-Barmbek.

On 18 October 1948, Brauchitsch died in the hospital. A series of British Army and Home Office medical boards followed, each coming to different conclusions and delaying proceedings against the surviving three men. In March 1949, a joint board of two British prison service doctors and two army doctors concluded Manstein alone was fit to stand trial. On 5 May 1949, there was a debate on German war crimes trials in the House of Lords.[12] The Lord Bishop of Chichester, George Bell, opened the debate with some well-rehearsed criticism of the British and

US war crimes trials. Bell was opposed to the Nazi regime that had existed in Germany, but believed the German elite could not possibly have been involved in war crimes. He told the House of Lords, 'It is very difficult for a defeated foe to appreciate the justice of punishing such crimes as the deportation of civilian populations in occupied territory, looting, murder of POWs and devastation not justified by military necessity, when similar charges could be brought against one or more of the Allies, but are not brought'. He may have had a point, but if trials against the Germans were losing momentum, trials of the victorious Allies were inconceivable.

Bell also disagreed with Article 8 of the Nuremberg Charter which read, 'The fact that the Defendant acted pursuant to order of his Government or of a superior shall not free him from responsibility, but may be considered in mitigation of punishment if the Tribunal determines that justice so requires'.[13] He thought the principle of *respondeat superior* (let the master answer) was most important and deeply believed the strongest guilt was with the makers of policy. He implied that these people should be tried and those who acted on the policy should not. He seemed unaware of the fallacy of this position – had these maxims applied, only Hitler could have been tried. In the House of Lords debate, 1st Baron Hankey was in absolute support of the bishop. He said, 'There was something cynical and revolting in the spectacle of British, French and American judges sitting on the Bench with colleagues who, however impeccable as individuals, represented a country which before, during and since the trials has perpetrated half the political crimes in the calendar', which appeared to support the childish *Tu quoque* defence. The baron would later provide a foreword to Reginald Paget's book *Manstein: His Campaigns and His Trial*.

Rundstedt was released on 26 May 1949 and died less than four years later. Strauss, released at the same time, lived until 1973. It was Manstein alone who faced justice in the Curiohaus on 23 August 1949 when the final Curiohaus British military trial opened in Court One. The court was presided over by General Sir Frank Simpson. He had served with the British Expeditionary Force and was involved in the Dunkirk evacuation. He became Lieutenant General Bernard Montgomery's Chief of Staff in 1940 and Director of Military Operations in 1943. In 1948, Simpson was appointed General Officer Commanding-in-Chief Western Command. The Judge Advocate was Charles Collingwood, a county court judge who had been Assistant JAG from 1943 to 1945.[14]

Manstein was fortunate that the IMT had not judged the general staff and the high command of the Wehrmacht to be a criminal organization.[15] Had they done so it would have been a straightforward job for the prosecution to show that he had been one of the most senior members and, therefore, automatically guilty. As it was, the prosecution needed to gather, present and *prove* individual charges against Manstein. The lead prosecutor was Arthur Comyns Carr, who had been a member of the British prosecution team at the International Military Tribunal of the Far East, was a Liberal Party politician and a barrister. Comyns Carr brought to the trial his knowledge of the arguments and findings of the military trials against senior commanders in the Japanese Imperial Army. He used this knowledge to suggest that a precedent had been set for finding commanders guilty of a 'breach of duty' when they did not protect POWs and civilian populations from violation of the laws of war by their soldiers.

Barrister Frederick Jones assisted Comyns Carr. He had ended his military service as a major in the Royal Artillery, had been a junior counsel at the Nuremberg trial and was a Labour Party politician. Colonel Gerald Draper also worked for the prosecution. He had prosecuted several war crimes trials and was seen as a specialist in the law of armed combat. The prosecution sought to bring a catalogue of charges, alleging crimes against humanity, the mistreatment of POWs and the orchestration of military actions leading to unspeakable suffering. It argued for individual accountability in the face of immoral directives.

The defence attempted to portray Manstein as a mere soldier following orders and bound by military hierarchy. It was funded by public subscription and even Churchill dipped into his pocket to donate. Manstein was represented by Dr Hans Laternser, whom he knew well from the IMT, and Dr Paul Leverkuehn. To help the defence team with British legal procedure, the German lawyers turned to Reginald Paget, Baron Paget of Northampton. He read law at Cambridge, but did not graduate. Nevertheless, he was called to the bar in 1934 and was first elected as Labour MP for Northampton in 1945. Paget's junior was Sam Silkin also a Labour MP and barrister. Both worked *pro bono*. Much of what is officially known about the Manstein trial comes from Paget's book, a sometimes inaccurate and rather shrill representation of the four-month hearing, which he described as 'a political circus'.[16]

On the first day of the trial, Paget argued that Manstein should not be tried under the Royal Warrant. He thought it was the first time the Royal Warrant had been objected to, but he was wrong. It had been repeatedly and unsuccessfully challenged, including at the first Belsen trial in September 1945. Paget also seemed to think Manstein was still a POW because 'A state of war still existed between Britain and Germany and we were in military occupation'. Presumably, he had missed the German Instrument of Surrender, the legal document of unconditional surrender of the German armed forces to the Allies, which ended WW2 in Europe. This misconception allowed Paget to claim Manstein was due the rights of a POW, particularly that a prisoner could be sentenced only by a fair trial. This was defined as one the captor considers fair for his own troops. One feature of such a military trial would be that Manstein could only be judged by officers of his rank (which the Curiohaus court members were not). Comyns Carr simply argued that Manstein, rather than being a POW, was an accused war criminal – this precedent had been established at the International Military Tribunal for the Far East. The legal argument was complex, but the court ruled that Manstein was not a POW and could be tried under the Royal Warrant.[17]

The next day, the Judge Advocate read the seventeen separate charges against Manstein, many having multiple counts. It appeared to some that the prosecution had got a list of the war crimes committed by the Germans in Eastern Europe and tried to see what might stick to the former field marshal. But the charges were not in the least generic or vague – they were entirely specific. The first, second and third charges related to war crimes in Poland which had led to 1,209 killings. The first charge was for authorizing and permitting twenty-three counts of killing and maltreatment of Polish citizens by troops of Army Group South and Army Group East or by forces under Manstein's command. The prosecution had detailed evidence for each of the twenty-three atrocities. This seemed to be the most damaging of the three so-called 'Polish charges' and included counts involving the deportation of Jews from Upper Silesia and the prevention of their return.

When the Germans overran the area in 1939, they attempted to drive the Jewish population across the River San to Rava-Ruska in the east. Syma Weikselbaum, the Jewish wife of an accountant from Tarnobrzeg, gave this account of the river crossing:

> The Germans drove the people, shouting 'schnell, schnell', not supplying any means for the crossing to the other side. The people themselves had to organize and hire boats.

> This crossing was improvised with the use of broken planks which did not guarantee any security on the water. Drowning accidents occurred. One could see people swimming to the other side. Mothers held their babies over their heads. One could hear the screams of the Jews being driven across in this method as well as the shouts and shots from the Germans who were shooting in the direction of the river.[18]

Especially incriminating for Manstein was an addendum he added to his order entitled, 'Returning of Jews fled to the East'. It read in part, 'the floating back to Eastern Upper Silesia of Jewish refugees will be prevented with all possible means'.[19] There was little doubt that everyone in his command understood that meant death for any Jewish men, women and children trying to return home.

Comyns Carr and Draper accepted that often the Polish eyewitnesses were unable to distinguish the uniforms of the Germans who were trying to kill them, but presented evidence that in some cases they could. Exhibit 37 was a sworn deposition from Polish Jew Adam Brandys who said, 'Afterwards, during the occupation, I learnt to tell the difference between the uniforms of the SS troops and those of the Wehrmacht, and on the basis of this I can confirm that the troops which entered Sosnowiec on 4 September 1939 were not SS troops, but were soldiers in the Wehrmacht'. He continued, 'On the next day German soldiers walked around the houses and dragged out all the Jewish males. These men were put in rows with their hands up, and driven to the Town Hall. All the men from boys to old men were taken, and as they were being driven to the Town Hall the old men were falling down. The men who fell were shot on the spot.'[20]

At the IMT, Manstein had tried to distance the Wehrmacht from the SS, SD and *Einsatzgruppen* so that he could not be accused of having any control over their excesses. He told the IMT, 'Himmler prohibited everything which could have exerted any influence on the SS by the Armed Forces'. At Manstein's Curiohaus trial, however, the prosecution had documents showing the police organizations and paramilitaries were *subordinate* to the army which even had the power of court martial over them. Exhibit 68 was part of a special regulation issued by General Headquarters of the 8th Army (Manstein was the Chief of Staff). Point eight concerns the chain of command of the police forces and read in translation, 'They are subordinate to the C.in C. 8. Army Gen.Maj.

of the uniformed police Becker and SS-Brigadeführer Streckenbach will report regularly to GHQ 8.Army/DGMG on the employment and activity of the police formations under their command . . .'[21] Exhibit 69 special regulation 15, also issued by General Headquarters of the 8th Army read, 'Members of the police formations, including also the SS-Deadhead-formations [*sic*], employed in the operational area will be regarded as attached personnel of the armed Forces and are subject to military jurisdiction.'[22]

If that was not clear enough, the prosecution also had documentary evidence from the 'Manual of the General Staff Services' which supported the entitlement of Manstein to issue orders to the other units. This led to the second charge that Manstein deliberately and recklessly disregarded his duty as Chief of Staff to take such steps as were within his power to prevent the killing and maltreatment referred to in the first charge. The third charge included six counts that Manstein deliberately and recklessly disregarded his duty as Chief of Staff to take steps within his power to secure the humane treatment of Polish POWs, resulting in many of them being killed or mistreated.[23] Exhibit 119 gave typical support to this charge. Farmer and local bailiff Stanislaw Gozdur said in a deposition,

> I looked in the direction and saw Polish soldiers kneeling on the highway. In front of them stood armed German soldiers with weapons in their hands . . . The commanding officer ordered them to shoot the Polish soldiers as he did not know what to do with them and he did not wish to take them across the Wisla [Vistula]. He ordered 'Fire.' There was a series of shots.[24]

In Exhibit 120, Roman Catholic Padre Leopold Jarosz said,

> Afterwards about 20 Wehrmacht soldiers brought into the yard a group of about 30 disarmed Polish soldiers, in uniforms but without belts. The German soldiers placed the Poles near a ditch dug for anti-aircraft precautions. One Wehrmacht soldier was shooting at random about every other Polish soldier aiming at the temple or at the back of the head. Standing at a window in the vicarage I blessed the dying soldiers.[25]

Part of the reason for adding Polish charges to Manstein's indictment was political. Inserting them justified the British refusal to hand him over to Poland, where they feared an unsatisfactory trial might end with Manstein being hanged. The atrocities described were all too believable and supported by thousands of others which were being revealed daily. The charges, however, were criticised for lack of evidence supporting the prosecution's case that Manstein could have and should have stopped them. With what we now know about the German occupation of Poland, it is difficult to accept Paget's defence of Manstein. He essentially dismissed all the Polish evidence as being invented by peasants. He thought there were perhaps half a dozen atrocities which were the work of the SS. The final sentence in the slim chapter in his book regarding the 'Polish charges' reads, 'So far as the Polish campaign was concerned the evidence established very clearly that the conduct of the German army had been correct'.[26] The court appeared to agree and acquitted Manstein of the first three charges.

The remaining charges concerned the conduct of Manstein's 11th Army in the Soviet Union between September 1941 and April 1944 – the so-called 'Russian charges'. Within these, the fourth to seventh charges related to Soviet POWs. He was found guilty of the fourth charge which accused him of deliberately and recklessly disregarding his duty and failing to take steps to ensure adequate treatment of Soviet POWs. There were 11 counts in the charge covering 7,393 deaths. Manstein was also found guilty of the fifth charge, six counts of ordering or permitting the carrying out of orders towards the execution of Soviet prisoners of war illegally as 'partisans'. Both the fourth and fifth charges, however, had the wording describing his actions as deliberate removed. The character of the crimes was softened from commission to omission – not that he acted in a specific way, but that he had failed to act.[27]

Manstein was found not guilty of permitting the forced conscription of Soviet POWs to fight for the Germans (the sixth charge), but was found guilty of ordering forces under his command to use Soviet POWs in prohibited or dangerous work (the seventh charge). The Hague Convention of 1907 explicitly stated that POW work 'shall not be excessive and shall have no connection with the operations of the war'.[28] The prosecution, however, had evidence this had been ignored including Exhibit 162, an order which read in part, 'No prisoner-of-war who is brought in, is to be transferred any more to prisoner-of-war camps situated outside the Divisional area but is to be assigned immediately to already existing PW detachments to work at the construction of field fortifications'.[29]

In May 1941, Hitler issued the 'Decree concerning the exercise of Military Jurisdiction in the "Barbarossa" area and concerning special measures of the troops'. It stripped the punishment of offences by civilians from courts martial and placed it in the hands of individual officers. Their usual solution was simply to shoot the civilians. Building on this murderous declaration were orders to 'liquidate' (kill) so-called 'Franc-tireurs' and enemy civilians who attacked German armed forces.[30] The high command added its own document to the Führer Decree regarding the treatment of 'political commissars' who, it stated, 'if apprehended when fighting or offering resistance, they will on principle be liquidated at once by means of arms'.[31] These two documents made it hard for Soviet citizens to live through the invasion of their country since just about any of them could be said by the Germans to fall into one of these categories. In consequence, millions of them were murdered.

A further document produced by the prosecution team showed that at least some of the Wehrmacht knew how the document ordering the killing of 'political commissars' would look if it fell into Allied hands. Point one of a letter to the Chief of Staff Panzer Group 4 (including Manstein's corps) from the Chief of the General Staff of Army Group North stated, 'I consider it necessary to destroy the decree of the High Command of the Army concerning the treatment of political commissars, in order to prevent it from falling into the hands of the enemy, and to make its exploitation for propaganda purposes impossible'.[32] The three documents formed part of the prosecution evidence for the eighth charge which accused Manstein of being responsible for fifteen summary executions of 'political commissars' by army units or of transfer to the SD leading to their deaths. He was found guilty of this charge with amendments.

Three charges (ninth to eleventh) related to the activities of *Einsatzgruppe* D, the mobile killing force tasked with eliminating perceived civilian enemies of Germany. In southern Ukraine and Crimea these enemies were Roma, Sinti, Slavs, disabled people, Jehovah's Witnesses, communists and most specifically Jews. SS Major General Otto Ohlendorf led this homicidal group. The activities of the *Einsatzgruppen* had featured in two earlier trials. Sir Hartley Shawcross, the lead British prosecutor, informed the judges at the IMT about its murderous campaign and the Americans had prosecuted the '*Einsatzgruppen* Trial'.[33]

When Ben Ferencz, a young American prosecutor, unearthed evidence of the huge number of Soviet civilians killed by the *Einsatzgruppen*, the Americans hastily added the case to their subsequent Nuremberg trials.[34] The trial revealed that relatively small teams of men had murdered around a million people (the final number would later be shown to be twice as many) and noted, 'these men were in the field actively superintending, controlling, directing, and taking an active part in the bloody harvest'.[35] By concentrating on the perpetrators, the trial had exposed members of the SS, SD and Gestapo, but provided little evidence regarding the role played in the mass slaughter by the Wehrmacht. In his opening statement to the American court, prosecutor Brigadier General Telford Taylor said,

> Nor were the commanders of the armed forces ignorant of the task of the *Einsatzgruppen*. Hitler himself instructed them that it was the mission of these special task forces to exterminate all Jews and political commissars in their assigned territories. The *Einsatzgruppen* were dependent upon the army commander for their billets, food, and transport; relations between armed forces and the Security Police and SD were close and almost cordial, and the commanders of the *Einsatzgruppen* reported repeatedly that the understanding of the army commanders for the task of the *Einsatzgruppen* made their operations considerably easier.[36]

But a prosecution statement is not evidence.

Those accused in the '*Einsatzgruppen* Trial' gave written and oral testimony that their units were supported by the German army and could not have operated otherwise. For example, Ohlendorf's affidavit of 24 April 1947 stated, 'The armies or army groups had to supply the Einsatzgruppen with quarters, food, repairs, gasoline, and the like. Each army group and the 11th Army, the latter as nucleus of another army group for the Caucasus, was assigned an Einsatzgruppe, which in turn was divided into Einsatzkommandos and Sonderkommandos.'[37]

In the Manstein trial, the prosecution used this evidence to infer he must have known about the *Einsatzgruppen* activities, which could not have been carried out without his consent and co-operation.

They showed the court a document which illustrated a secondary line of command (a dotted line) between General HQ of the 11th Army, which Manstein commanded, and Ohlendorf's *Einsatzgruppe* D.[38] Manstein's defence, however, pointed out that the convicted criminals in the '*Einsatzgruppen* Trial' had, 'kept themselves alive by giving evidence for the prosecution at the trials of various German generals'.[39] The court decided to disregard the evidence as unsound and acquitted Manstein on these charges. They found him guilty of the tenth charge, but that he did not 'deliberately and recklessly' disregard his duty to prevent the actions of the *Einsatzgruppen*. The severity of the sentence Manstein could be given for being found guilty of this charge was also reduced by recasting it as a 'crime of omission'. Proof would be needed that Manstein had a legal obligation to act and that he consciously failed to fulfil that obligation. Such proof was thin on the ground.

The twelfth charge accused Manstein of directly instigating troops under his command to commit brutalities against the Jewish population in his area of operations. It appeared to be hard for Manstein to deny this as the prosecution produced a command from him saying, 'The soldier must appreciate the necessity for harsh punishment of Jewry, the spiritual bearer of the Bolshevist terror'.[40] Seven counts made up this charge which included killing tens of thousands of Jews. One example involved the murder of thousands of Jews in Kerch in Eastern Crimea. Between 1 and 3 December 1941, Sonderkommando 10b assigned to the 3rd Romanian Army, which was under Manstein's command,[41] shot about 2,500 Jews in an anti-tank trench close to the city. Later that December, the Germans killed every remaining Jew they could find.[42] Manstein's defence introduced doubt into the court about the numbers. Paget could not imagine the large numbers claimed to have been killed by the *Einsatzgruppen*, writing, 'I do not myself believe that the Jews murdered in the Crimea number more than 2000 to 3000', acknowledging, however that whatever the numbers, the crime was appalling.[43] Despite the prosecution evidence, Manstein was acquitted of this charge.

The thirteenth to sixteenth charges related to crimes against Soviet civilians. Manstein was acquitted on the fourteenth charge of issuing orders permitting executions of Soviet citizens without a trial, but guilty on the other three charges (the thirteenth with amendments). These charges had a total of forty-five counts detailing killings, forced labour on military-related works and deportation to Germany for slave labour. The prosecution had copies of many orders authorizing the use of slaves. Exhibit 397 read in part, 'The units after agreement with the sector leaders, will also employ all civilians in the age groups between 16 – 60 on construction work . . . Officers are authorized to hang civilians who refuse.'[44] Incredibly, Manstein's defence seemed to think that slave labour was acceptable. Paget wrote, 'Compulsory labour was no new experience to the Ukrainian peasant and the conditions provided by the Germans were better . . . '.[45]

The final charge (seventeenth) was thirteen counts of 'scorched earth' orders during his retreat, commanding deportation of populations, seizure of foodstuffs and destruction of all objects of value. Manstein could hardly deny this as he had admitted it to the IMT. During that trial, he had been asked, 'Was large-scale destruction carried out within the areas of your army or army group?' to which Manstein had answered, 'Yes, in the Ukraine particularly, there were very considerable destructions'. Later he elaborated, 'In 1943, during the retreat beyond the Dnieper, I myself saw that planned destruction to a considerable extent had been carried out by order of Hitler. Hitler had ordered that the territories east of the Dnieper should be made useless for the Russians.'[46] He was found guilty of the charge with amendments.

After four months, on 19 December 1949, Court One assembled to hear on which charges Manstein had been found guilty. There were nine (some of which were amended to reduce his responsibility) and he was sentenced to 18 years' imprisonment. He was taken to Werl Prison where he protested in letters to Paget and Liddell Hart, insisting that he had done nothing wrong and could accept no guilt whatsoever. In January 1950, Lieutenant General Sir Charles Keightley, GOC-in-C BAOR, confirmed the guilty findings, but inexplicably reduced Manstein's sentence to 12 years. In less than a month, a third of his sentence had been removed.

Manstein had been tried and convicted while Clement Attlee led a Labour government in the UK. Attlee lost a snap election in 1951 to the Conservatives who took control led by Churchill. Within a month, Prime Minister Churchill wrote to the Foreign Secretary, Anthony Eden, suggesting all German officers remaining in British custody should be released. Eden resisted and instead implemented a legal device to count pretrial custody against sentences imposed. Thus, Manstein's sentence was further reduced by four and a half years.[47] The seven and a half years he then expected to serve was again reduced for 'good conduct.' In August 1952, he was granted medical parole to be treated in Kiel for a cataract in his left eye. He stayed in Kiel until February 1953 and was then allowed to convalesce in Allmendingen, close to where his wife was staying with relatives. It was from here he was 'released' on 7 May 1953. The local Bürgermeister gave children the day off school and there was a festive procession through the town.[48] He died 20 years later and was buried with full military honours in Dorfmark, Lower Saxony.

There had been a determination, at least immediately after the end of the war, to bring to justice all those responsible for crimes against peace, crimes against humanity, war crimes and conspiracy to commit the criminal acts referred to in these charges. But the most that could be said of this massive effort was there had been a 'symbolic reckoning'.[49] It was planned for many trials to be heard by an international court (the IMT), but this commitment floundered in the morass of geopolitics after just one trial. The IMT was followed by a programme of trying the accused in separate zones of occupation, but waning enthusiasm, dwindling resources and political resistance rapidly eroded official enthusiasm. The Allied governments tried to wriggle out of their stated responsibility to prosecute war criminals before the trials had even begun. So, when the Cold War presented a chance to end them in the 1950s, the Americans, British and French seized the advantage and dismantled the trial machinery. It was paramount that the new Federal Republic of Germany (FRG) contributed to Western defence against the Soviet bloc. But for the FRG to be on the side of the Western Allies, German politicians and people alike called for a further demonstration of goodwill – let the incarcerated war criminals free. British military courts had tried 937 people for war crimes with 269 acquitted.[50] A meagre 668 were made to pay in some way for their crimes. Less than 200 of the guilty were executed. Those imprisoned were all free by the mid-1950s. Tens, perhaps hundreds, of thousands remained untried and simply got away with their crimes.

The British war crimes trials did help to establish the principle that individuals, including military leaders, could be held culpable for their actions, even if those actions were taken in the name of the state. The fairness of the trials can be challenged for their undue reliance on written deposition, which made it impossible for a witness to be cross-examined. Confidence in written evidence, however, was essential. Frequently witnesses moved away from the area where a crime had occurred and left behind only their affidavit. Who can blame a Czech or French person for wanting to go home rather than stay in the land of their former oppressor? Sometimes they were willing to return to give evidence, but often they were not. Many had disappeared or even died. Hearsay evidence was allowed, but the court was warned in the Royal Warrant, 'It shall be the duty of the Court to judge of the weight to be attached to any evidence given in pursuance of this Regulation which would not otherwise be admissible'. Written and hearsay evidence was not accepted without question.

British military trial judging panels comprised, mainly, British soldiers leading to the accusation of 'victors' justice'. This line was taken by many of the accused, not least by Hermann Göring at the IMT. The Allies did challenge themselves to consider whether the charge was valid. In a paper read before the Edinburgh University Law Faculty Society on 5 February 1946, Professor Arthur L Goodhart examined it. He did not share the view that the IMT, and by extension the British military courts, lacked the impartiality which is essential in all judicial procedure because its members represented only the victorious Allied nations. Attractive as this argument may sound in theory, he said, it ignored the fact that it runs counter to the administration of the law in every country. The prisoner has a right to demand that his judges shall be fair, but not that they shall be neutral. Goodhart quoted Lord Wright, who pointed out that the same principle applies to ordinary criminal law, 'a burglar cannot complain that he is being tried by a jury of honest citizens'.[51]

Finally, we must ask whether the tripartite aims of criminal justice, deterrence, rehabilitation and punishment were served. Regarding deterrence, the answer must be a resounding 'no' as there continued to be war crimes throughout the rest of the twentieth century. As for rehabilitation, some convicted war criminals were subject to denazification in the same way as other German citizens, but for most the programme had been abandoned long before they were released. There was a surprising lack of remorse – prisoners commonly cited ill-health as grounds for remission of their sentences rather than showing repentance for their crimes. That leaves the question of punishment. Those executed paid the highest price possible for their crimes, but those imprisoned escaped the common definition of justice. Nibbling away at the sentences of German war criminals ensued. British politicians hoped the erosion of penalties would hardly be noticed by the British public who they predicted didn't care much anyway. They were right, the last convicted war criminal left British custody in 1957.[52]

Even the corpses of those executed by the British were a problem. The usual British practice was to bury the bodies of hanged prisoners within prison grounds. On 11 December 1945, General Brian Robertson, Deputy Military Governor of the British Occupation Zone of Germany, confirmed that this would also be the British policy in Germany despite the procedure in German law which was to release bodies to the next-of-kin for burial. This caused some friction. The families of the dead pleaded for information on the last resting places of their loved ones only to find that they were within prison grounds and could not be visited.[53]

Despite burying them three-deep, after hanging ninety convicted war criminals Hameln Prison ran out of space for graves within its grounds. Ludwig Ramdohr, a brutal interrogator in Ravensbrück, was the last to be interred there in May 1947. But the British trials were far from over at this time and it was expected that there would be many more hangings. What were the British authorities to do with the bodies? The solution chosen was to transport newly-hanged corpses by night to the nearby Friedhof am Wehl cemetery for burial in plot CIII. This had the unfortunate consequence of laying the criminals to rest in the same grounds as some of their victims. The last person to be hanged by the British in Hameln Prison was Jerza Andzeak, a displaced Polish man convicted for illegal use of a firearm and murdering a policeman. He was laid in the mass grave in December 1949. In early 1954, the problem of burying war criminals in a marked area where they might be martyred was compounded when the government of Lower Saxony decided to exhume the remains in the Hameln Prison yard and add them to the bodies already in the mass grave.

Plot CIII now holds the bodies of all the convicted war criminals hanged by the British. Over the years, Hameln politicians have vacillated on how to deal with this part of their cemetery. Sometimes the graves were marked and at one time there was even talk of a memorial stone.[54] Now the area is once again unmarked and has become overgrown, the veiled resting place of the convicted merging with the obscurity of the Curiohaus trials that put them there.

NOTES

Introduction

1. Phillips, R, *Trial of Josef Kramer and Forty-Four Others (The Belsen Trial)* (1949) William Hodge & Co Ltd, p. 174.
2. Two of those indicted were not tried by the IMT. German industrialist Gustav Krupp was too infirm and excluded from the proceedings. Robert Ley, Head of the German Labour Front, committed suicide before the trial began. Nazi Party Secretary Martin Bormann was tried *in absentia*.
3. For example, Charlesworth, Lorie, 'Forgotten justice: forgetting law's history and victims' justice in British "minor" war crime trials in Germany 1945-8' (2008) *Amicus Curiae*, 74, pp. 2–10.
4. Hassel, Katrin, *Kriegsverbrechen vor Gericht* (2008) Nomos.
5. Phillips, R, *Trial of Josef Kramer and Forty-Four Others (The Belsen Trial)* (1949) William Hodge & Co Ltd.
6. I owe a debt to the KZ-Gedenkstätte Neuengamme as this was inspired by their approach in excellent summary materials available online at https://www.kz-gedenkstaette-neuengamme.de/en/curiohaus/ (Retrieved 15 Oct 2023).

Chapter 1: The Beginning of War Crimes Trials

1. There are good accounts of the Leipzig Trials in Mullins, Claude, *The Leipzig Trials* (1921) H F G Witherby, and in Creel, George, *War Criminals and Punishment* (1944) Hutchinson & Co Ltd, pp. 57–64.
2. Winston Churchill's broadcast on the Soviet-German War, 1941, https://www.nationalchurchillmuseum.org/winston-churchills-broadcast-on-the-soviet-german-war.html (Retrieved 22 Nov 2023).

3. https://www.presidency.ucsb.edu/documents/statement-warning-neutral-nations-against-asylum-for-war-criminals (Retrieved 16 Apr 2022).
4. Overy, Richard, *Interrogations* (2001) Penguin Group, p. 8.
5. Churchill, Winston S, *The Second World War* (1951) Chartwell Edition, Volume 5, The Educational Book Company Ltd, p. 286.
6. United Nations War Crimes Commission, *History of the United Nations War Crimes Commission and the Development of the Laws of War* (1948) HMSO, Chapter 6.
7. Davidson, Eugene, *The Trial of The Germans* (1997) University of Missouri Press, p. 8.
8. United Nations War Crimes Commission, *History of the United Nations War Crimes Commission and the Development of the Laws of War* (1948) HMSO, p. 6.
9. The War Office, 18 June 1945, Royal Warrant 0160/2498, A. O. 81/1945 *Regulations for the Trial of War Criminals.*
10. Mullins, Claud, *The Leipzig Trials* (1921) H F G Witherby, pp. 109–12.
11. *The American Journal of International Law*, Volume 16, No. 4 (Oct 1922), pp. 721–3.
12. Statement by Justice Jackson on War Trials Agreement (12 August 1945) https://archive.ph/A3IC (Retrieved 11 Oct 2022).
13. Author's conversation with RAF Lancaster navigator, Leslie Blaza, 1978.
14. Total RAF aircrew flying combat missions was around 125,000. RAF casualties are detailed in http://www.rafinfo.org.uk/bcww2losses/BC-RoH-casstats.htm (Retrieved 30 Jan 2024).
15. Borch, Fred L, 'Lore of the Corps: War Crimes in Sicily Sergeant West, Captain Compton, and the Murder of Prisoners of War in 1943', *Army Lawyer* (2020), Issue 5, pp. 1 –17.
16. Hassel, Katrin, *Kriegsverbrechen vor Gericht* (2008) Nomos pp. 21–22.
17. Nuremberg Trials Final Report Appendix D: Control Council Law No. 10, 20 December 1945, https://avalon.law.yale.edu/imt/imt10.asp (Retrieved 8 Oct 2022).
18. https://encyclopedia.ushmm.org/content/en/article/subsequent-nuremberg-proceedings (Retrieved 8 Oct 2022).
19. United Nations War Crimes Commission, *Law Reports of Trials of War Criminals* (1947) HMSO. United Nations War Crimes Commission,

History of the United Nations War Crimes Commission and the Development of the Laws of War (1948) HMSO.

20. BAOR Administrative Instruction No.104, definitions of war crimes, August/September 1945, TNA WO 311/857.
21. For a good discussion of judicial precedent, see Keenan, Denis, *Smith & Keenan's English Law* (2001), 13th Edition, Longman, pp. 168–79.
22. The court composition for the *Peleus* trial was:
    President – Brigadier C I V Jones CBE (106 Anti-aircraft Brigade)
    Members – Brigadier R M Jerram, Commodore D Young-Jamieson (Royal Navy), Captain Sir Roy Gill (Royal Naval Reserve), Lieutenant-Colonel H E Piper (Royal Artillery), Captain E Matpheos (Royal Hellenic Navy), Commander N I Sarris (Royal Hellenic Navy)
    Judge Advocate – A Melford Stevenson (Barrister)
    Prosecutor – R C Halse (Military Department, Judge Advocate General's Office)
    Defence Counsel for Eck – Captain Meckel (German Navy)
    Defence Counsel for Eck – Dr Todsen (German Barrister)
    Defence Counsel for Hoffmann, Weisspfennig & Schwender – Dr Pabst (German Barrister)
    Defence Counsel for Hoffmann – Dr Wulf
    Defence Counsel for Lenz – Major N Lermon (British Barrister HQ 8 District)
    Defence Counsel for all accused – Professor A Wegner
    TNA WO 235/5.
23. Cameron, John, *Trial of Heinz Eck et al (The Peleus Trial)* (1949) William Hodge and Company Limited, p. 3.
24. Ibid., pp. 4–6.
25. Ibid., p. 11.
26. Ibid., p. 16.
27. Ibid., p. 23.
28. Ibid., pp. 31–3.
29. Ibid., pp. 44–6.
30. Ibid., pp. 52–4.
31. Statements of Hoffmann and Weisspfennig, TNA WO 235/5.
32. Cameron, John, *Trial of Heinz Eck et al (The Peleus Trial)* (1949) William Hodge and Company Limited, pp. 85–6.
33. Ibid., pp. 89–90.

34. Judge Advocate's summing up speech, TNA WO 235/5.
35. As noted by Hugh Scott-Barrett, DJAG 21st Army Group, North-West Europe, TNA WO 235/5.
36. Release notes for Lenz and Schwender, TNA WO 235/604.
37. https://phdn.org/archives/holocaust-history.org/auschwitz/zyklonb/ (Retrieved 28 Sept 2023).
38. https://history.evonik.com/en/ns-era/degussa-ns (Retrieved 28 Sept 2023).
39. The Cyanide Code – International Cyanide Management Institute – archived from the original https://web.archive.org/web/20121130094124/http://www.cyanidecode.org/cyanide_environmental.php (Retrieved 28 Sept 2023).
40. https://www.auschwitz.org/en/history/auschwitz-and-shoah/gas-chambers/ (Retrieved 8 Oct 2023).
41. Summary of sales of Zyklon B, TNA WO 309/1602.
42. Copy of second letter from Emil Sehm, TNA WO 309/1602.
43. The court composition for the Zyklon B trial was:
    President – Brigadier R B L Persse
    Members – Lieutenant-Colonel Sir Geoffrey Palmer (Coldstream Guards) and Major S M Johnstone (Royal Tank Regiment)
    Judge Advocate – C L Stirling (Barrister)
    Prosecutor – Major G I A D Draper (Irish Guards, Judge Advocate General's Branch, HQ. BAOR)
    Defence Counsel for Tesch – Dr O Zippel
    Defence Counsel for Weinbacher – Dr C Stumme
    Defence Counsel for Drosihn – Dr A Stegemann
    TNA WO 235/83.
44. United Nations War Crimes Commission, *Law Reports of Trials of War Criminals* (1947), Volume I, HMSO, p. 95.
45. Article 46 of the Hague Regulations of 1907 reads, 'Family honour and rights, the lives of persons, and private property, as well as religious convictions and practice, must be respected. Private property cannot be confiscated.' https://avalon.law.yale.edu/20th_century/hague04.asp#art46 (Retrieved 29 Sept 2023).
46. Testimony of Wilhelm Bahr, TNA WO 235/83.
47. Testimony of Emil Sehm, TNA WO 235/83.
48. Testimony of Kate and Wilhelm Pook, TNA WO 235/83.
49. Testimony of Erna Eliza Biagini and Anna Ünzelmann, TNA WO 235/83.

50. Testa control books pages for supply of Zyklon B to Auschwitz, TNA WO 309/1602.
51. Judge Advocate's summary, TNA WO 235/83.

Chapter 2: Trials for Murdering Captured British Soldiers

1. https://avalon.law.yale.edu/19th_century/hague02.asp#art1 (Retrieved 27/08/22).
2. The numbers from each regiment are still unclear. There were probably sixty-two from the 1st Battalion Royal Norfolks together with men from the 1st Battalion Royal Scots, 2nd Battalion Manchester Regiment and 6th Battalion Argyll and Sutherland Highlanders.
3. Sharpe, W J, *Massacre and Murder in Le Paradis* (2015) FeedARead.com Publishing.
4. The London District Cage in Kensington was one of several British military intelligence facilities where German POWs (particularly members of the SS and NSDAP) were interrogated.
5. The court composition for the Le Paradis trial was:
   President – Lieutenant Colonel E C Van Der Kiste (Essex Regiment)
   Members – Major P Witty (Hamburg Garrison Unit), Major C Champion (Royal Pioneer Corps), Captain J E Tracey (Royal Army Ordnance Corp), Captain A Preston (Royal Tank Regiment)
   Judge Advocate – F Honig (Barrister)
   Prosecutor – T G Field-Fisher (Barrister)
   Defence Counsel – Dr G Uhde (German Barrister)
   TNA WO 311/927.
6. Knöchlein proceedings, TNA WO 311/927 p. 12.
7. Ibid., p. E10.
8. Ibid., p. 18.
9. Ibid., p. 21.
10. Ibid., p. A3.
11. Signatories to the Hague Convention of 1899, which included the UK and Germany, agreed not to use 'bullets which expand or flatten easily in the human body' (commonly called dum-dum bullets) in any war between them.

12. Knöchlein proceedings, TNA WO 311/927 p. A17.
13. Ibid., p. J3.
14. Ibid., pp. B6 & B7.
15. Report of Captain the Hon. R A D Woodhouse, Royal Norfolk Regiment observer at the Knöchlein trial p. 4 http://www.leparadismassacre.com/trial-description.html (Retrieved 22 Sept 2022).
16. Knöchlein proceedings TNA WO 311/927 p. B25.
17. Ibid., p. D15.
18. Ibid., p. D13.
19. Sharpe, W J, *Massacre and Murder in Le Paradis* (2015) FeedARead.com Publishing.
20. TNA WO 235/572A Exhibit 19. This degree of removal from the original would normally be challenged in court. That it was not might demonstrate acceptance of the difficulties involved in cooperation between the Allied judiciary rather than unreliability of the evidence.
21. TNA WO 235/572A Exhibit 19.
22. Knöchlein proceedings TNA WO 311/927 pp. E18–E19.
23. TNA WO 235/571.
24. Donnell, Clayton, *Eben-Emael and the Defence of Fortress Belgium, 1940* (2021) Pen & Sword Military.
25. *Trial of the Major War Criminals Before the International Military Tribunal, Nuremberg, 14 November 1945 – 1 October 1946* (1947) Volume 15, p. 328.
26. Operation MUSKETOON was a combined British-Norwegian commando raid. Ten men from British Army No. 2 Commando and two men from the Norwegian Armed Forces in exile (part of the SOE) attacked and damaged the Glomfjord hydroelectric power plant. The plant supplied electricity to an aluminium factory vital to the German production of aircraft. Although the operation was a success as the plant was destroyed, seven captured British commandos were subsequently murdered in Sachsenhausen concentration camp. The second charge against Colonel General Paul Nikolaus von Falkenhorst in his Braunschweig trial accused him of being responsible for forces under his command handing over to the SD two British officers and six British other ranks, all POWs who had taken part in commando operations, with the result that the prisoners were

killed. The men referred to in charge two were all from No.2 Commando: Captain Graeme Delamere Black DSO, MC, Captain Joseph Blundell J. Houghton MC, Company Sergeant Major Miller Smith, Lance Sergeant William Henry Albert Chudley, Rifleman Cyril Henry Abram, Private Eric Gordon Curtis and Private Reginald Henry Makeham. The court may not have known at the time that Corporal Erling Djupdraet had died of his wounds. Falkenhorst was found not guilty of this charge.

27. Operation GROUSE began on 18 October 1942, when an SOE advanced party of four commandos of the Norwegian Independent Company were parachuted into Norway. Warrant Officer Jens Anton Poulsson, Warrant Officer Knut Haugland, Sergeant Arne Kjellstrup and Sergeant Clause Helberg had an exhausting trek through the snow to reach the proposed landing zone between the east arm of the Mosvatn Lake and the Rauland Road. When they reached the Vemork area, they transmitted reports on the weather conditions and German defences.
28. The full story of Operation GROUSE is well covered in Mears, R, *The Real Heroes of Telemark* (2003) Hodder & Stoughton.
29. TNA AIR 39/45.
30. Ibid.
31. Ibid.
32. https://www.qsl.net/pe1ngz/airforce/airforce-raf/raf-eureka-rebecca.html (Retrieved 8 Nov 2022).
33. The full story can be found in Wiggan, R, *Operation Freshman* (1986) William Kimber & Co. London.
34. http://aircrewremembered.com/operation-freshman.html(Retrieved 29 Aug 2022).
35. Probst died as a result of parotid gland cancer on 14 May 1946 in No.6 Civilian Internment Centre at the former Neuengamme concentration camp.
36. The court composition for the Behren trial was:
President – Major-General N A Coxwell-Rogers (Royal Engineers)
Members – Colonel L C C Harrison, Lieutenant-Colonel J C de F Sleeman (Royal Tank Regiment), Major M A Gibbs (Coldstream Guards), Captain P D Agnew (Irish Guards)
Judge Advocate – Wing-Commander O C Barnett (Barrister)
Prosecutor – Captain R G Dromgoole (Judge Advocate General's branch – War Crimes Section)

Defence Counsel – Dr R G Muller (German Barrister)
TNA WO 235/119.

37. A *lensmann* is a Scandinavian term for the leader of a rural police district.
38. Sworn statement of Hovland. The initials were RE for Royal Engineers. This was strong evidence that the soldiers were in uniform. Hovland repeated this statement when giving evidence for the prosecution, TNA WO 235/119.
39. Benestad statement, TNA WO 235/119.
40. Varden testimony, TNA WO 235/119.
41. Dromgoole's cross-examination of Behren, TNA WO 235/119.
42. Wiggan, R, *Operation Freshman* (1986) William Kimber & Co. London, pp. 145–6.
43. Ibid., p. 151.
44. Fylgjesdal statement, TNA WO 309/2056.
45. Dr Bjonness statement, TNA WO 309/2056.
46. More information about the men is at http://ww2talk.com/index.php?threads/operation-freshman.19590/ (Retrieved 29 Aug 2022).
47. The court composition for the Seeling *et al* trial was:
    President – Major-General C H Miller
    Members – Lieutenant-Colonel J M Ripley (Royal Artillery), Lieutenant-Colonel H J Wright (Royal Army Service Corps), Major R J Palmer, Major H J Jennings
    Judge Advocate – Major Edward Steel (Pioneer Corps, Barrister)
    Prosecutor – Major A Burnett (Royal Artillery)
    Defence Counsel for Seeling – Captain L Irving (Royal Artillery, Law Student)
    Defence Counsel for Hoffmann & Feuerlein – Captain F R Miller (Royal Artillery – Solicitor)
    TNA WO 235/29.
48. Proceedings, Seeling *et al*, TNA WO 235/29.
49. Pierrepoint flew several times to Germany between December 1945 and December 1949 to hang convicted war criminals and others found guilty of a capital crimes in the British Occupied Zone. See https://www.capitalpunishmentuk.org/hameln.htm (Retrieved 07 Jan 2024).
50. Letter from Brig. H Shapcott, TNA WO 235/216A.
51. The court composition for the first Trandum trial was:
    President – Brigadier E Fitz H Lynch

Members – Lieutenant Colonel J E L Corbyn (5 Duke of Cornwall's Light Infantry), Major F E Woolnough (7 Somerset Light Infantry), T/Major E C Gray (2 Seaforths), Captain P Wellesly-Colley (2 Irish Guards)
Judge Advocate – Sir Shirley Worthington-Evans (Barrister)
Prosecutor – Captain R G Dromgoole (BAOR Judge Advocate General's Office)
Defence Counsel – Dr Walter Grimm
TNA WO 235/216A.

52. The thirteen accused in the first Trandum trial were: Siegfried Bahlinger, Otto Baldauf, Hermann Bölck, Friedrich Wilhelm Engel, Werner Möller, Erich Penning, Herbert Peuker, Karl Rönnefeldt, Josef Schneider, Ludwig Bieber, Alexander Etling, Peter Göttling & Willi Korneffel.
53. The sworn statements of the accused and Oscar Hans make up Exhibits 8 to 43 of the trial proceedings, TNA WO 235/216A.
54. The Trandumskogen War Memorial records the number of people killed.
55. Wiggan, R, *Operation Freshman* (1986) William Kimber & Co. London, pp. 99–106.
56. Hans statement, TNA WO 235/216A.
57. Affidavit of Lindboe Nordtomme (Oslo Police) on exhumation of bodies, TNA WO 309/2056. The bodies were recovered in August 1945 and buried with full military honours at Vestre Gravlund in Oslo.
58. Schnieder statement (Exhibit 18), TNA WO 235/216A.
59. Statements of Bahlinger (Exhibit 20), Baldauf (Exhibit 21), Engel (Exhibit 33), Möller (Exhibit 13), Peuker (Exhibits 15 & 31) and Rönnefeldt (Exhibit 24), TNA WO 235/216A.
60. Dr Grimm, TNA WO 235/216A.
61. Esser statement, TNA WO 235/216A.
62. The six others sentenced to 14 years' imprisonment were Siegfried Bahlinger, Otto Baldauf, Friedrich Wilhelm Engel, Werner Möller, Herbert Peuker & Karl Rönnefeldt.
63. TNA WO 309/678.
64. Report of Norwegian trials of Oscar Hans, TNA WO 235/539.
65. The court composition for the second Trandum trial was: President – Lieutenant Colonel J A Glendinning (Royal Artillery)

Members – Major G Frampton (1st Manchester Regiment), Captain J A Randall (Royal Signals Regiment), Captain J B Vasey (1st York and Lancaster Regiment), Captain B S Walker (No.1Wireless Regiment Royal Signals)
Judge Advocate – A A H Marlowe MP (Barrister)
Prosecutor – S O Olson (Barrister)
Defence Counsel – Dr Werner Schoen
TNA WO 309/215 & WO 309/678.

66. Hovland statement, TNA WO 309/215.
67. Prosecution opening statement, TNA WO 235/539.
68. Hans trial evidence, TNA WO 235/539.
69. Compare this with the search terms 'Belsen' (204 files), 'Ravensbrück' (156 files) and 'Neuengamme' (96 files). Figures correct on 16 February 2024.
70. https://hansard.parliament.uk/Commons/1944-05-19/debates/db46d142-0fe7-4a61-81c9-b6acc840edd8/CommonsChamber (Retrieved 04 Sept 2022).
71. https://api.parliament.uk/historic-hansard/commons/1944/jun/23/officer-prisoners-of-war-germany-shooting (Retrieved 04 Sept 2022).
72. Andrews, Allen, *Exemplary Justice* (1978) Corgi, pp. 273–4.
73. For the story of the hunt for the killers, their arrests and interrogations, see Read, Simon, *Human Game* (2012) Constable & Robinson Ltd.
74. The court composition for the first Stalag Luft III trial was:
    President – Major General H L Longden
    Members – Air Commodore F H Ware (RAF), Colonel R H Gordon (Royal Engineers), Lieutenant Colonel E C Van Der Kiste (Essex Regiment), Lieutenant Colonel E J Inkson (South Staffordshire Regiment), Wing Commander G S Taylor (RAF), Wing Commander C M C Woodroffe (RAF)
    Judge Advocate – C L Stirling (Barrister)
    Prosecutor – Colonel R C Halse (Judge Advocate General's Office)
    TNA WO 235/424.
75. (1) Committing a war crime in that they at diverse places in Germany and German-occupied territory, between 25 March, 1944, and 13th April, 1944, were concerned together and with SS Gruppenführer Müller and SS Gruppenführer Nebe and

other persons known and unknown, in the killing in violation of the laws and usages of war of prisoners of war who had escaped from Stalag Luft III.

(2) Committing a war crime in that they at diverse places in Germany and German-occupied territory, between 25 March, 1944, and 13th April, 1944, aided and abetted SS Gruppenführer Müller and SS Gruppenführer Nebe and each other and other persons known and unknown, in carrying out orders which were contrary to the laws and usages of war, namely, orders to kill prisoners of war who had escaped from Stalag Luft III.

The court charged Max Wielen with these two counts only.

76. (3) The court accused Emil Schulz and Walter Breithaupt of killing Squadron Leader R J Bushell and Pilot Officer B W M Scheidhauer, both of the Royal Air Force.

(4) The court accused Alfred Schimmel of killing Flight Lieutenant A R H Hayter (Royal Air Force).

(5) The court accused Josef Albert Andreas Gmeiner, Walter Herberg, Otto Preiss and Heinrich Boschert of killing Flying Officer D H Cochran (Royal Air Force).

(6) The court accused Emil Weil, Eduard Geith and Johann Schneider of killing Lieutenant H J Stevens and Lieutenant J S Gouws, both of the South African Air Force.

(7) The court accused Johannes Post, Hans Kahler and Artur Denkmann of killing Squadron Leader J Catanach (Royal Australian Air Force), Pilot Officer H Espelid (Royal Air Force), Flight Lieutenant A G Christensen (Royal New Zealand Air Force) and Pilot Officer N Fuglesang (Royal New Zealand Air Force).

(8) The court accused Oskar Schmidt, Walter Jacobs and Wilhelm Struve of killing Pilot Officer H Espelid (Royal Air Force), Flight Lieutenant A G Christensen (Royal New Zealand Air Force) and Pilot Officer N Fuglesang (Royal New Zealand Air Force).

(9) The court accused Erich Hermann August Zacharias of killing Flying Officer G A Kidder (Royal Canadian Air Force) and Squadron Leader T G Kirby-Green (Royal Air Force).

77. Charge sheet of Max Wielen and seventeen others, TNA 235/424.

78. The British had requested the extradition of Scharpwinkel from the Soviet Union, but the Soviets wanted to try him for killing their

POWs. They allowed him to be interviewed in Moscow on 31 August 1946 and 19 September 1946, TNA AIR 40/2269.

79. *Law Reports of Trials of War Criminals, The United Nations War Crimes Commission* (1949), Volume 11, HMSO London, p. 36.
80. https://media.nationalarchives.gov.uk/index.php/the-great-escape-youve-seen-the-film-now-hear-the-truth/ (Retrieved 04 Sept 2022).
81. *Law Reports of Trials of War Criminals, The United Nations War Crimes Commission* (1949) Volume 11, HMSO London, p. 39.
82. Ibid.
83. Ibid., p. 45.
84. For full details of which Germans were charged for shooting which airmen, see *Law Reports of Trials of War Criminals, The United Nations War Crimes Commission* (1949) Volume 11, HMSO London, pp. 32–3.
85. Franz Schmidt never made it to a war crimes trial. During interrogation, at Neuengamme, he confessed to shooting the airmen and later committed suicide. Read, Simon, *Human Game* (2012) Constable & Robinson Ltd, p. 269.
86. Oskar Schmidt statement (Exhibit 35), TNA WO 235/424.
87. Oskar Schmidt testimony, TNA WO 235/427.
88. Jacobs statement (Exhibit 36), TNA WO 235/424.
89. Jacobs testimony, TNA WO 235/428.
90. Post testimony, 5 Aug 1947, TNA WO 235/427.
91. Post testimony, 6 Aug 1947, TNA WO 235/427.
92. *Law Reports of Trials of War Criminals, The United Nations War Crimes Commission* (1949), Volume 11, HMSO London, p. 47.
93. Ibid., p. 51.
94. *Law Reports of Trials of War Criminals, The United Nations War Crimes Commission* (1949), Volume 1, HMSO London p. 103. Also in the Hadamar Trial of October 1945, the court had held that, 'the laws and customs of war are addressed not only to combatants but also to civilians, and that civilians, by committing illegal acts against nationals of the opponent, may become guilty of war crimes.' Ibid., p. 54.
95. *Law Reports of Trials of War Criminals, The United Nations War Crimes Commission* (1949), Volume 11, HMSO London pp. 40–5.
96. Ibid., p. 46.
97. For full details of sentences, see *Law Reports of Trials of War Criminals, The United Nations War Crimes Commission* (1949)

Volume 11, HMSO London pp. 44–6. Note this source wrongly states that the court sentenced Walter Breithaupt to death. He received a sentence of life imprisonment.

98. The court composition for the second Stalag Luft III trial was:
President – Lieutenant Colonel B G Melsom (East Lancashire Regiment)
Members – Major C L A Hall (208 CRASC), Captain A B Houston (Royal Dragoons), Captain F G Robson (Royal Horse Artillery), Captain J W Smith (SRF)
Judge Advocate – A A H Marlowe (Barrister)
Prosecutor – Lieutenant Colonel G Barratt
Defence – Dr Hübbe, Frau Dr Kruger-Nieland and Dr Weber
TNA WO 235/573.
99. The list of the airmen killed is at http://aircrewremembered.com/stalag-luft-sagan-and-belaria-the-fifty.html (Retrieved 26 Oct 2022).
100. 14 January 1949 letter from Lord Russell of Liverpool to GOC-in-C BAOR, TNA WO 235/798.
101. 30 December 1948 letter from Lord Russell of Liverpool to GOC-in-C BAOR, TNA WO 235/798.

Chapter 3: Trials for Murdering and Mistreating Forced Labourers

1. Harvey, Elizabeth, 'Last Resort or Key Resource? Women Workers from The Nazi-Occupied Soviet Territories, The Reich Labour Administration and The German War Effort' (2016) *Transactions of the RHS* 26, p. 150.
2. Fried, John H E, *The Exploitation of Foreign Labour by Germany* (1945) International Labour Office, Montreal.
3. The lives of several women who passed through the Neugraben and Tiefstack camps are commemorated by stumbling blocks (*stolpersteine*) in Neugraben-Fischbek, including Ruth Frischmannová, Zuzana Glaserová, Nina Müller and Elisabeth Polach (née Adler) https://www.stolpersteine-hamburg.de/en.php (Retrieved 5 Sept 2023).
4. 'Über das Außenlager des KZ Neuengamme in Tiefstack' (2021) *Italienische Militärinternierte von 1943 bis 1945 in Hamburg* https://imiinhamburg.wordpress.com/2021/08/02/uber-das-

ausenlager-des-kz-neuengamme-in-Tiefstack/ (Retrieved 15 Jul 2023).

5. In April 1945, Landsberger was transported to Bergen-Belsen concentration camp, which was liberated by British troops on April 15, 1945. Sick with tuberculosis, she took almost two years to recover in a sanatorium. She then emigrated to the USA and married, becoming Anita Lobel.
6. Donat deposition, TNA WO 235/121.
7. Letters between Czechoslovak War Crimes Mission and the JAG, TNA WO 309/407.
8. The court composition for the Neugraben Tiefstack trial was:
President – Major T A Wigglesworth (102nd Northumberland Hussars, Anti-Tank Regiment, Royal Artillery)
Members – Major D C Stewart-Smith (Barrister & DJAG) and Lieutenant W C Brokfield (sometimes written Brookfield – 8th King's Royal Irish Hussars)
Judge Advocate – None appointed as Stewart-Smith was legally qualified
Prosecutor – Captain C G Butcher
Defence for Kliem – Dr H E Mevert (there is confusion in the record and Kliem's defence counsel may have been Dr G Robert)
Defence for Josef Müller – Dr Walter Huxdorff
Defence for Erich Hugo Schulz – Dr Papendiek
Defence for Christian Koopmann – Dr F Stemmann
Defence for Albert Runkel – Dr Kleffel
Defence for Anita Frank – Dr K H Konig
Defence for Julius Zederkopf – Dr R Schulz
Defence for Christol Dibbern – Dr E Schoendienst
Defence for Herta Sürth – Dr A Phillipp
Defence for Georg Heidtmann – Dr Adolf F Gerken
Defence for Gertrud Schulz – Dr H Lappenberg
Defence for Maria Szaroletta – Dr H Fritze
Defence for Erhardt Hauenstein – Dr H Gabein
Defence for Gustav Rosoli – Dr H Soll
Defence for Eva Maria Borowski – Dr H H Meyer
TNA WO 235/149.
9. TNA WO 235/122.
10. Details of the trial of Maria Szaroletta, TNA WO 235/121. Four other guards were also acquitted: Erhardt Hauenstein and Eva

Maria Borowski (TNA WO 235/108), Gertrud Schulz and Gustav Rosoli (TNA WO 235/109).

11. TNA WO 235/143A.
12. Donat deposition, TNA WO 235/121 and Seeliger deposition (foreman at Diago-Werke Müller & Co), TNA WO 309/407.
13. TNA WO 235/122.
14. Donat deposition, TNA WO 235/121.
15. TNA WO 235/117.
16. Neumann testimony, TNA WO 235/149.
17. Prof. Dr Hopf (Head Doctor of the University Skin Clinic in Hamburg-Eppendorf) deposition, TNA WO 309/407.
18. Fuchs testimony, TNA WO 235/149.
19. Dr Klewansky deposition, TNA WO 309/407.
20. Neumann testimony, TNA WO 235/149.
21. A kapo was a prisoner assigned by camp guards to supervise groups of other prisoners either in accommodation blocks or during forced labour. Kapos often received more food and were sometimes spared the worst abuses in a camp. To maintain their privileged position, they often treated fellow prisoners more brutally than did the guards.
22. Exhibit C was the names of 226 prisoners who died at Alter Banter Weg and who were buried in Friedhof in Aldenburg, Wilhelmshaven, TNA WO 235/298.
23. The court composition for the first Alter Banter Weg trial was:
    President – Lieutenant Colonel G J James (Royal Artillery)
    Members – Major R A Archer-Shee (10th Hussars), Captain J H Harding (7th Hussars), Captain D J Browne (2nd Royal Tank Regiment), Captain W H Simister (Royal Army Ordnance Corps)
    Judge Advocate – R A Romain (Barrister)
    Prosecutor – Captain H W E Cleaver (Royal Artillery, Office of JAG)
    Defence for Drossen & Günther – Dr Peelig
    Defence for Hoffmann & Horstmann – Dr Breymeier
    Defence for Jepsen – Dr Schön
    Defence for Sürig & Thümmel – Dr Schlüter
    TNA WO 235/296.
24. The first Alter Banter Weg trial (4 February 1947 to 6 March 1947) indicted Rudolf Franz Georg Günther, Ernst Hoffmann, Gustav Alfred Jepsen, Heinrich Wilhelm Sürig, Otto Thümmel, Gottfried

Drossen, Hans Horstmann, Ernst Johann Franz Pingel and Georg Karl August Radatz.

25. 12 October 1947 report by Captain Russell Jones, TNA WO 309/879.
26. Jepsen was tried in Lüneburg together with Joachim Freitag and Otto Muller, TNA 235/229.
27. Jepsen's behaviour is described in depositions in TNA WO 235/298.
28. 2 April 1947 report to GOC-in-C from Lord Russell of Liverpool, TNA WO 235/300.
29. Payen deposition, TNA WO 235/298.
30. The court composition for the Georg Radatz trial (second Alter Banter Weg trial) was:
    President – Lieutenant Colonel S C Auld (Royal Artillery)
    Members – Major J N Goodwyn (Welsh Regiment), Captain P E du Vivier (Royal Engineers), Captain D A Livingstone (Royal Scots Fusiliers), Captain A Clarke (Essex Regiment)
    Judge Advocate – Not appointed
    Prosecutor – Captain W H Nicholson (HQ BAOR)
    Defence – Dr Meyer-Labastille
    TNA WO 235/517.
31. Jenvresse testimony, TNA WO 235/517.
32. Gybels testimony, TNA WO 235/517.
33. Schmidt deposition (Exhibit 13), TNA WO 235/492.
34. Schwarz deposition (Exhibit 8), TNA WO 235/492.
35. Kruse deposition (Exhibit 7), TNA WO 235/492.
36. 4 December 1947 letter from Lieutenant Colonel G I A D Draper to Judge Advocate General's Office, TNA 311/505.
37. The court composition for the Steinbergen Quary trial was:
    President – Lieutenant Colonel B G Melsom (East Lancashire Regiment)
    Members – Major R J N Bartlett (7th Parachute Battalion), Captain B J Rimmer (15th Medium Regiment, Royal Artillery), Captain A J Duncan (1st Battalion Worcestershire Regiment), Captain D M McLeod (1st Battalion Gordon Highlanders)
    Judge Advocate – F Honig (Barrister)
    Prosecutor – A Vollmar (Barrister)
    Defence for Schmidt – Dr Meyer-Labastille
    Defence for Rinne – Dr Krueger-Nieland
    Defence for Koch – Dr H Burchard-Motz
    TNA WO 235/491.

38. Möller deposition, TNA WO 311/505.
39. Schmidt deposition (Exhibit 11), TNA WO 235/492.
40. Opening address of Dr Mayer-Labastille for Schmidt (Exhibit 14), TNA 235/492.
41. Closing addresses of Dr Krueger-Nieland for Rinne (Exhibit 34) and Dr Burchard-Motz for Koch (Exhibit 35), TNA WO 235/493.
42. Outline of prosecution closing address (Exhibit 36), TNA WO 235/493.
43. TNA WO 235/495 and FO 371/109726.
44. Ref: https://www.yadvashem.org/docs/nuremberg-law-for-protection-of-german-blood-1935.html (Retrieved 14 June 2022).
45. Szobar, Patricia, 'Telling Sexual Stories in the Nazi Courts of Law: Race Defilement in Germany, 1933 to 1945', *Journal of the History of Sexuality*, Volume 11, Number 1 and 2, January/April 2002, pp. 131–63.
46. Herbert, Ulrich, *Hitler's Foreign Workers* (1997) Cambridge University Press, pp. 73–4.
47. Report of No.2 WCIT 2WCIT/C/13 – TNA WO 235/230.
48. Summary of examination of Hildegard Lütten by Captain P R Nixon 2WCIT, TNA WO 309/128.
49. Lord Russell of Liverpool, *The Scourge of The Swastika* (1954) Cassell & Co. Ltd, p. 142.
50. Testimony of Jan Kardacz, TNA WO 235/232.
51. Summary of examination of Hildegard Lütten by Captain P R Nixon 2WCIT, TNA WO 309/128.
52. Hamburg Stumbling Stones archive https://www.stolpersteine-hamburg.de/en.php?&MAIN_ID=7&BIO_ID=5210 (Retrieved 14 Jun 2022).
53. Originally, seventeen people had been accused. In addition to the eleven discussed the British considered trying Hamburg SS Lieutenant Colonel Seetzen, his deputy SS Major Kuhl and SS Sergeant Major Josef Weiss, Kaufmann, Eggers and Tesenfitz – Cover of file WO 309/128 – TNA WO 309/128.
54. Letter to DJAG BAOR 18 April 1946, TNA WO 309/128.
55. The court composition for the first Poppenbüttel trial was:
    President – Major J A Glendinning (Royal Artillery)
    Members – Captain K M Hore (Welsh Regiment) and Captain Z Zienkiewicz (Polish Forces)
    Judge Advocate – None appointed

Prosecutor – Captain Dromgoole
TNA WO 235/232.

56. Lütten Eyewitness for prosecution notes, TNA WO 309/128.
57. Carsten statement to Captain James Warburton 2WCIT 2 October 1945, TNA WO 235/230.
58. Sworn statements of Janiak and Zawidzki to Captain Peter Roycroft Nixon 2WCIT 3 October 1945, TNA WO 235/230, and prosecution statement of Kardacz in Poppenbüttel Case 1, TNA WO 235/232.
59. Interrogation of Grimm in Neumünster 5 October 1945, TNA WO 235/230.
60. Interrogation of Mumm in Altona 6 October 1945, TNA WO 235/230.
61. Poppenbüttel Case 1 Court Proceedings, TNA WO 235/230.
62. https://www.capitalpunishmentuk.org/hameln.htm (Retrieved 15 June 2022).
63. Message from EXFOR to HQ8 Corps District, TNA WO 309/128.
64. TNA WO 309/128.
65. Deposition of Albert Adolf Schweim, TNA WO 235/232.
66. The security police (*Sicherheitspolizei* or SiPo) were made up of the criminal police (Kripo) and the secret state police (*Geheime Staatspolizei* or Gestapo). The security service (*Sicherheitsdienst* or SD) was the intelligence agency of the 'protective echelon' political soldiers (*Schutzstaffel* or SS) and the NSDAP. Some ranks and equivalents can be found here https://en.wikipedia.org/wiki/Kriminalpolizei_(Nazi_Germany) (Retrieved 18 June 2022).
67. The court composition for the second Poppenbüttel trial was:
President – Lieutenant Colonel J A Glendinning (Royal Artillery)
Members – Captain H W G Pawson (Somerset Light Infantry) and Lieutenant J A Turner (Suffolk Regiment)
Judge Advocate – None appointed
Prosecutor – Captain Dromgoole (DJAG)
Defence for Thiele – Dr Johannes Balfanz
Defence for Hinze – Dr Guido Adler
Defence for Rehmke – Dr Heinz Sander
TNA WO 235/230.
Glendinning presided over thirty-eight British military trials. Hassel, Katrin, *Kriegsverbrechen vor Gericht* (2008) Nomos, p. 167.
68. File record of Thiele statement to Forbes, TNA WO 235/230.
69. Dr Belfanz petition 7 August 1946, TNA WO 235/230.

70. Dr Sander petition 7 August 1946, TNA WO 235/230.
71. Cancelled death warrant and note from Lord Russell of Liverpool – TNA WO 235/230.

Chapter 4: Trials for The Deaths of Children

1. Person, Katarzyn and Steinert, Johannes-Dieter, *Przemysłowa Concentration Camp: The Camp, the Children, the Trials* (2022) Palgrave Macmillan.
2. Kestin, Robert W, 'They Cry No More: A Case Of War Crimes Against Newborns' (1992) *The Polish Review*, Vol. XXXVII, No. 3, p. 315.
3. *Schwangerschaft von Ostarbeiterinnen* https://perspectives.ushmm.org/item/memo-on-pregnancies-among-forced-laborers (Retrieved 23 Jun 2022).
4. Kestin, Robert W, 'They Cry No More: A Case Of War Crimes Against Newborns' (1992) *The Polish Review*, Vol. XXXVII, No. 3, p. 315.
5. German NDR TV programme *Panorama* report by Andrea Röpke and Volker Steinhoff 'Death Camps for babies – US lawyers accuse VW of genocide' first broadcast 6 May 1999 https://daserste.ndr.de/panorama/archiv/1999/Todeslager-fuer-Babys-US-Anwaelte-beschuldigen-VW-des-Voelkermordes,erste7242.html (Retrieved 6 Jan 2023).
6. Bently presided over sixty-one British military trials – the most of any officer. Hassel, Katrin, *Kriegsverbrechen vor Gericht* (2008) Nomos, p. 167.
7. Walter Heinrich Wilhelm Schulz, the Lefitz Bürgermeister, was arrested himself on 11 November 1947 and held in No.2 CIC at Fischbeck. 1WCIT could not find enough evidence to charge him on the same terms as Machel and Grönitz, so he was released on 25 November 1947 and used by Grieve as a prosecution witness instead.
8. Koopman testimony, WO TNA 235/447.
9. The court composition for the Lefitz Children's Hostel trial was: President – Lieutenant Colonel H R Bently OBE (Cheshire Regiment) Members – Major A L C Marriot (RAMC), Captain The Viscount Savernare (Royal Horse Guards), Captain F O Lestrange (10th Royal Hussars), Captain D E R Kelsey (RAMC)

Judge Advocate – J H L Aubrey-Fletcher (Barrister)
Prosecutor – W P Grieve (Barrister)
Defence for Machel – Dr Eissner
Defence for Grönitz – Dr Meissner
TNA WO 235/447.

10. Proceedings, TNA WO 235/447 pp. 2.
11. Emma Schulz testimony, TNA WO 235/447.
12. Pietrowska testimony, TNA WO 235/447.
13. Wiazdzyk testimony, TNA WO 235/447.
14. The children's death certificates were Exhibit C, TNA WO 235/447.
15. Gibbons, H L & Hebdon, C K, 'Teething as a Cause of Death: A Historical Review', *The Western Journal of Medicine* (December 1991) 155, 6, pp. 658–9.
16. Kleim (née Zündt) deposition, TNA WO 311/507.
17. Zimmermann testimony, TNA WO 235/447.
18. Judge Advocate summation, TNA WO 235/447.
19. DJAG report from R C Halse to Hamburg District Commander, TNA WO 235/447.
20. The lower figure comes from Helm, Sarah, *If This Is a Woman* (2015) Abacus, p. xii. The higher figure can be found in Saidel, Rochelle G, *The Jewish Women of Ravensbrück Concentration Camp* (2006) Terrace Books, p. 3.
21. The 'Hohenlychen group' included doctors Karl Gebhardt, Fritz Fischer, Karl Brunner, Herta Oberheuser, Percival Treite, Rolf Rosenthal, Karl Brandt and Nurse Hingst.
22. Dr Nedvedova-Nedjedla deposition, TNA WO 235/318.
23. Salvesen deposition, TNA WO 235/318.
24. Seidemann deposition, TNA WO 235/318.
25. Karl Brandt, Karl Gebhardt, Herta Oberhauser and Fritz Fischer were handed over to the Americans.
26. The court composition for the first Ravensbrück trial was:
President – Major-General V J E Westropp CBE (General Staff)
Members – Colonel Henri de Bonnechose (Juge du Tribunal de la Seine), Lieutenant-Colonel J A Glendinning (Royal Artillery), Major Kasimierz Olszewski (Polish Forces), Major D S Bowling-Smith MC (Royal Tank Regiment), Captain E H Buckland (The Duke of Wellington's Regiment), Captain W H Scott (Royal Army Service Corps)

Judge Advocate – C L Stirling CBE KC (Deputy Judge Advocate General of the Forces)
Prosecutors – Major S M Stewart (JAG's Branch HQ BAOR), Captain J W da Cunha (23rd Hussars), Madame Aline Chalufour (Docteur en Droit)
There were eleven defence counsellors representing the sixteen accused in court and four who were absent, TNA WO 235/305.

27. Helm, Sarah, *If This Is a Woman* (2015) Abacus, p. 704.
28. Dr Nedvedova-Nedjedla testimony, TNA WO 235/305.
29. Siedemann testimony, TNA WO 235/306.
30. Benedict, Susan, 'The Nadir of Nursing: Nurse-Perpetrators of the Ravensbrück Concentration Camp', *Nursing History Review* (2003), Volume 11, p. 197.
31. Post-mortem report of Treite, TNA WO 309/689.
32. https://encyclopedia.ushmm.org/content/en/article/josef-mengele (Retrieved 7 Mar 2023).
33. Experiments by Bayer AG beginning in 1932 showed that the sulphonamide Prontocil was effective against a range of bacterial infections inside the body, particularly streptococci https://www.chemeurope.com/en/encyclopedia/Prontosil.html (Retrieved 17 Oct 2022).
34. Silver, J R, 'Karl Gebhardt (1897–1948): A lost man' (2011) *Journal of the Royal College of Physicians*, Edinburgh; 41, pp. 366–71.
35. Helm, S, *If This is A Woman* (2016) Abacus, pp. 233–5.
36. Kutschera-Aichbergen, H, 'Der Heilende Einfluss von Hauttuberkulosen auf die Tuberkulose der Lungen und des Kehlkopfes' (1943) *Klin Wochenschr* 22, pp. 566–8.
37. https://womenofeverycomplexionandcomplexity.weebly.com/gertrud-scholtz-klink-female-fuhrer-breathed-her-nazi-beliefs.html (Retrieved 17 Oct 2022).
38. Schwarberg, G, *The Murders at Bullenhuser Damm* (1980) Indiana University Press, pp. 18–19.
39. Heißmeyer, K, 'Grundsätzlichesüber Gegenwarts- und Zukunftsaufgaben der Lungenheilstätte' (1943) *Zeitschrift fur Tuberkulose*; 90, pp. 34–6.
40. TNA WO 235/167.
41. Kowalski deposition, Wiener Holocaust Library, Collection 2162 Neuengamme Trials: J C Giffin Papers, p. 22.
42. Czekala deposition, Ibid., p. 23.

43. Klein denied any knowledge of the source of the lymph nodes or any joint enterprise with Heißmeyer and was not tried for war crimes. He became an instructor of forensic medicine at the University of Heidelberg. See Schwarberg, G, *The Murders at Bullenhuser Damm* (1980) Indiana University Press, p. 169.
44. Williams, A T, *A Passing Fury* (2017) Vintage.
45. https://www.frankfallaarchive.org/prisons/neuengamme-concentration-camp/ (Retrieved 20 Jan 2023).
46. Schwarberg, G, *The Murders at Bullenhuser Damm* (1980) Indiana University Press, pp. 95–6.
47. Ibid., p. 97.
48. Ibid.
49. The court composition for the first Neuengamme trial was:
President – Brigadier R B L Persse
Members – Lieutenant Colonel J B M Stanton (King's Own Scottish Borderers), Major P L Curnock (Royal Artillery), Major J C Giffen (Royal Fusiliers)
Judge Advocate – C L Stirling (Barrister)
Prosecutors – S M Stewart & P S Wein (JAG Branch BAOR)
There were nine defence counsellors, TNA WO 235/189.
50. TNA WO 235/162.
51. TNA WO 235/163.
52. *SS-Obergruppenführer* Oswald Ludwig Pohl was head of the SS Main Economic and Administrative Office and the lead administrator of the Nazi concentration camps. He was tried in 1947, *The United States of America vs. Oswald Pohl, et al*, found guilty and hanged on 7 June 1951.
53. TNA WO 235/164.
54. Professor Prenant deposition, Wiener Holocaust Library, Collection 2162 Neuengamme Trials: J C Giffin Papers, p. 48.
55. TNA WO 235/162.
56. TNA WO 235/165.
57. Trzebinski testimony, TNA WO 235/165.
58. The cover of WO 309/396 lists FLIEGE, THOMSEN, LORENTZEN, ZIMMERMANN and FICKERS as well as the defendants that were tried. Strippel was also listed, but not tried as he was not in custody.
59. Die Gedenkstätte Bullenhuser Damm.
60. Eggebrecht deposition, TNA WO 309/388.

61. Hoevelborn deposition, TNA WO 309/388.
62. Frahm deposition, TNA WO 309/396.
63. Jauch deposition, TNA WO 235/189.
64. Lüdke deposition, TNA 309/396.
65. Brake deposition, TNA 309/396.
66. The court composition for the third Neuengamme trial was:
    President – Lieutenant Colonel J P Archer-Shee MC (10th Hussars)
    Members – Major R A Readman (Scots Guards) and Captain J Hardiment (Seaforths)
    Judge Advocate – Edward Steel (Barrister)
    Prosecutor – Captain H Cleaver
    Defence for Frahm – Dr Schöndienst
    Defence for Jauch – Dr Cappelle
    Defence for Brake – Dr Beermann
    TNA WO 235/681.
67. Petition for Frahm, TNA WO 235/189.
68. Petition for Jauch, TNA WO 235/189.
69. Cleaver report to Lieutenant Colonel J Leicester-Warren, TNA WO 309/396.
70. https://www.tracesofwar.com/articles/5383/Floating-concentration-camps-in-the-Bay-of-Lubeck (Retrieved 18/10/22).
71. Schattner, Thomas, *Strippels Blutspur durch Europas KZs – Sie begann vor 70 Jahren hier in Unshausen, im heutigen Schwalm-Eder-Kreis*, pp. 57–62. https://web.archive.org/web/20070109175135/http://www.gedenkstaette-breitenau.de/rundbrief/RB-24-57.pdf (Retrieved 20 Dec 2023).
72. Schwarberg, G, *The Murders at Bullenhuser Damm* (1980) Indiana University Press, p. 132. Schwarberg goes after Münzberg in Chapter 8, pp. 120–38.

Chapter 5: Trials for Murder in Work Education Camps

1. https://www.bundesarchiv.de/zwangsarbeit/haftstaetten/index.php?tab=20 (Retrieved 23 Dec 2022).
2. https://www.documentatiegroep40-45.nl/dwangarbeid_oud/camps.htm (Retrieved 23 Dec 2022).
3. Ryan testimony, TNA WO 235/441 and Bryan & Ryan deposition 8, TNA WO 309/37.

4. TNA WO 309/37.
5. The court composition for the AEL Bremen-Farge trial was:
   President – Lieutenant Colonel B G Melsom (East Lancashire Regiment)
   Members – Major C V Watson-Gandy (Black Watch), Captain J D P Milne (York and Lancaster Regiment), Captain G Sutherland (Royal Artillery), Captain N J Bath-Jones (Royal Artillery)
   Judge Advocate – Guy Sixsmith (Barrister)
   Prosecutor – P Wien (Barrister)
   Defence Counsel for Heidreder – Dr Henzel
   Defence Counsel for Hasse – Dr Schmidt
   Defence Counsel for Van der Veen – Dr Funke
   Defence Counsel for Sauer and Zehntner – Dr Möller
   Defence Counsel for Walhorn & Meyer – Dr Jonas
   Defence Counsel for Gärtner – Dr John
   Defence Counsel for Grauer-Carstensen – Dr Hartmann
   Defence Counsel for Velke – Dr Bruckmann
   Defence Counsel for Voss, Breckner & Plothe unknown
   TNA WO 235/441.
6. Bryan & Ryan deposition 8, TNA WO 309/37.
7. Hasse testimony, TNA WO 235/441.
8. Sauer testimony, TNA WO 235/441.
9. Walhorn testimony, TNA WO 235/441.
10. Schramm testimony, TNA WO 235/441.
11. Niemeyer testimony, TNA WO 235/441.
12. Knott testimony, TNA WO 235/441.
13. Plothe testimony, TNA WO 235/441.
14. Sixsmith, Guy, *Bremen-Farge War Crimes Trial Observations by The Judge Advocate* 4th April 1948, TNA WO 235/442.
15. Lofti, Gabriele, *KZ Der Gestapo: Arbeitserziehungslager in Dritten Reich* (2000) Deutsche Verlags-Anstalt, p. 191.
16. Reiter, Martin, *Das Arbeitserziehungslager Wilhelmsburg* https://www.kurt-und-herma-roemer-stiftung.de/wp-content/uploads/Reiter-Martin_Das-AEL-Wilhelmsburg.-Aktuelle-Forschungen.pdf (Retrieved 25 Nov 2023).
17. The court composition for the AEL Hamburg-Wilhelmsburg trial was:
    President – Lieutenant Colonel H R Bently OBE (Cheshire Regiment)

Members – Major B D Witty (East Yorkshire Regiment), Captain A P McArthur (Royal Norfolk Regiment), Captain L H Wilshaw (Royal Artillery), Captain J D R Vokes (Royal Engineers)
Judge Advocate – F Honig (Barrister)
Prosecutor – C E B Roberts (Barrister)
Defence Counsel for Schmidt and Kreuzer – Dr Heber
Defence Counsel for Hungerberg and Oehmke – Dr Adler
Defence Counsel for Hamel and Sommerfeld – Dr Eichler
Defence Counsel for Staben and Koopmann – Dr Müller
Defence Counsel for Klimkeit and Behnke – Dr Brügmann
Defence Counsel for Paudert – Dr Bunsen
Defence Counsel for Broadkorb and Ohlmeyer – Dr Lang
Defence Counsel for Weinhert and Obernhuber – Dr Krüger-Niedland
TNA WO 235/770 & WO 235/507.

18. AEL Hamburg-Wilhelmsburg trial testimony, TNA WO 235/507.
19. Nikolic deposition, TNA WO 311/497.
20. Testimony regarding shooting Frenchman TNA WO 235/507 & WO 235/508.
21. Oehmke testimony, TNA WO 235/508.
22. Professor Koopman testimony, TNA 235/507.
23. On 1 August 1942, Schmidt was assigned to Sonderkommando 4a of Einsatzgruppe C. He became its leader in January 1943. In the autumn of 1943, he moved to the RSHA in Berlin. On 1 February 1944, he became a Gestapo leader in Kiel. At the end of the war, Schmidt obtained false papers and fled. He escaped justice for war crimes until 1963 when he was held on remand while his involvement in AEL Nordmark and the 1944 murders of four Allied airmen were investigated. In 1965, unwell, he was released from detention. In 1968 the Kiel Regional Court sentenced Schmidt to two years in prison for aiding and abetting the murder of the Allied aviation officers, but his period of pretrial detention was taken into account and he was released. He was not tried for his part in the Einsatzgruppen murders and died a free man in Munich in 1983.
24. Dr A K Mant Preliminary Report, TNA WO 309/1068.
25. Hölzel statement, TNA WO 311/492.
26. The court composition for the first AEL Nordmark trial was: President – Lieutenant Colonel B G Melsom (East Lancashire Regiment)

Members – Major E J A Pettman (3rd Royal Tank Regiment), Captain O C Berger (The Greys), Captain R W Herbert (7th Hussars), Captain M P Dixon (2nd Royal Tank Regiment)
Judge Advocate – F Honig (Barrister)
Prosecutor – A Vollmar (Barrister)
Defence Counsel for Müller – Dr Gustav Uhde
Defence Counsel for Baumann – Dr Wolfgang Hensel
Defence Counsel for Kleinsteuber and Stender – Dr Erich Brügmann
Defence Counsel for Klostermann and Forck – Dr Walter Block
Defence Counsel for Jensen and Eickhoff – Dr Hubert Rull
Defence Counsel for Unruh – Dr Fritz Rüss
Accused first charge: Bruno Müller, Otto Baumann, Willy Stender, Gustav Klostermann, Hans Forck, Heinrich Unruh, Ruth Kleinsteuber, Herman Eickhoff and Orla Jensen
Accused second charge: Müller, Baumann, Stender, Forck and Jensen
Accused third charge: Klostermann
TNA WO 235/481.

27. Braitmann testimony, TNA WO 235/481.
28. Klostermann & Unruh depositions, TNA WO 235/483.
29. Scoor testimony, TNA WO 235/481.
30. The court translation of the German ‘maschinenpistole’ into ‘machine pistol’ is incorrect. The correct translation is ‘submachine gun’.
31. Vollmar’s hand-written notes p. 258, TNA WO 235/481.
32. Dr Hensel’s closing statement for Baumann, TNA WO 235/484.
33. Jensen testimony, TNA WO 235/482.
34. Stender testimony, TNA WO 235/482.
35. Baumann testimony, TNA WO 235/482.
36. Dr A K Mant Preliminary Report, TNA WO 309/1068.
37. Dr Hensel’s closing statement for Baumann, TNA WO 235/484.
38. Braitmann testimony, TNA WO 235/481.
39. Ibid.
40. Baumann deposition, TNA WO 235/483.
41. Baumann testimony, TNA WO 235/481.
42. Jensen testimony, TNA WO 235/482.
43. Ibid.
44. TNA WO 235/482.

45. The court composition for the first two minor accused AEL Nordmark trials was:
President – Lieutenant Colonel S C Auld (Royal Artillery)
Members – Major V Dunne MBE (Royal Army Ordnance Corps), Captain B D Chapman (Royal Norfolk Regiment), Captain M H Broadway (Kings Own Scottish Borderers), Captain F L W Cole (Oxfordshire & Buckinghamshire Light Infantry)
Judge Advocate – I C Baillieu (Barrister)
TNA WO 235/437.
46. The court composition for the Emil Dier trial was:
President – Lieutenant Colonel B G Melsom (East Lancashire Regiment)
Members – Major T A Berrigan (Royal Artillery), Captain K H Sutherland (Black Watch), Captain R Knox (11th Air Formation Signal Regiment), Captain E Phillips (98th Group Royal Pioneer Corps)
Judge Advocate – None appointed.
TNA WO 235/774.
47. Hölzel testimony, TNA WO 235/519.

Chapter 6: Trials for Killings During the 'End Phase'

1. The *Volkssturm* was a militia established by the NSDAP towards the end of the war in a last-ditch effort to fight the encroaching Allies. It comprised men aged between 16 and 60 who had not already been conscripted. *Volkssturm* units were under the direct command of the NSDAP *Gauleiter* and *Kreisleiter*.
2. Kershaw, Ian, *The End* (2012) Penguin, Chapter 6.
3. 25 August 1947 Progress Report re: Rheinmetall Borsig, War Crimes Group (NWE) No.3 Team, TNA WO 309/1135.
4. https://steinwache-rombergparkkomitee.org/mahnmal-bittermark/ (Retrieved 4 Jun 2023).
5. Kleine Vennekate, Erik, *1945 – Luftangriff, Mord und Einmarsch. Die letzten Wochen des Zweiten Weltkriegs in Ratingen* p. 32.
6. https://www.kz-gedenkstaette-neuengamme.de/en/history/satellite-camps/satellite-camps/hannover-ahlem-a-12/ (Retrieved 18 Jun 2023).

7. Exhibit A, Extract of Report by Medical Commission, TNA WO 235/444.
8. The court composition for the first Hannover Gestapo trial was:
   President – Lieutenant Colonel E C Van der Kiste (Essex Regiment)
   Members – Major R S Griffith (Royal West Kent Regiment), Major V H McCalmont (Royals), Major C M Price-Owen (Royal Artillery), Captain M P S Truell (Dorset Regiment)
   Judge Advocate – Sir Shirley Worthington-Evans (Barrister)
   Prosecutor – Major S Stewart
   TNA WO 235/433.
9. Wolters deposition, TNA WO 235/444.
10. Peek deposition, TNA WO 235/444.
11. Methfessel deposition, TNA WO 235/444.
12. Rasche deposition, TNA WO 235/444.
13. Plünnecke deposition, TNA WO 235/444. This deposition was taken in Prison de Namur, Belgium, where Plünnecke was being held by the Belgian Ministry of Justice in anticipation of being tried for the ill-treatment and torture of Belgians. They were keen to have him back, TNA WO 309/824.
14. Plünnecke deposition, TNA WO 235/444.
15. DJAG summary to the GOC-in-C BAOR for confirmation of court findings and sentences, TNA WO 235/715.
16. The court composition for the second Hannover Gestapo trial was:
    President – Lieutenant Colonel H R Bently (Cheshire Regiment)
    Members – Major E N Dominy (Royal Horse Artillery), Captain A F Stephen (Gordon Highlanders), Major G E Wheeler (Wiltshire Regiment), Captain R Z H Montgomery (Royal Army Service Corps)
    Judge Advocate – Not appointed
    Prosecutor – F W I Barnes (Barrister)
    TNA WO 235/419.
17. Plünnecke testimony, TNA WO 235/419.
18. Joost deposition, TNA WO 235/419.
19. Rasche deposition, TNA WO 235/419.
20. Joost testimony, TNA WO 235/419.
21. Joost defence counsel summing up, TNA WO 235/419.
22. Joost proceedings, TNA WO 235/419.
23. 8 March 1948 letter from Halse to McCreery, TNA WO 235/715.

24. 8 March 1948 letter from McCreery to Robertson, TNA WO 235/715.
25. 24 March 1948 letter from acting DCOS (Execution) to McCreery, TNA WO 235/715.
26. 22 March 1948 reply from Robertson to McCleery. TNA WO 235/715.
27. Letter from Eden to ER II, TNA FO 371/109723.
28. 18 July 1947 Note from Lieutenant Colonel Dr J P G van Velzen, Netherlands War Crimes Commission to Officer In Charge Executive Trial & Extradition Section, War Crimes Group (NWE), HQ BAOR, TNA WO 309/824.
29. The court composition for the Seelhorst Cemetery trial (the third Hannover Gestapo trial) was:
    President – Lieutenant Colonel S C Auld (Royal Artillery)
    Members – Major C E Hind (Border Regiment?), Captain A T Cripps (10th Hussars), Captain H S Adair (Cheshire Regiment), Captain G M Lewis (10th Hussars)
    Judge Advocate – R A Romain (Barrister)
    Prosecutor – Captain A W H Nicolson
    Defence – Dr Östmann
    TNA WO 235/498.
30. Nicolson summing up, TNA WO 309/313.
31. Kleine Vennekate, Erik, *1945 – Luftangriff, Mord und Einmarsch. Die letzten Wochen des Zweiten Weltkriegs in Ratingen* https://docslib.org/doc/12955922/1945-luftangriff-mord-und-einmarsch-die-letzten-wochen-des-zweiten-weltkriegs-in-ratingen-von-erik-kleine-vennekate (Retrieved 4 Jan 2024).
32. The third Düsseldorf case was for alleged killings at Rheinmetall Borsig. The fourth was for crimes committed in the Schiess work education camp. The fifth was an attempt to bring to justice SS Colonel Dr Walter Albath, the leader of the Gestapo for the whole region. Instead, he faced trial in the Curiohaus later in 1948 for the crimes committed in the Burgholz forest, near Wuppertal, see list of cases being investigated by War Crimes Group (NWE) in Wehrkreis IV, TNA WO 309/1133.
33. 29 April 1947 Progress Report by Captain W Ellery Anderson, TNA 309/1134.
34. Neuss statement to German Police, TNA WO 309/1134.
35. Reinarz statement to German Police, TNA WO 309/1134.

36. Rohde statement to German Police, TNA WO 309/1134.
37. List of cases being investigated by War Crimes Group (NWE) in Wehrkreis IV, TNA WO 309/1133.
38. Exhibit U, 24 January 1947 Preliminary autopsy report by Dr Kurt Böhmer, TNA WO 309/1134.
39. William (Bill) Ellery Anderson was a genuine British hero. Born in 1919 in Headington, Oxfordshire, (as William Ellery McMahon Anderson) he attended the prestigious Beaumont College.
    In 1939, he began a 15-year career in the British military by joining the Royal Gloucestershire Hussars. In 1940, he was commissioned into the Worcestershire Regiment. He joined the Parachute Regiment and SAS, where he served in North Africa (earning the Military Cross), Sicily, Italy and Holland. He then joined the Royal Ulster Rifles in 1947 and worked in the British War Crimes Group (North West Europe). Between 1950 and 1951, he fought in Korea where he was an instructor in the 29th Brigade Battle Training School and the only British special forces operative to work behind the enemy lines. He received a bar for his MC. He left the British Army in 1954 with the rank of major. From 1954 to 1956 he was part of the Falkland Islands Dependencies Survey Expedition where he led a team in Hope Bay exploring one of the least-known sectors of the Antarctic. His book *Expedition South* is an account of his time there.
    He was a Fellow of the Royal Geographical Society and later Governor of Durham Prison. Ellery Anderson died in 1992 in London.
40. Reinarz deposition, TNA WO 309/1134.
41. Rohde deposition, TNA WO 309/1134.
42. Harnischfeger deposition, TNA WO 235/390.
43. Hamburger, another policeman mentioned in early reports in connection with the Kalkumer Forest murders, was killed in an air raid.
44. The court composition for the trial of Harnischfeger & Ochs (the second Düsseldorf case) was:
    President – Lieutenant Colonel H R Bently (Cheshire Regiment)
    Members – Major A M Evans (Royal Artillery), Captain J Williamson (Royal Scots Fusiliers), Captain R J Towers (Royal Artillery), Captain B E Keble (Royal Army Service Corps)
    Judge Advocate – None assigned

Prosecutor – R D L Kelly (Barrister)
Defence Counsel for Harnischfeger – Dr Burchard-Motz
Defence Counsel for Ochs – Dr Meyer-Labastille
TNA WO 235/390.

45. Arrangements for trial of Harnischfeger and Ochs, TNA WO 309/788.
46. Dr Burchard-Motz's defence closing speech, TNA WO 235/390.
47. The Queen v Tolson (1889) 23 QBD 168, 181 Cave J.
48. Dr Meyer-Labastille's defence closing speech, TNA WO 235/390.
49. R D L Kelly prosecution closing speech, TNA WO 235/390.
50. 21st Oct 1947 report from Captain A W H Nicolson to HQ BAOR, *War Crimes Group (NWE) Execution of Allied Nationals for lootings and offences committed with violence in Germany*, TNA WO 311/495.
51. The court composition for the subsequent trial of Harnischfeger (the first Düsseldorf case) was:
President – Lieutenant Colonel J A Glendinning (Royal Artillery)
Members – Major W A Dickson (Royal Army Ordnance Corps), Captain R D Anderson (Royal Norfolk Regiment), Captain I R C Greenlees (Ox & Bucks), Captain C B J Oldrini (Foresters)
Judge Advocate – None assigned
Prosecutor – R H Murphy (Barrister)
Defence – Dr Burchard-Motz
TNA WO 235/504.
52. Brillo deposition, TNA WO 309/812.
53. Hake deposition, TNA WO 309/812.
54. Harnischfeger deposition, TNA WO 309/812.
55. Partial record of Harnischfeger defence testimony and cross-examination, TNA WO 235/504.
56. Report of Düsseldorf CID on recovery of bodies, pathology report of Dr Kurt Böhmer and skull photographs, TNA WO 309/812.
57. Brillo deposition, TNA WO 309/812.
58. Schaefer deposition, TNA WO 309/812.
59. Harnischfeger deposition, TNA WO 309/812.
60. Report by Lord Russell of Liverpool, TNA WO 235/504.
61. There are references to both 'Camp Bertha' and 'Camp Berta' in the files connected to the third Düsseldorf case (TNA WO 309/370 & 309/1135). 'Bertha' would be pronounced as 'Berta' in German and may be the source of the confusion.

62. 28 January 1948 Report from Lieutenant Colonel R A Nightingale to HQ BAOR, TNA WO 309/1135.
63. Ibid.
64. 12 February 1948 letter to Mr Mead, Legal Division, HQ 65 CCG (BE) BAOR 15 from Lieutenant Colonel Draper, TNA WO 309/370.
65. Pohlmann deposition, TNA WO 235/414.
66. Ernst deposition, TNA WO 235/414.
67. Spaethe deposition, TNA WO 309/344.
68. The court composition for the trial of Wilhelm Brinkmann (first Rheinhausen case) was:
    President – Lieutenant Colonel H R N Bently OBE (Cheshire Regiment)
    Members – Major W A M Chippindale (Worcestershire Regiment), Captain F O L'Estrange (10th Hussars), Captain B J A Hargreaves (Rifle Brigade), Captain G H Brazier (Royal Artillery)
    Judge Advocate – W Russell-Lawrence (Barrister)
    Prosecutor – F W I Barnes (Barrister)
    Defence – Dr Harald Matthiessen
    TNA WO 235/414.
69. Exhibit C, translation of Public Enemy Decree 'Looting in freed territory', TNA WO 235/414.
70. Exhibit J, final pleadings for Brinkmann by Dr Matthiessen, TNA WO 235/414.
71. 5 February 1948 summary of first Rheinhausen case by Brig R C Halse for the DJAG, TNA WO 235/414.
72. 14 October 1947 briefing letter to Office of the Judge Advocate General from Major S M Stewart, TNA WO 309/334.
73. Schubert deposition, TNA WO 311/235.
74. Dikty deposition, TNA WO 311/235. Note: Dikty's first name may have been Gottlieb as hand-corrected on the Curiohaus schedule of proceedings.
75. 'APPENDIX to Case RHEINHAUSEN II', WO 309/334.
76. Exhibit G, autopsy report, TNA WO 311/235.
77. The court composition for the trial of Gottfried Dikty (second Rheinhausen case) was:
    President – Lieutenant Colonel H R Bently OBE (Cheshire Regiment)

Members – Major T C Palmer (15th Medical Regiment Royal Artillery), Captain F H Chandler (Royal Army Ordnance Corps), Captain V R W Mountford (Worcestershire Regiment), Captain B Stubbs (Royal Artillery)
Judge Advocate – Deemed unnecessary
Prosecutor – Major W T Fielding (Barrister – Intelligence Corps)
Defence – Dr Wolfgang Graener
TNA WO 235/542.

78. 19 October 1948 letter to General Officer Commanding-in-Chief of the BAOR from DJAG Lord Russell of Liverpool, TNA WO 235/780.
79. 13 October 1947 Captain F N Potts brief for investigation of third Rheinhausen case, TNA WO 309/1277.
80. 28 June 1948 Field Investigation Report from Major J A McKee, TNA WO 309/334.
81. 8 July 1948 note to Officer Commanding Field Investigation Section War Crimes Group (NWE) from Major J M Ratcliffe (Commander No.2 Field Investigation Team), TNA WO 309/1277.

Chapter 7: The End of British Military Trials in Germany

1. Jones, P D, 'Nazi Atrocities Against Allied Airmen: Stalag Luft III and The End of British War Crimes Trials' (1998) *The Historical Journal*, 41, 2, p. 548.
2. TNA WO 32/12197.
3. Jones, P D, 'Nazi Atrocities Against Allied Airmen: Stalag Luft III and The End of British War Crimes Trials' (1998) *The Historical Journal*, 41, 2, p. 550.
4. Ibid., p. 554.
5. Förster, Jürgen, 'The relation between Operation Barbarossa as an ideological war of extermination and the Final Solution' in David Cesarani (ed.), *The Final Solution: Origins and Implementation* (2002) Taylor & Francis e-Library, p. 85.
6. Officially, *The United States of America vs. Wilhelm von Leeb, et al.*
7. Taylor, Telford, *Final Report to the Secretary of the Army on the Nuernberg War Crimes Trials Under Control Council Law No.10* (1949) US Government Printing Office, p. 82.

8. Bower, Tom, *Blind Eye To Murder* (1995) Little, Brown & Co., pp. 281–2.
9. Bloxham, D, 'Punishing German Soldiers during the Cold War: The Case of Erich von Manstein' (1999) *Patterns of Prejudice* 33: 4, p. 33.
10. House of Commons Debate, 18 October 1948. *Hansard Parliamentary Debates*, fifth series (House of Commons), Vol. 457, c. 257.
11. Melvin, Mungo, *Manstein: Hitler's Greatest General* (2011) Phoenix, pp. 432–5.
12. House of Lords Debate, 5 May 1949. *Hansard Parliamentary Debates*, fifth series (House of Lords), Vol. 162, c. 377.
13. https://ihl-databases.icrc.org/en/ihl-treaties/nuremberg-tribunal-charter-1945/article-8 (Retrieved 03 Feb 2024).
14. The court composition for the Manstein trial was:
President – Lieutenant General Sir Frank Ernest Wallace Simpson (Royal Engineers)
Members – Major General D A L Wade, Brigadier C A Dixon, Brigadier R B Lambe, Colonel R F Wilson, Colonel E T Henlop, Colonel L A Liddell.
Judge Advocate – Judge Charles Arthur Collingwood
Prosecution – Sir Arthur Comyns Carr (Barrister), Elwyn Jones (Barrister), Mr Honig, Colonel G I A D Draper, Major S Smith
Defence – R T Paget (Barrister), S C Silkin, Dr Laternser, Dr Leverkuehn
TNA FO 1060/1289.
15. Nuremberg Trial Proceedings Volume 22, Day 217, 30 September 1946 pp. 520–3 https://avalon.law.yale.edu/imt/09-30-46.asp (Retrieved 6 Aug 2023).
16. Paget, R T, *Manstein: His Campaigns and His Trial* (1970) Natraj Publishers (India) – my copy was published in India, but it was first published by Collins in 1951.
17. Record of the first day of the Manstein trial, TNA FO 1060/1289.
18. Exhibit 555, Weikselbaum deposition, Book 6/11, Liddell Hart Centre for Military Archives, King's College London.
19. Exhibit 84, 23 September 1939 document signed by Manstein, Book 6/2, Liddell Hart Centre for Military Archives, King's College London.

20. Exhibit 37, Brandys deposition, Book 6/2, Liddell Hart Centre for Military Archives, King's College London.
21. Exhibit 68, Part Translation of Document No. MAR 1501 War Crimes Unit, Book 6/2, Liddell Hart Centre for Military Archives, King's College London.
22. Exhibit 69, Part Translation of Document No. MAR 1523 War Crimes Unit, Book 6/2, Liddell Hart Centre for Military Archives, King's College London.
23. Prosecution details on the 'Polish Counts', TNA WO 311/644.
24. Exhibit 119, Gozdur deposition, Book 6/2, Liddell Hart Centre for Military Archives, King's College London.
25. Exhibit 120, Jarosz deposition, Book 6/2, Liddell Hart Centre for Military Archives, King's College London.
26. Paget, R T, *Manstein: His Campaigns and His Trial* (1970) Natraj Publishers (India), p. 133.
27. The full text of the charges is in TNA WO 311/664 – they are précised here.
28. Laws and Customs of War on Land (Hague IV); 18 October 1907, Annexe to The Convention, Article 6.
29. Exhibit 162, Translation of Document No. NOKW-2785, Office of Chief of Counsel for War Crimes, Book 6/4, Liddell Hart Centre for Military Archives, King's College London.
30. Exhibit 200, Translation of Document C-50, Führer Decree, Book 6/5, Liddell Hart Centre for Military Archives, King's College London.
31. Exhibit 199, Translation of Document NOKW 1076, Book 6/5, Liddell Hart Centre for Military Archives, King's College London.
32. Exhibit 204, Translation of Document NOKW 3136 (WB 4047), Book 6/5, Liddell Hart Centre for Military Archives, King's College London.
33. Officially, *The United States of America vs. Otto Ohlendorf, et al.*
34. https://judicature.duke.edu/articles/last-living-nuremberg-trial-prosecutor-recalls-his-work-on-the-einsatzgruppen-trial/ (Retrieved 6 Aug 2023).
35. *Trials of War Criminals before the Nuernberg Military Tribunals under Control Council Law No.10*, Volume IV (1949) US Government Printing Office, p. 412.
36. Ibid., p. 37.

37. Ibid., p. 92.
38. Exhibit 241, Translation of Document No. NO 2295, War Crimes Unit, Book 6/6, Liddell Hart Centre for Military Archives, King's College London.
39. Paget, R T, *Manstein: His Campaigns and His Trial* (1970) Natraj Publishers (India), p. 97.
40. Exhibit 33, Translation of Document No. 4064 – PS, Office of U.S. Chief Counsel, Book 6/1, Liddell Hart Centre for Military Archives, King's College London.
41. Melvin, Mungo, *Manstein: Hitler's Greatest General* (2011) Phoenix, p. 230.
42. Killing of Jews in Kerch https://collections.yadvashem.org/en/untold-stories/killing-site/14626711-Bagerovo-Anti-Tank-Trench (Retrieved 25 May 2023).
43. Paget, R T, *Manstein: His Campaigns and His Trial* (1970) Natraj Publishers (India), p. 172.
44. Exhibit 397, Part Translation of Document No. WB 3530 NOKW 2894, Book 6/9, Liddell Hart Centre for Military Archives, King's College London.
45. Paget, R T, *Manstein: His Campaigns and His Trial* (1970) Natraj Publishers (India) pp. 175.
46. Nuremberg Trial Proceedings Volume 20, Day 200, 10 August 1946 pp. 612–13 https://avalon.law.yale.edu/imt/08-10-46.asp (Retrieved 25 May 2023).
47. Bloxham, D, 'British War Crimes Trials Policy in Germany, 1945 – 1957: Implementation and Collapse' (2003) *Journal of British Studies*, 42, p. 116.
48. Melvin, Mungo, *Manstein: Hitler's Greatest General* (2011) Phoenix, p. 494.
49. Bloxham, D, 'British War Crimes Trials Policy in Germany, 1945 – 1957: Implementation and Collapse' (2003) *Journal of British Studies*, 42, p. 118.
50. In the British zone, a total of 3,265 people were prosecuted and 1,223 acquitted; 937 people had been tried for war crimes by a British military court with 269 acquitted; 148 had been tried for crimes against humanity by Control Commission courts with 88 acquitted; and 2,180 had been tried by German District Courts with 866 acquitted. Statistics given by the Under-Secretary of State for Foreign Affairs (Mayhew) in reply to a Parliamentary

question, 28 March 1949. *Hansard Parliamentary Debates*, fifth series (House of Commons), Vol. 463, c. 829.

51. Goodhart, Arthur L, 'The Legality of the Nuremberg Trials' in Mettraux, G (ed.), *Perspectives on the Nuremberg Trial* (2008) Oxford University Press, pp. 626–37.
52. Some war criminals found guilty by the IMT remained in 'international' custody.
53. Sharples, Caroline, 'What do you do with a Dead Nazi? Allied Policy on the Execution and Disposal of War Criminals, 1945-55' in Erlichman, C & Knowles, C, *Transforming Occupation in the Western Zones of Germany* (2018) Bloomsbury Publishing, pp. 97–112.
54. Sharples, Caroline, 'Burying the Past? The Post-Execution History of Nazi War Criminals' in Ward, R, *A Global History of Execution and the Criminal Corpse* (2015) Palgrave Macmillan, pp. 249–71.

BIBLIOGRAPHY

Primary Sources

The National Archives (UK) – abbreviated herein to TNA – Records series WO 235, WO 309, WO 311.

Twelve bound indexed volumes of typescript documents referred to by counsel and used as evidence in Manstein's trial, Liddell Hart Centre for Military Archives, King's College London.

Brand, George, *Trial of Heinrich Gerike et al – The Velpke Baby Home Case* (1950) William Hodge & Co.

Cameron, John, *Trial of Heinz Eck et al (The Peleus Trial)* (1949) William Hodge & Co.

Höss, Rudolf, *Commandant of Auschwitz* (1959) The World Publishing Company.

Stevens, E H, *Trial of Nikolaus von Falkenhorst* (1949),William Hodge & Co.

Trial of the Major War Criminals Before the International Military Tribunal, Nuremberg, 14 November 1945 – 1 October 1946 (1947).

Trials of War Criminals before the Nuernberg Military Tribunals under Control Council Law No.10 (1949) US Government Printing Office.

United Nations War Crimes Commission, *History of the United Nations War Crimes Commission and the Development of the Laws of War* (1948) HMSO.

United Nations War Crimes Commission, *Law Reports of Trials of War Criminals* (1947) HMSO.

Wiener Holocaust Library, Collection 2162 Neuengamme Trials: J C Giffin Papers.

Secondary Sources

Andrews, Allen, *Exemplary Justice* (1978) Corgi.

Bazyler, M J and Tuerkheimer F M, *Forgotten Trials of The Holocaust* (2014) New York University Press.

Bower, Tom, *Blind Eye To Murder* (1995) Little, Brown & Co.

Butler T R F and Garsia, M, *Archbold's Criminal Pleading, Evidence and Practice* (1943) 31st Edition.

Carruthers, Bob, *The Gestapo On Trial* (2014) Pen & Sword Military.

Churchill, Winston S, *The Second World War* (1951) 'Chartwell' Edition Volume 5 The Educational Book Company Ltd.

Davidson, Eugene, *The Trial of The Germans* (1997) University of Missouri Press.

Donnell, Clayton, *Eben-Emael and the Defence of Fortress Belgium, 1940* (2021) Pen & Sword Military.

Fried, John H E, *The Exploitation of Foreign Labour by Germany* (1945) International Labour Office, Montreal.

Hassel, Katrin, *Kriegsverbrechen vor Gericht* (2008) Nomos.

Helm, Sarah, *If This Is a Woman* (2015) Abacus.

Jervis, Sir John, *Archbold Pleading, Evidence and Practice in Criminal Cases* (1922) 26th Edition, Sweet & Maxwell Ltd.

Kershaw, Ian, *The End* (2012) Penguin.

Longden, Sean, *To the Victor the Spoils* (2005) Arris Books.

Mears, R, *The Real Heroes of Telemark* (2003) Hodder & Stoughton.

Melvin, Mungo, *Manstein: Hitler's Greatest General* (2011) Phoenix.

Mullins, Claud, *The Leipzig Trials* (1921) H F G Witherby.

Overy, Richard, *Interrogations* (2001) Penguin Group.

Paget, R T, *Manstein: His Campaigns and His Trial* (1970) Natraj Publishers (India).

Person, Katarzyn & Steinert, Johannes-Dieter, *Przemysłowa Concentration Camp: The Camp, the Children, the Trials* (2022) Palgrave Macmillan.

Read, Simon, *Human Game* (2012) Constable & Robinson Ltd.

Russell of Liverpool, Lord, *The Scourge of the Swastika* (1989) Macmillan Publishing Company.

Saidel, Rochelle G, *The Jewish Women of Ravensbrück Concentration Camp* (2006) Terrace Books.

Schwarberg, G, *The Murders at Bullenhuser Damm* (1980) Indiana University Press.

Sharpe, W J, *Massacre and Murder in Le Paradis* (2015), FeedARead.com Publishing.

Taylor, Telford, *Final Report to the Secretary of the Army on the Nuernberg War Crimes Trials Under Control Council Law No.10* (1949) US Government Printing Office.

The People's Verdict: A Full Report of the Proceedings at the Krasnodar and Kharkov German Atrocity Trials (1944) Hutchinson & Co.

Wachsmann, Nikolaus, *KL – A History of the Nazi Concentration Camps* (2015) Little, Brown

Wiggan, R, *Operation Freshman* (1986) William Kimber & Co. London.

Williams, A T, *A Passing Fury* (2017) Vintage.

INDEX